Effective Writing

TENTH EDITION

Effective Writing

A Handbook for Accountants

Claire B. May, Ph.D.

Gordon S. May, Ph.D.

University of Georgia, Emeritus

Boston   Columbus   Indianapolis   New York   San Francisco   Upper Saddle River
Amsterdam   Cape Town   Dubai   London   Madrid   Milan   Munich   Paris   Montreal   Toronto
Delhi   Mexico City   São Paulo   Sydney   Hong Kong   Seoul   Singapore   Taipei   Tokyo

Editor in Chief: Donna Battista
Sponsoring Editor: Nicole Sam
Editorial Project Manager:
  Heather McNally
Editorial Assistant: Christine Donovan
Marketing Manager: Alison Haskins
Managing Editor: Jeff Holcomb
Senior Production Project Manager:
  Roberta Sherman
Manufacturing Buyer: Carol Melville

Creative Director: Jayne Conte
Text and Cover Designer:
  Suzanne Behnke
Cover Photo: Fotolia
Full-Service Project Management:
  Aptara®, Inc.
Composition: Aptara®, Inc.
Printer/Binder: STP/RRD/Harrisonburg
Cover Printer: STP/RRD/Harrisonburg
Text Font: Times Ten Roman (10/12)

Credits and acknowledgments borrowed from other sources and reproduced, with permission, in this textbook appear on the appropriate page within text.

Library of Congress Cataloging-in-Publication Data

May, Claire Arevalo.
  Effective writing: a handbook for accountants / Claire B. May, Ph.D., Gordon S. May, Ph.D.—Tenth edition.
    pages cm
  Includes index.
  ISBN 978-0-13-357949-9
  1. Business report writing. 2. Communication in accounting. I. May, Gordon S. II. Title.
  HF5719.M375 2015
  808.06'6657—dc23

                                           2013045794

10 9 8 7 6 5 4

ISBN 10:   0-13-357949-2
ISBN 13: 978-0-13-357949-9

Brief Contents

Preface   xv

PART 1: COMMUNICATION STRATEGIES   1

Chapter 1   Accountants as Communicators   1

Chapter 2   The Writing Process: An Overview   17

Chapter 3   The Flow of Thought: Organizing for
             Coherence   35

Chapter 4   A Sense of Style: Writing with Conciseness
             and Clarity   59

Chapter 5   Standard English: Grammar, Punctuation,
             and Spelling   85

Chapter 6   Format for Clarity: Document Design   110

Chapter 7   Critical Thinking   125

Chapter 8   Accounting Research   138

PART 2: BUSINESS DOCUMENTS   168

Chapter 9   Letters   168

Chapter 10   Memos   192

Chapter 11   Reports   204

Chapter 12   E-Communication and Social Media   224

PART 3: WRITING AND YOUR CAREER   241

Chapter 13   Writing for Exams: CPA, CMA, and
             Academic Exams   241

Chapter 14   Writing for Employment: Résumés and
             Letters of Application   254

Chapter 15   Writing for Publication   270

Chapter 16   Oral Communication: Listening and
             Speaking   277

Index   291

Contents

Preface   xv

PART 1: COMMUNICATION STRATEGIES   1

Chapter 1   Accountants as Communicators   1

What Do Accountants Write?   3

How Well Do Accountants Write?   4

What Makes Writing Work?   4

Effective Writing: An Example   6

You Can Become a Good Writer   6

Writing and Other Forms of Communication   8
  Reuding   8
  Listening   8
  Speaking   9

Writing and Problem Solving   9

Writing and Critical Thinking   10

Communications and Ethics   10

Conclusion   12

Exercises   12

Notes   15

Chapter 2   The Writing Process: An Overview   17

Getting Started: Identifying Purpose   18

Thinking Critically about the Issues   20

Analyzing the Readers   20

Getting Your Ideas Together   22
  Gathering Information   23
  Generating Ideas   23
  Arranging Ideas: Organization   24

Writing the Draft   26

Revising the Draft   26

The Final Draft   28

Dealing with Writer's Block   28

Writing under Pressure   29

Writing and Electronic Media   29

Help from Colleagues: Critiquing   30

Exercises   30

**Chapter 3   The Flow of Thought: Organizing for
Coherence   35**

Writing with Unity   35

Using Summary Sentences   36

Responding to Readers' Questions and Concerns   37

Transitions   38
Transitional Words and Phrases   39
Repetition of Key Words and Phrases   41
Pronouns Used to Achieve Coherence   42
Problems with Transitions   43

Paragraphs   44
Length   44
Structure   44
Paragraph Development   47

Organizing Answers to Discussion Questions
and Essays   48
Discussion Questions   48
Essays   49
Applying Essay Techniques to Other Kinds of Writing   52
Sample Essay   52

Test Yourself   54

Test Yourself: Answer   54

Exercises   54

**Chapter 4   A Sense of Style: Writing with Conciseness
and Clarity   59**

Conciseness   59
Unnecessary Words   59
Simplicity   61
Verbs and Nouns   64

Clarity   66
Jargon   66
Precise Meaning   67
Concrete, Specific Wording   70

Readable Writing   72
Passive and Active Voice   72
Variety and Rhythm   75
Tone   76

Test Yourself   79

Test Yourself: Answers   79

Exercises   80

Notes   84

Chapter 5   Standard English: Grammar, Punctuation, and Spelling   85

Major Sentence Errors   85
Fragments   86
Comma Splices   86
Fused Sentences   87

Problems with Verbs   88
Tense and Mood   88
Subject-Verb Agreement   89

Problems with Pronouns   90
Pronouns and Gender   91

Problems with Modifiers   92

Parallel Structure   93

Apostrophes and Plurals   93

Commas   94
Comma Guide Sheet   95

Colons and Semicolons   97

Direct Quotations   98

Spelling   100

Help from the Computer   101

Test Yourself   102

Test Yourself: Answers   103

Exercises   104

Notes   109

Chapter 6   Format for Clarity: Document Design   110

Good Design: An Illustration   110

A Professional Appearance   114
Paper and Print   114
White Space and Margins   114
Neatness Counts!   115

Formatting   115
Headings   115
Lists and Set-Off Material   116
Pagination   117

Graphic Illustrations   117

Exercises   122

Note   124

Chapter 7 Critical Thinking 125

Making an Argument: The Process 126
*Reaching Sound Conclusions: Two Approaches to
Logic 129*
Fallacies: Mistakes in Reasoning 131
Critical Thinking and Ethical Dilemmas 133

Exercises 134

Note 137

Chapter 8 Accounting Research 138

Research: Basic Guidelines 138
FASB Accounting Standards Codification® 139
Electronic Sources of Information 140
Printed Sources of Information 141
Note Taking 142
Direct Quotation and Paraphrase 143
Plagiarism 143
Organizing Your Notes and Ideas 144
Writing Your Research Report or Memo 144
Integrating Notes into Your Writing 144
Revising 145
Documentation 145

Critical Thinking and Technical Accounting
Research 147
Financial Accounting Research 147
Steps in the Financial Accounting Research Process 147

Exercises 150

Notes 153

Appendix 8-A: Sources of Accounting and Financial
Information on the Internet 155

Appendix 8-B: Online Database Services 159

Appendix 8-C: Other Printed Sources of Accounting and
Financial Information 161

Appendix 8-D: Internal Documentation Style 162

Appendix 8-E: Endnotes or Footnotes and Bibliography
Style 165

PART 2: BUSINESS DOCUMENTS 168

Chapter 9 Letters 168

Principles of Letter Writing 168
Planning a Letter 168
Organization 169
Conciseness and Clarity 170

Tone   170
Form and Appearance   170
Parts of the Letter   173

Responding to Correspondence   175

Typical Accounting Letters   176
Engagement Letters   176
Management Advisory Letters   179
Tax Research Letters   179

Standardized Letters: A Caution   184

Letters Sent by Email   184

Exercises   184

Notes   191

Chapter 10   Memos   192

Memos: Some Basic Principles   192
The Parts of a Memo: Organizing for Coherence   192
Concise, Clear, Readable Memos:
  Style and Tone   194
Formats   194

Sample Memos   198
Memos to Clients' Files   198

Memos Sent by Email   198

Exercises   199

Notes   203

Chapter 11   Reports   204

Planning a Report   204

The Parts of a Report   207
Transmittal Document   208
Title Page   208
Table of Contents   208
List of Illustrations   209
Summary Section   209
Introduction   209
Body of the Report   210
Conclusion   210
Appendices (Optional)   210
Notes and Bibliography   210
Graphic Illustrations   211

Appearance   211

Style and Tone   211

Exercises   220

Note   223

Chapter 12   E-Communication and Social Media   224

Email   225
Composing the Email   225
Uses for Email: Informal or Formal?   228
Email within an Organization   228
External Email   229
Email—a Few More Cautions   229

Use of Electronic Media in Job Searches and Job
Applications   231
Use of Social Media for Job Searches   231
Electronic Submission of Résumés   231
LinkedIn Profiles   232

Social Media Used in the Accounting Profession   232
Social Media Policies   233
Blogs   234
Instant Messaging and Texting   235

Telephone Etiquette   236
Cell Phones   237

A Final Word: Sometimes Face-to-Face Is Better   237

Exercises   237

Notes   240

PART 3:   WRITING AND YOUR CAREER   241

**Chapter 13   Writing for Exams: CPA, CMA,
and Academic Exams   241**

Writing for the CPA Exam   241

Writing for the CMA Exam   244

Preparing for and Taking the CPA Exam or CMA
Exam   246
Manage Your Time   246
Use the Exam Questions to Organize the Response   247

Writing Responses for Academic Exams   247
Preparation   247
Taking the Exam   247
Qualities of a Good Written Response   249

Effective Writing and Technical Mastery:
Both Important   249

Exercises   250

Notes   252

Chapter 14   Writing for Employment: Résumés and Letters of Application   254

Starting the Job Search: Researching Possible Employers   254

Preparing Your Materials   255
Follow Instructions   255
Prepare Your Résumé   256
What Not to Put on a Résumé   260
Write a Letter of Application   260
Write a Thank-You Letter   262
Electronic Submissions   263

Exercises   264

Notes   269

Chapter 15   Writing for Publication   270

Planning Your Article   270

Research   273

Drafting and Reviewing the Article   274

Submitting the Article   274

Exercises   275

Chapter 16   Oral Communication: Listening and Speaking   277

Listening Skills   277
For Conversations with Another Person or in a Small Group   277
For Large Group Discussions, Lectures, and Meetings   278

Oral Presentations   278
Preparing to Speak   279
Making the Presentation: Poise and Confidence   284
Special Considerations in Presentations of Financial Information   287

A Final Word   288

Exercises   288

Index   291

Preface

Effective Writing: A Handbook for Accountants, 10th edition, is designed to help accounting students and practitioners improve their communication skills. It can be used as a supplementary text for regular accounting courses, as a text in an accounting communication course, or as a text in a business communication or technical writing course when these courses include accounting students. The handbook is also a useful desk reference or self-study manual for accountants in practice.

   Effective Writing guides the writer through all the stages of the writing process: planning, including analysis of audience and purpose; critical thinking about the problem to be solved or the job to be accomplished; generating and organizing ideas; writing the draft; revising for readable style and correct grammar, and designing the document for effective presentation. In addition to these basic writing principles, the book covers letters, memos, reports, and other formats used by accountants in actual practice, including email, social media, and other forms of electronic communication. Throughout the text, *Effective Writing* stresses coherence, conciseness, and clarity as the most important qualities of the writing done by accountants.

NEW TO THIS EDITION

- Expanded coverage of writing for the CPA Exam and the CMA Exam, in addition to general principles of effective writing as practiced by professional accountants.
- Assignment material has been extensively revised in all chapters. Many chapters now include exercises labeled "Current Professional Issues" to indicate assignments that are particularly useful in introducing students to current domestic or international issues with which the accounting profession is concerned.
- Chapter 8, Accounting Research
  - Sources for electronic accounting research have been extensively updated.
- Chapter 12, E-Communication and Social Media
  - New to this edition, this chapter covers the impact of electronic communication technology on communications and writing in the accounting profession, including email, texting, instant messaging,

cell phones, use of social media in job searches, and the general impact of social media on the accounting profession. The chapter also covers telephone etiquette.

- Chapter 13, Writing for Exams: CPA, CMA, and Academic Exams
  - This chapter has been revised to cover the new writing requirement on the CMA Exam. Coverage of the CPA Exam has also been expanded.
- Chapter 15, Writing for Publication
  - Revised to cover blogs and responses to online publications

In addition to its focus on effective writing and speaking, *Effective Writing* stresses other "soft skills" accountants need to be successful practitioners, such as the ability to listen attentively, read carefully, think critically, and interact with others in a respectful, professional way. Chapter 16 includes an extensive discussion of listening skills and also discusses the preparation of an oral presentation, including audience analysis and organization of materials, as well as techniques of effective delivery and the use of visual aids.

Effective Writing also includes sections on the ethics of communication. Chapter 1 introduces students to ethical issues related to accounting communication, and Chapter 7 shows them how to use critical thinking skills to resolve ethical dilemmas.

Critical thinking is the focus of Chapter 7, which introduces the principles of critical thinking and shows how careful reasoning can help students and professionals solve accounting problems. The chapter discusses inductive and deductive reasoning, the construction of an argument, and fallacies students will learn to recognize and eliminate.

Another special feature of this book is Chapter 8, which discusses accounting research. Here you will find valuable reference material on such topics as

- Where to find accounting information (including Internet sites)
- How critical thinking can help you solve problems and write persuasive documents
- How to write citations of accounting sources, including the *FASB Accounting Standards Codification*® and Internet sources

Chapter 13 covers writing for professional and academic examinations, including the CPA exam and the CMA exam, both of which contain questions requiring candidates to demonstrate their writing ability. Chapter 14 provides additional guidance on writing for employment.

This edition of *Effective Writing* includes many new and revised assignments that reinforce the concepts covered in the text. Some exercises have answers within the text for independent review. The *Instructor's Manual* contains answers to many other exercises. Most chapters also include topics for writing or speaking assignments. The assignments, like the illustrations in the text, are concerned with accounting concepts and situations and thus will seem relevant and familiar to those studying and practicing accounting. In addition, many chapters in the 10th edition of *Effective Writing* contain assignments that will introduce students to currently emerging national and international topics affecting the profession. These assignments are labeled "Current Professional Issues" in the chapters.

Effective Writing can be used in conjunction with traditional accounting courses. Instructors can assign cases and topics for research based on the accounting concepts being studied in class, or they can use the assignments provided in this handbook. Students then analyze the accounting problem, research the literature if necessary, and prepare answers according to an assigned format such as a letter, technical memo, formal report, or oral presentation. The handbook guides students toward principles of effective writing and speaking. Instructors can then evaluate students' performance based on the criteria discussed in the text and the *Instructor's Manual*.

The *Instructor's Manual* contains suggestions for everyone wishing to improve the communication skills of accounting students, whether in a regular accounting course or in a course devoted to communication. It includes topics such as motivating students to improve their communication skills, designing assignments, and evaluating performance, as well as chapter commentaries and masters for slides and handouts.

The *Instructor's Manual* can be downloaded through Pearson's Instructor Resource Center, online at http://www.pearsonhighered .com/irc.

We hope that this book will help those preparing to enter the profession, as well as those already in practice, to achieve greater success through effective communication.

Claire B. May
Gordon S. May

CHAPTER

Accountants as Communicators

T he ability to communicate effectively, whether through speaking or writing, is essential to success in the accounting profession and in the business world in general.[1] Writing and speaking, interpersonal skills, leadership skills, and the ability to think critically and to listen carefully are sometimes referred to as "soft skills," as opposed to the "hard skills" of technical knowledge and ability. The major differences among competitors may often be found in the degree to which employees have mastered writing, speaking, and other non-technical skills.

Soft skills are generally regarded as the key to business success and more important than technical accounting skills. One highly successful accountant has pointed out the importance of both writing and thinking:

> Some of the smartest accountants I have ever known are not the ones who knew standards backwards and forwards, but the ones that knew how to write and think.[2]

These skills are especially important in today's global environment. According to the International Accounting Education Standards Board (IAESB), successful accountants must be able to "present, discuss, report and defend views effectively through formal, informal, written and spoken communication; and . . . listen and read effectively."[3]

As you can see, to achieve your career goals in accounting, you may need to improve your communication skills. The American Institute of Certified Public Accountants (AICPA) believes that communication skills are now and will continue to be as important as professional knowledge, analysis and organization skills, technological skills, and research skills —all of which are essential for entry-level accountants (Figure 1–1). Among the personal attributes listed by the AICPA for competency in public accounting is "effective business writing." An AICPA report says that the writing of entry-level professionals should demonstrate standard grammar, appropriate style and tone, logical organization, clarity, and conciseness.[4]

FIGURE 1–1 Knowledge and Skills Required of Entry-Level CPAs

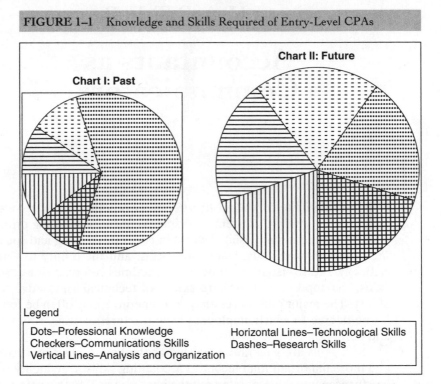

Legend

Dots–Professional Knowledge
Checkers–Communications Skills
Vertical Lines–Analysis and Organization

Horizontal Lines–Technological Skills
Dashes–Research Skills

Source: American Institute of Certified Public Accountants, Briefing Paper No. 2, *Computerizing the Uniform CPA Examination—Issues, Strategies, and Policies: An Update,* 5 March 2001.

Effective writing skills are essential for accountants in all areas of professional practice, including managerial accounting. The IMA (formerly known as the Institute of Management Accountants) has stated that "written communication is a critically important skill set for the management accountant and for the effective functioning of accounting and finance teams."[5]

So to be successful as well as competent, accountants must be good communicators, showing that they can use words effectively. Many colleges and universities now stress effective writing in accounting coursework. The AICPA evaluates candidates' writing skills on the CPA exam,[6] and the IMA evaluates writing skills on the CMA exam.[7]

Unfortunately, some students and accountants lack the skills they need to be effective communicators. Accounting firms are on record as being dissatisfied with the communication skills of entry-level accountants,[8] and a high percentage of accounting firms have reported poor writing skills as one reason for job terminations.[9]

Accountants need communication skills to get a good job and to keep that job after they are hired. Of course, "communication skills" is a broad area that includes formal and informal oral presentations, interpersonal communication, reading, listening, and skills in other related areas, including the ability to think carefully and critically. Ethical issues can also affect communication, both what accountants say and how they say it. Because this text is primarily about writing, we will now look at some of the documents accountants write on the job.

WHAT DO ACCOUNTANTS WRITE?

In every type of accounting practice, writing is an essential part of the job. Whether in public accounting, management accounting, not-for-profit accounting, or government accounting,[10] and whether specializing in tax, auditing, systems, or some other area, accountants write almost every day.

Examples in three specialized areas—tax, auditing, and systems—suggest a few of the many occasions that require accountants to write.

Tax accountants in accounting firms often write memos to other members of the firm that describe the results of their research. These memos become part of the clients' files. A tax accountant might also write a letter advising the client about the best way to handle a tax problem. Tax accountants must also write letters to the Internal Revenue Service (IRS) on behalf of clients, and occasionally may even write a judicial brief.

Auditors write memos to be included in a client's audit files that describe the work done on the audit. They may also write memos to their colleagues to request advice or to report research results. After the audit engagement, auditors may write advisory letters to management that suggest ways to improve accounting and internal control procedures.

Systems specialists write documents for readers with varying degrees of computer expertise. They may write a beginners' guide on how to use a software package or a highly technical report on a complex accounting system application. They may also write a narrative description of an accounting information system, as we will see later in this chapter.

No matter what their specialty, all accountants write memos to their supervisors, subordinates, and co-workers to request or provide information. They also write letters to clients, agencies, and a variety of other readers.

Technical reports and memos, both formal and informal, are also important ways in which accountants communicate. For instance, an accountant working for a corporation might write a report for management on alternative accounting treatments for a particular kind of business transaction. An accountant working for an accounting or business services firm might write a technical memo on how best to handle a client's unusual accounting problem.

Yet another kind of writing prepared by accountants is the narrative portion of financial statements. Footnote disclosures communicate information that users may need to interpret the statements accurately. Unfortunately, the meaning of some footnote disclosures is not always clear to many financial statement readers. Several years ago, the Securities and Exchange Commission (SEC) issued a "plain English" disclosure rule requiring companies filing registration statements to write those statements in "plain English" so that readers would find them easier to understand. The rule enumerates several principles of "plain English," including the use of short sentences and clear, concise language.[11]

Not all professional writing appears on paper. Email is nearly universal, and other forms of electronic communication have become increasingly important in recent years.

To be effective, letters, memos, emails, reports, and other business documents must be well written. How will clients react if, after reading a letter from their CPA, they are still confused about their income tax problem? How will management or one's supervisors react to a report that is poorly organized and hard to follow?

HOW WELL DO ACCOUNTANTS WRITE?

Earlier we noted that many entry-level accountants lack adequate writing skills, even though the ability to write well is essential for success in the business world. Some people believe the problem is getting worse, in part because we have become an online society in which a large part of everyday communication occurs via email and other forms of electronic communication. Electronic communication often emphasizes brevity over completeness, clarity, or attention to style. Therefore, we are being conditioned to use a type of writing that is not effective in many business situations. Yet even email and other forms of electronic communication can be written effectively, as Chapter 12 of this text shows.

WHAT MAKES WRITING WORK?

What is good writing? The list of tips for writers in Figure 1–2 summarizes many qualities of effective business writing, including the writing done by accountants. These qualities are stressed throughout this text. Let's examine these tips in a little more detail.

The first tip concerns the *content* of the document. You must know what you are talking about, and the information you give should be accurate and relevant. The second tip is *critical thinking*. You must analyze the issues with which you are dealing, including the questions and concerns of your readers. Can the issues be resolved in more than one way? If so, you will have to evaluate the alternatives carefully.

FIGURE 1–2   Tips for the Effective Writer

1. *Content:* Be sure that the accounting content is correct and complete. Have you addressed all relevant accounting issues?
2. *Critical Thinking:* Think carefully and critically about the issues with which you're dealing. Anticipate questions and objections your readers might raise.
3. *Appropriateness for Readers:* Write the document with a particular reader in mind. Check that issues are discussed on a level the reader can understand. For most documents, it is better to focus on practical, explicit information and advice related to the case you are discussing rather than general accounting theory.
4. *Conciseness:* Write as concisely as possible, given the reader's needs and the issues to be addressed.
5. *Clarity:* Develop a style that is clear and readable. Choose words that convey your meaning with precision and clarity.
6. *Coherence:* Structure the document so that it is coherent. The organization should be logical and the train of thought easy to follow. Summarize main ideas near the beginning of the document, and begin each paragraph with a topic sentence.
7. *Revision:* Revise the document so that it is polished and professional. It should be free of all spelling errors and typos; grammatical errors should not detract from the message.

The third tip for effective writing is *to write appropriately for your readers.* Your writing should be suitable for readers in several ways: It should be written on a level they understand and find meaningful, and it should anticipate and answer their questions.

The fourth tip is *conciseness.* Say what needs to be said in as few words as possible. To keep your writing concise, avoid digressions, unnecessary repetition, and wordiness.

Clarity is the next tip. Write as simply as possible, using words and phrases with which the reader is familiar. To improve the clarity of your writing, choose words that mean precisely what you intend so that your sentences convey only one meaning: the meaning you want to convey. Well-structured sentences also contribute to clear writing.

Coherence is the logical, orderly relationship of ideas. Coherent writing is, simply, writing that is well organized. The flow of thought is easy to follow, and important ideas stand out. To write coherently, you must carefully think through the ideas you want to convey. The ideas must be arranged logically and then written in a way readers can comprehend. Coherence is the sixth tip for effective writers.

The final tip is to *revise* your writing so that it is polished and professional. Documents should look attractive and be free of grammatical and mechanical errors.

EFFECTIVE WRITING: AN EXAMPLE

You will find many examples of the kinds of documents accountants write throughout this text. One such document is the narrative
description of an accounting information system (AIS). Figure 1–3
is an example of such a narrative description, in this case the payroll
processing system of a hypothetical company, S&S, a small retail business owned by Scott and Susan. This description illustrates many of
the characteristics of effective writing introduced here and explained
more fully in later chapters of this text.

If you read the description, you will notice that it is organized logically, following the steps of the payroll process, so that the narrative
is *coherent*. That is, readers will be able to understand how this system functions. Paragraphs are short and easy to follow. Sentences are
clear and *concise*. The language is *correct*—written following the conventions of Standard English. The document is also written at a level
appropriate to the readers, whom we assume to be the owners, managers, and other professionals who work with the payroll system at S&S.

YOU CAN BECOME A GOOD WRITER

With all this talk about the importance of good writing to a successful career in accounting, you may feel overwhelmed or discouraged.
Many people believe that they can never become good writers.

A word of encouragement is in order. Virtually anyone who suc-
ceeds in college work has the education and the skills to become at least
an adequate writer, and probably even a good one. Problems with writing are often the result of two factors, both of which can be corrected:
lack of adequate training in writing skills, and lack of self-confidence.

Let's address the latter problem—the poor image some people
have of themselves as writers. One reason to be optimistic about your
writing ability is that you've already learned quite a bit about how to
write from English courses and other writing classes, as well as from
personal experience. Most people are better writers than they realize.
They have the potential to become even more effective after they've
mastered a few strategies such as the ones we'll cover in this text. As
you read this text, note the techniques and principles you already use
in your writing. Don't lose sight of your strengths while you work to
improve the areas that could be better.

Another reason you should be able to write well as an accountant
is that you will be writing about topics you understand and find interesting. If you have had unpleasant experiences with writing in courses
other than accounting, the problem may have been that you were
writing about topics you weren't particularly interested in or didn't

FIGURE 1–3 Narrative Description of Payroll Processing at S&S[12]

When employees are hired, they complete a new-employee form. When a change to an employee's payroll status occurs, such as a raise or a change in the number of exemptions, the human resources department completes an employee change form. A copy of these forms is sent to payroll. These forms are used to create or update the records in the employee/payroll file and are then stored in the file. Employee records are stored alphabetically.

Some S&S employees are paid a salary, but most are hourly workers who record their time on time cards. At the end of each pay period, department managers send the time cards to the payroll department. The payroll clerk uses the time card data, data from the employee file (such as pay rate and annual salary), and the appropriate tax tables to prepare a two-part check for each employee. The clerk also prepares a two-part payroll register showing gross pay, deductions, and net pay for each employee. The clerk updates the employee file to reflect each employee's current earnings. The original copy of the employee paychecks is forwarded to Susan. The payroll register is forwarded to the accounts payable clerk. The time cards and the duplicate copies of the payroll register and paychecks are stored by date in the payroll file.

Every pay period, the payroll clerk uses the data in the employee/payroll file to prepare a payroll summary report for Susan so that she can control and monitor labor expenses. This report is forwarded to Susan, with the original copies of the employee paychecks.

Every month, the payroll clerk uses the data in the employee/payroll file to prepare a two-part tax report. The original is forwarded to the accounts payable clerk, and the duplicate is added to the tax records in the payroll file. The accounts payable clerk uses the tax report to prepare a two-part check for taxes and a two-part cash disbursements voucher. The tax report and the original copy of each document are forwarded to Susan. The duplicates are stored by date in the accounts payable file.

The accounts payable clerk uses the payroll register to prepare a two-part check for the total amount of the employee payroll and a two-part disbursements voucher. The original copy of each document is forwarded to Susan, and the payroll register and the duplicates are stored by date in the accounts payable file.

Susan reviews each packet of information she receives, approves it, and signs the checks. She forwards the cash disbursements vouchers to Ashton, the tax reports and payments to the appropriate governmental agency, the payroll check to the bank, and the employee checks to the employees. She files the payroll report chronologically.

Ashton uses the payroll tax and the payroll check cash disbursement vouchers to update the general ledger. He then cancels the journal voucher by marking it "posted" and files it numerically.

feel qualified to discuss. When you write about subjects you like and understand, it's much easier to write clearly and persuasively.

Finally, you may find it much easier to do the kind of writing recommended in this text because it is simple, direct writing. Some people believe that they must write in long, complicated sentences filled with difficult, "impressive" vocabulary. In fact, just the opposite is true: Effective business writing is written as simply as possible. It is therefore easier to do.

WRITING AND OTHER FORMS OF COMMUNICATION

Writing is only one of several forms of communication, along with such skills as reading, listening, speaking, and interpersonal communication. In fact, all these forms of communication work together to determine how well a person gives and receives information. Let's look at how reading, listening, and speaking skills can help you improve your writing.

Reading

Reading affects writing in several ways. Often you will write a memo or letter in response to a written communication from someone else. In public practice, for example, you might write a letter to clients to answer questions they have posed in a letter to your firm. The ability to read the earlier correspondence carefully is essential to an effective response.

Careful reading is also important when you research accounting literature as background for the documents you write. The tax code, government regulations, financial accounting standards, articles in professional journals, and *The Wall Street Journal* are examples of the material you must read to stay informed on accounting issues and procedures. You will need to understand this material and be able to apply it to particular situations.

You will also read information circulated and stored within your own firm or company, such as client files and memos or emails from colleagues. Reading this material carefully will provide many of the insights and facts you need to deal effectively with situations for which you are responsible.

Thus, careful reading, with an understanding of important ideas and key facts, can contribute to effective writing.

Listening

Along with reading, the ability to listen carefully determines how well you receive information from others. On the job, you interact with colleagues, supervisors, subordinates, or clients; at school, you interact with professors and other students. Listening carefully to these people provides important information you can use as the basis of your writing. Listening gives you facts about projects you are working on, along with insights into other people's expectations and concerns.

In many situations, listening skills contribute to effective writing. Instructions given by the professor in class, interviews with clients, requests from supervisors, and phone conversations with colleagues are a few examples. In all these situations, attentive listening is necessary to hear what people are saying. It's often a good idea to take notes and, when necessary, ask questions for clarification or additional information.

Careful listening to what others say is often a key ingredient in effective writing. By listening carefully, you learn much about what others know about a situation, what their concerns are, and what they expect from you.

Speaking

Oral communication is one of the soft skills we mentioned earlier as important to success in the accounting profession. Writing and speaking will often overlap in your professional activities. Informally, you may have meetings and conversations to discuss reports or memos you've written. You may use what you've written as the basis for formal oral presentations before a group. You might make a presentation to a board of directors, senior managers, or members of a professional organization.

WRITING AND PROBLEM SOLVING

The nation's largest public accounting firms are unanimous in calling for improved communication skills for those entering the profession. These firms also identify problem-solving skills as essential to successful accounting practice:

> Individuals seeking to be successful in the diverse world of public accounting must be able to use creative problem-solving skills in a consultative process. They must be able to solve diverse and unstructured problems in unfamiliar settings. They must be able to comprehend an unfocused set of facts; identify and, if possible, anticipate problems; and find acceptable solutions.[13]

Problem solving requires many skills, such as identifying key issues, researching relevant literature, and thinking critically and analytically. At each step of the problem-solving process, writing can help you reach sound conclusions.

You can generate ideas on a topic by writing down what you know about that topic, as well as what you have yet to find out. The act of writing about a subject can actually help you clarify your thinking. As one wit put it, "How do I know what I think until I see what I say?" There's more truth in this quip than might at first be apparent. Research into how people think and learn has shown that writers often generate ideas and improve their insights into a subject as they write down their thoughts.

Writing can help you solve problems in other ways as well. For example, as you research accounting literature, you take notes. You might also write requests to other people for additional information you need to solve the problem.

Writing that you use to solve problems and make decisions is writing for yourself. After the problems have been solved, or at least clearly defined, you can put your insights and conclusions into writing that will help you and others make decisions. Writing, problem solving, and decision making are often inseparable, interactive processes that are essential to the practice of accounting.

WRITING AND CRITICAL THINKING

We've seen that problem solving and decision making, like writing and other forms of communication, are significant parts of an accountant's job. But before you can solve a problem or make a decision, you need to think carefully and critically about the issues at hand.

What is critical thinking? It can be defined as fair, open-minded thinking that asks appropriate questions and considers all relevant information before reaching a conclusion. A critical thinker considers a situation from multiple points of view and evaluates the pros and cons of an argument before reaching a conclusion. Critical thinkers are careful to avoid errors, or fallacies, in their thinking and analyses. Chapter 7 discusses the critical thinking process in more detail.

Critical thinking and effective writing go hand in hand: As you take notes and write down your ideas about an accounting problem, the issues and alternative solutions will become clearer. This critical thinking becomes important as you prepare to write the final document.

COMMUNICATIONS AND ETHICS

Accounting communication, including writing, may involve ethical considerations as well as critical thinking and problem solving. In fact, these three processes—analyzing ethical and other accounting issues, thinking critically, and solving problems—are often essential components of effective communication.

Ethics may be defined broadly as the standards we use to determine what is right and wrong—a set of moral principles or values that govern how we act. We learn these ethical principles in a variety of ways, from our families, religious communities, schools, or in general from the society of which we are a part. Professional people, including accountants, also acquire ethical standards as part of their professional training.

Accountants must adhere to very high ethical standards as they perform their professional responsibilities. CPAs must follow reporting rules established by the SEC and other governmental agencies, and they must adhere to ethical standards established by nongovernmental entities such as the Financial Accounting Standards Board (FASB) and the AICPA. In fact, the AICPA's Code of Professional Ethics is a major source of ethical standards for all accounting professionals, not just CPAs. Management accountants also adhere to ethical requirements established by the IMA, as well as by federal, state, and local laws. Individual firms and corporations may also have ethical codes for their employees.

Legal requirements and codes of professional conduct provide standards of ethical behavior for accountants as they perform their professional responsibilities. Yet these laws and codes alone may not always provide enough guidance for specific ethical dilemmas. Accountants sometimes face situations for which ready-made answers are not available. When you are faced with such a dilemma, you will need to think critically about the issues in light of your own personal ethical standards in order to make an ethical decision. Remember, too, that there may be a gap between what is legal and what is ethical. For many years, discrimination against ethnic minorities and women was legal in this country, but such discrimination was never ethical.

Ethical considerations often affect the way we communicate in a professional situation, whether orally or in writing. Remember that accounting is a process of measuring and reporting financial information. Ethical issues can relate to what we say and how we say it. The AICPA's Code of Professional Ethics requires that its members report all the information needed for a user of the information to make a reasonable decision; the Code also requires that financial data not be misrepresented. Thus, information must be reported in an honest, reasonably complete manner. Moreover, the information must be communicated clearly so that users can understand it. Accuracy, clarity, and completeness are all qualities of the ethical communication of accounting information.

Ethics also affects the attitude with which we regard other people, whether the public at large, our clients, or colleagues and co-workers. An important principle here is that other people deserve to be treated with courtesy and respect. Later chapters discuss such ethical considerations as writing with a courteous tone, the respectful use of titles and pronouns, and the need to write clear and concise documents so that readers can find the information they need as quickly as possible. We will also discuss analyzing readers' interests and needs as an essential step in the writing process. Finally, sections of this text that discuss critical thinking and accounting research show how to analyze ethical dilemmas. You will learn how to decide what information to provide, and how to provide it in a way that not only adheres to professional and legal standards, but also shows respect for the people who will use the information.

CONCLUSION

To be a successful accountant, you must master many skills. You must understand and be able to apply accounting principles, of course, but you must also be able to think critically and ethically and to communicate effectively. A competent, ethical accountant who is also a critical thinker and an effective communicator usually is rewarded with professional success.

EXERCISES

Exercise 1–1 [General]

Consider the writing you find in one or two articles in *The Wall Street Journal* or the business section of another major newspaper or magazine. How effective, or ineffective, do you find the writing? If you have trouble reading or understanding what you read, is the problem due to ineffective writing? If you find the material understandable and interesting to read, what qualities of the writing contribute to this effectiveness? You might consider the Tips for Effective Writing in Figure 1–2 as the basis of your evaluation.

Exercise 1–2 [Financial]

Look at some published corporate SEC Forms 10-K or annual reports for the most recent year and evaluate the financial statement disclosures they contain. Find examples of disclosures that are not written as clearly or concisely as they could be and rewrite them to be more clear and concise. Share your results with the class and discuss them. (Hint: You can access many 10-Ks and annual reports on the Internet by following the links to listed companies at the New York Stock Exchange (NYSE) Web site at https://nyse.nyx.com.)

Exercise 1–3 [General]

Prepare a written report on why the SEC is so concerned that corporations use "plain English" in their filings and what it is doing about the issue. Among the materials you consult, be sure to look at the following SEC publications, but do not limit your sources to just these:

- *A Plain English Handbook: How to Create Clear SEC Disclosure Documents* at www.sec.gov/news/extra/handbook.htm
- *Updated Staff Legal Bulletin No. 7* at www.sec.gov/interps/legal/cfslb7a.htm
- *Plain English Disclosure Final Rules* at www.sec.gov/rules/final/33-7497.txt

Exercise 1–4 [General]

Research the topic of "soft skills" and prepare an article for your school's newspaper on their definition and importance in the accounting and business world.

Exercise 1–5 [Ethics]

Do you believe ethical considerations are an important part of an accountant's professional responsibilities? Why or why not? Think about this question, and then write notes according to the following outline. Use only the sections of the outline that are relevant to your position on this issue.

1. Ethical considerations are important to accountants because: (list your reasons)
2. Ethical considerations are not very important to accountants because: (list your reasons)
3. Accountants find guidance in making ethical decisions from the following sources: (list the sources you find)

Exercise 1–6 [Managerial]

Management Accounting Quarterly (MAQ) contains articles related to managerial accounting. Search a few recent editions to find an article that may interest you. Critique the writing using each of the Tips for Effective Writing in Figure 1–2. How effective or ineffective do you find the writing? Does the writing style contribute to your understanding of the article? Why or why not? (You can access MAQ on line at http://www.imanet.org/resources_and_publications/management_accounting_quarterly.aspx. Access is on a subscription basis, so you may have to gain access through your school's library.)

Exercise 1–7 [Auditing]

AccountingWEB (www.accountingweb.com) contains articles related to many areas in accounting including auditing. Search *AccountingWEB* to find an auditing article that may interest you. Critique the writing using each of the Tips for Effective Writing in Figure 1–2. How effective or ineffective do you find the writing? Does the writing style contribute to your understanding of the article? Why or why not?

Exercise 1–8 [Systems]

Smart Brief (www.smartbrief.com/industry/accounting) is a source for newsletters that publish articles on various topics. One of these newsletters is *InfoTech Update*, which addresses topics relating to information technology in accounting. Search *InfoTech Update* on *Smart Brief* to find an information technology article that may interest you. Critique the writing using each of the Tips for Effective Writing in Figure 1–2. How effective or ineffective do you find the writing? Does the writing style contribute to your understanding of the article? Why or why not?

Exercise 1–9 [Tax]

Journal of Accountancy (published by the American Institute of Certified Public Accountants) and *The CPA Journal* (published by the New York State Society of CPAs) publish articles on many topics of interest to practicing accountants. Search these publications to find an article on tax that may interest you. Critique the writing using each of the Tips for Effective Writing in Figure 1–2. How effective or ineffective do you find the writing? Does the writing style contribute to your understanding of the article? Why or why not?

Exercise 1–10 [International]

The International Journal of Accounting, published by the University of Illinois, contains articles explaining international accounting practices. Search this publication to find an article on international accounting that may interest you. Critique the writing using each of the Tips for Effective Writing in Figure 1–2. How effective or ineffective do you find the writing? Does the writing style contribute to your understanding of the article? Why or why not?

Exercise 1–11 [General]

The chair of the accounting department at your school has asked you to address beginning accounting students at an orientation session. The topic of your presentation is to be "A Competitive Edge: The Importance of Writing Skills for Accountants." Your purpose is to convince the students to take the need for good writing skills seriously.

Write an outline you can use as a basis for your presentation. As steps in preparing your outline, follow these guidelines:

- Analyze your audience for this presentation. How will you present your topic so that they find it meaningful and interesting?
- Think critically about the objections your audience might raise to your arguments. How will you respond to their objections?
- What material will you include in your presentation? Remember to anticipate your audience's objections, and the way you will respond. Also remember to arrange your ideas in a logical order.
- Using the guidelines found in Chapter 16—Oral Communication: Listening and Speaking, practice and present your talk. Your instructor may ask you to make your presentation in class. As an alternative, you may ask a few friends to listen to your presentation.

Exercise 1–12 [General]

Assume that the talk you presented for Exercise 1–11 was very success-ful. In fact, the chair of your accounting department has asked you to write an article based on your talk for the departmental website, which is available to all accounting majors.

Using the guidelines given in Chapter 15—Writing for Publication, write the article.

Exercise 1–13 [Current Professional Issues]

The AICPA has listed fraud control as an emerging professional issue. Read what the institute has to say about "Managing the Business Risk of Fraud" at http://www.acfe.com/uploadedFiles/ACFE_Website/Content/documents/managing-business-risk.pdf. Critique the writing using each of the Tips for Effective Writing in Figure 1–2. How effective or ineffective do you find the writing? Does the writing style contribute to your understanding of the article? Why or why not?

NOTES

1. This is true not only in account-ing but also in almost any business occupation including the areas of finance, marketing, and consult-ing. As pointed out in an article in *Business Week*, even new employees in these areas may have to prepare long reports or presentations as well as shorter forms of writing on the job. See Julie Gordon, "Memo to Students: Writing Skills Matter," *Business Week*, 26 April 2006. http://www.businessweek.com/stories/2006-04-25/memo-to-students-writing-skills-matter (9 April 2013).

2. Don Pfluger of CPA and business advisory firm Gallina as quoted in Bill Carlino, "The new breed of audi-tors," *accountingTODAY*, 1 May 2012. http://www.accountingtoday.com/ato_issues/26_5/Auditor-Landes-AICPA-Enron-Worldcom-audit-62448-1.html (9 April 2013).

3. International Accounting Education Standards Board (IAESB), *IES 3: Professional Skills and General Education.* (New York: IAESB, 2004), pars. 13, 17; reprinted in *Handbook of International Education Pronouncements 2010 Edition.* (New York, IAESB, 2010), 48–49.

4. American Institute of Certified Public Accountants, Invitation to Comment, *AICPA Competency Model for the New Finance Professional.* (New York: AICPA, 7 October 1997), 5.

5. William Cordes, Director of Exam Administration for the IMA, personal email (15 May 2013).

6. The Business Environment and Concepts (BEC) section of the exam contains three written communica-tions tasks. See "A Guide to CBT-e: The New 2011 Uniform CPA Examination," https://www.aicpa.org/BecomeACPA/CPAExam/ForCandidates/HowToPrepare/DownloadableDocuments/New_2011_CPA_exam_guide_to_CBTe.pdf (9 April 2013).

7. The exam contains two 30-minute essay questions on each of the two parts of the exam. See "Become a CMA®," www.imanet.org/cma_certification/become_a_cma.aspx (10 May 2013).

8. *The Wall Street Journal*, 16 July 1986, "Words Count," 1.

9. Alan A. Cherry and Lucy A. Wilson, "A Study of the Writing Skills of Accounting Majors in California" (unpublished study, 1987).

10. In a 2006 survey of its members in government conducted by the AICPA, 80% of respondents indicated written and oral communication skills were essential. See "AICPA Survey—Phase II: Government Members Foresee 'Brain Drain' in the Government Workforce," Government E-News, American Institute of Certified Public Accountants, 17 May 2006. http://fmcenter.aicpa.org/NR/rdonlyres/FA53AA12-25AF-4BCC-A25E-4281FCC56DBB/0/GPAC_NEWS_15.pdf (21 May 2007).

11. "Plain English Disclosure." Securities and Exchange Commission. *Staff Legal Bulletin No. 7(CF)*. www.sec.gov/interps/legal/slbcf7.htm (9 April 2013): 1–2.

12. Marshall B. Romney and Paul J. Steinbart, *Accounting Information Systems*, 12th ed., © 2012, p. 53. Reprinted and Electronically reproduced by permission of Pearson Education, Inc., Upper Saddle River, New Jersey.

13. Duane R. Kullberg, William L. Gladstone, Peter R. Scanlon, J. Michael Cook, Ray J. Groves, Larry D. Horner, Shaun F. O'Malley, and Edward A. Kangas, *Perspectives on Education: Capabilities for Success in the Profession* (Big Eight Accounting Firms, 1989), 6.

CHAPTER

The Writing Process:
An Overview

E ffective writing, like accounting, is a process. One step in the
accounting process is to analyze transactions to determine
how to record them. Several questions basic to the accounting system underlie your analysis of financial transactions and their
treatment. What is the purpose of the information recorded and ultimately reported? Who are the users of this information, and what
are their needs? Do the readers expect this information to be presented in a certain form, such as the typical presentations found in
annual reports? How can the information be most fairly and effectively presented?

These questions are as important to good writing as they are to
good accounting. Planning, which emphasizes both the purpose of the
writing and the needs and expectations of the readers, is the first step
in the writing process.

In this chapter, we discuss the writing process from beginning to
end: planning for purpose and audience, including critical thinking
about the issues; gathering information; generating and organizing
ideas; drafting; revising; and proofreading. (Figure 2–1 summarizes
the steps of the writing process.) You will learn how to apply this
process to overcome much of the anxiety you may feel about writing,
including the problem of writer's block. Throughout the chapter, we
also discuss how computer technology can help you at every stage of
the writing process.

In the previous chapter, we identified seven tips for effective
writing that focus on content, critical thinking, appropriateness
for readers, conciseness, clarity, coherence, and revision (see
Figure 1–2 in Chapter 1). In this and following chapters, we discuss specific guidelines and techniques that will help you achieve
these goals.

FIGURE 2–1   The Writing Process

Plan
- Read the assignment or consider the task carefully.
- Analyze the purposes of the document.
- Identify the accounting issues, including different ways those issues might be addressed.
- Analyze the issues from the readers' point of view. What are their interests, needs, and expectations?
- Gather and organize material.

Draft
- Write down your ideas.
- Don't stop to edit.
- Write the parts of the paper in whatever order you want.
- Keep your readers in mind as you compose.

Revise
- Reread the document from the readers' point of view. Is your treatment of the accounting issues fair, thorough, and persuasive?
- Revise the document so that it is clear, coherent, and concise.
- Proofread for grammatical, mechanical, and typographical errors.

GETTING STARTED: IDENTIFYING PURPOSE

One of the first stages in the writing process—analyzing the purpose of the document—is easy to overlook. When you think about purpose, you decide what you want to accomplish with your letter, memo, or other document. Do you want to provide your readers with information about some topic, answer their questions, recommend a course of action, persuade them to do something, or convince them to agree with you on some point?

These are just a few of the purposes a document can have. You should think carefully about the purpose *before* beginning to write. It might be helpful to think of your purpose in terms of three categories: to give information about something, to propose a course of action, or to solve a problem. The purpose of most writing tasks falls into one of these categories, or perhaps a combination of them.

As an example, assume you are the controller for Franklin Electrical Supplies. Franklin is considering purchasing stock in SolLite, Inc., one of Franklin's major suppliers of lighting fixtures. A report on this possible purchase could have any of the following purposes:

- To inform management of the advantages (or disadvantages) of the purchase
- To recommend that Franklin purchase (or not purchase) the stock
- To suggest a way to finance the purchase

The purpose of the report, or of any writing, determines what material it should contain. Consider another example. Your client, Coastal Development, is faced with a lawsuit that could result in a large loss. You might write a letter to Coastal's controller about the disclosure requirements for contingent loss liabilities as a result of pending litigation. In such a letter, you would not discuss gain contingencies or loss contingencies from bad debts. You would analyze the specific purpose of the letter to decide what information was relevant for this situation.

Another way to think about the purpose of a document is to identify the accounting issues it will address. Sometimes these issues are obvious, but at other times you must analyze the situation carefully before all the issues become apparent. For example, a client might seek your help on the best way to record a transaction to minimize income tax liability. As you analyze the transaction, you might become aware of accounting issues that would never occur to the client, such as the need to record the transaction consistently with generally accepted accounting principles (GAAP). You might also become aware of ethical or legal issues that the client had not considered.

Identifying the issues can help you define the purposes of the document you are writing, because one purpose might be to explain the accounting issues in a way your reader can understand.

After you have analyzed your purposes carefully, you should write them down. Be as specific as possible and try to define the purposes in a sentence. This sentence might later become part of the document's introduction.

When you analyze your purpose, *be specific*. Remember that you are writing to particular individuals in a particular situation. Relate the purpose of your writing to these people and their concerns. That is, state the purpose in the context of this specific situation rather than in broad, general terms. In the Franklin Electrical Supplies example, suppose you were writing a report on how to finance the purchase of SolLite, Inc., stock. You would limit your discussion to the financing alternatives available to Franklin that are practical for the company to consider.

Sometimes, to determine the purpose of a document, you need to read previous correspondence on the subject, such as a letter or email from a client. Be sure to read this correspondence carefully, noting important information and questions you've been asked to address. You may also receive an oral request to write something, perhaps from your supervisor. If you receive such a request to write, listen carefully to the directions. If the purpose of the document is not clear, ask questions until you're sure what the document should include.

THINKING CRITICALLY ABOUT THE ISSUES

If the purpose for your writing involves analyzing complex accounting issues, think carefully about your topic as you plan your document, gather information, and write. Sometimes the issues are complex: A problem might have more than one reasonable solution, and some people might disagree with the course of action you recommend. As you plan your writing, keep alternative points of view in mind. Consider not only the reasons for your own opinion, but also the reasons other people might have a different view. How will you support your opinion, and how will you respond to the arguments of people who disagree with you? Critical thinking about the issues throughout the writing process helps ensure that the document you write is persuasive. Your readers will regard you as knowledgeable and fair, and they will take seriously what you write. (Chapter 7 discusses critical thinking in more detail.)

ANALYZING THE READERS

When you are planning a writing task, it is important to consider who the readers will be. A memo on a highly technical accounting topic might be written one way for an accounting colleague, but another way for a client or manager with only limited knowledge of accounting procedures and terminology.

Effective writers analyze the needs and expectations of their readers before they begin to write. In writing a letter or memo, you will probably be writing to a limited number of people, perhaps to only one person. You also know, or can find out, important information about the reader or readers. Again, you must ask certain questions: How much do the readers know about the subject being discussed? What else do they need to know? Have they already formed opinions on the accounting issues? The answers to these questions, and perhaps others, will suggest the level at which you will write, including the terms and procedures you will explain, the background you will provide, and the arguments you will make.

Accountants who deal with the public should be particularly careful in analyzing the needs of their readers. A tax specialist, for example, might have clients with widely varying experience and knowledge of tax terminology. A corporate executive would probably understand such concepts as depreciation and accruals, but a small shopkeeper might not be familiar with this terminology. Business letters to these two clients, even on the same topic, should be written differently.

Consider the readers' attitudes and biases. Are your readers likely to be neutral to your recommendations, or will they need to be convinced? The critical thinking about the issues you have already done will help you write to your readers in a convincing way. Remember your readers' interests and concerns as you write. How will they benefit, directly or indirectly, from what you propose? How can you present your arguments to overcome their objections and biases? To answer this last question, you must anticipate readers' questions, research the issues, and then organize your arguments into a convincing sequence.

Other important considerations when analyzing your readers' needs and expectations are tone and style. What are their attitudes and biases? Some readers react well to an informal, friendly style of writing, but other readers believe that professional writing should be more formal. Whoever your readers are, remember always to be courteous. Whether you write in a technical or conversational style, all readers appreciate (and deserve) consideration, tact, and respect. Treating your readers with courtesy and respect will help ensure that your writing is ethical, as well as effective.

Word choices also contribute to an effective and responsible writing style. For example, many readers might find the following sentence troubling:

A successful *CEO* will treat *his* subordinates with respect.

Some readers might argue that the choice of pronouns (*CEO/his*) implies a gender bias. Use plural nouns and pronouns so that your language will be more inclusive:

Successful *CEOs* will treat *their* subordinates with respect.

Sometimes your readers will have additional expectations about your documents. In a classroom situation, the instructor usually gives directions about different aspects of your papers, such as format and due date. The instructor expects you to follow these directions. How well you do so usually affects your grade.

Readers' expectations are also important when you write on the job. Managers in some firms expect in-house memos and reports to follow certain conventions of format, organization, and style. If you work for such a firm, your memos and reports will seem more professional— and be more effective—if they are consistent with these expectations.

In fact, meeting readers' expectations might actually be a matter of company policy. Policies often govern how certain documents are written and what procedures they must go through for approval. Many professional services firms do not let new staff members send letters to clients unless a manager or partner first approves them. If you were a new staff member in such a firm, you might draft the client letter, but a manager or partner would review it and possibly ask you to make revisions. Moreover, for certain documents, such as some engagement letters and auditing reports, the actual language used in the letter might be determined by company policy. The partner will expect you to follow these policies with great care.

> **FIGURE 2–2**   Planning a Paper

> *Consider these questions as you plan the documents you write:*
>
> **1.** Answer after you read and analyze the assignment or consider the task:
>
> - What are the accounting issues in this case?
> - Are there ethical issues I should consider?
> - What literature will I research to resolve these issues?
> - Who will read this document?
> - What different opinions might readers have about the issues?
> - What are the readers' concerns?
> - What are the purposes of this document?
>
> **2.** Answer after you research and analyze the case:
>
> - What are the main points (conclusions) I need to make in this document?
> - What material should I include to make these conclusions clear and meaningful to the reader(s)?
> - How will I support my conclusions and respond to readers' objections?

In the example of the client letter just discussed, there are actually two or three readers: the manager and/or partner who reviews and approves the letter, and the client who receives it. This letter should be written on a technical level that is appropriate for the client, and it should address the client's concerns, but it should also meet the expectations of the manager and partner. Analyzing readers' needs, interests, and expectations is obviously more complex when there are several readers. Think carefully about the different readers and use your best judgment to meet the expectations of them all.

Analyzing readers' needs, expectations, and opinions is an important part of the preparation for writing. Planning, during which you think carefully about both your audience and your purpose, is the first guideline for effective writing. We'll add more to this list throughout the chapter.

1. Analyze the purpose of the writing, the accounting issues involved, and the needs and expectations of the readers.

Figure 2–2 summarizes questions you can ask yourself to help plan your writing.

GETTING YOUR IDEAS TOGETHER

After you have evaluated the purpose of the writing and the needs of the readers, you are ready for the second stage in the writing process: gathering information and organizing the ideas you want to present. This step might be quick and simple. For a short letter, you may not need to do further research; organizing your ideas may involve only a short list of the main topics you want to include in the letter—perhaps one topic for each paragraph.

For much of the writing you do, gathering information and organizing might be a more complicated process that involves much thought and perhaps some research as well. Let's look at some techniques you can use.

Gathering Information

Before you begin to write the document, be sure you have complete, accurate information. You can check the work that has already been done and then locate new information you'll need.

For many projects, some information might already be available. If you're working on an audit, for example, information might be available from other members of the audit team as well as from the files from the previous years' audits. Explore these sources of information fully. Review the files carefully and, when necessary, talk with the people who have already worked on the project.

Sometimes you might need to do additional research. This task can involve background reading on a technical topic or a careful review of professional standards or law, such as Financial Accounting Standards Board (FASB) publications, the tax code, IRS publications, or SEC publications. As you read this material, take notes carefully and be alert for information that might be helpful when you write. Remember also that accounting issues often have more than one possible solution. As you research, look for material that supports more than one point of view.

This research may require you to interview people who will be affected by the project that you are working on. Suppose you intend to propose in a report a new accounting information system for your company. You can gain important insights into topics your report should cover by talking with the people who would be affected by the proposed system. You can learn what they want the system to accomplish, what they might need to know about it, and whether they have already formed opinions that should be considered when you write your report.

Generating Ideas

After you have gathered the information you need, you are ready to begin the next phase of the writing process: deciding exactly what to say.

If you have not already written your statement of purpose, now is the time to do so. Try to break up the purpose into several subtopics. Suppose the purpose of a client letter is to recommend that the client company update its accounting system. The statement of purpose for this letter could specify the different accounting jobs for which the expanded system would be useful, outline its major advantages, and respond to questions and objections the client might have.

Another useful technique for generating ideas is brainstorming. With this technique, you think about your topic and write down all your ideas, in whatever order they come to you. Don't worry about organizing the ideas or evaluating them; later, you can consider how these ideas fit into the outline you developed when you analyzed the purposes of the document.

Brainstorming is often easier to do at the computer. As you type in the keywords and phrases that occur to you, the phrases might start to become sentences and the sentences might flow together to become paragraphs. You may find that the faster you record your ideas, the more freely the ideas flow. Thus, using a computer can be valuable when you need to generate ideas quickly.

Arranging Ideas: Organization

After you've decided what you want to say, it's important to consider how best to arrange these ideas so that the readers will find them easy to follow. In other words, it's time to think about how the document will be organized.

Much of the work you've already done will help you decide on the best pattern of organization. You may be able to use your statement of purpose as the basis of your organization, or your paper may be structured so that the readers' major concerns are your principle of organization—that is, each concern might be a major division of your paper. Some documents can be organized according to the accounting issues they address.

When considering all these approaches to organization, and possibly deciding among them, remember this principle: The needs and interests *of your readers* should determine the document's organization. Arrange your ideas in the order that they will find most helpful and easiest to follow. Anticipate when your readers are likely to raise objections or ask questions, and respond to those needs when they are likely to occur.

There are a few other points of organization to consider. First, most writing has the same basic structure: an introduction, a concise summary of important ideas, development of the main ideas, and a conclusion. This structure is shown in Figure 2–3. In later chapters of this handbook, we will discuss more fully this basic structure as it is used for particular kinds of writing.

Another point is that ideas should be arranged in a logical order. To describe how to reconcile a bank statement, for instance, you would discuss each step of the procedure in the order in which it is performed.

Finally, you can often organize ideas according to their importance. In business writing, always arrange ideas from the most to the

FIGURE 2–3   Basic Writing Structure

- *Introduction:* identifies the subject of the document and tells why it was written. Sometimes the introduction also provides background information about the topic or stresses its importance. You may also use the introduction to build rapport with your reader, perhaps by mentioning a common interest or concern or referring to previous communication on the topic.
- *Concise statement of the main ideas:* summarizes explicitly main ideas, conclusions, or recommendations. This part of a document may be part of the introduction or a separate section. It can be as short as a one-sentence purpose statement or as long as a three-page executive summary.
- *Development of the main ideas:* Includes explanations, examples, analyses, steps, reasons, arguments, and factual details. This part of an outline or paper is often called the body.
- *Conclusion:* Brings the paper to an effective close. The conclusion may restate the main idea in a fresh way, suggest further work, or summarize recommendations, but an effective conclusion avoids unnecessary repetition.

least important. Note that this principle means you start with the ideas that are most important *to the reader.*

Suppose you are writing a report to recommend that your firm purchase new software for maintaining its accounting records. Naturally, you will want to emphasize the advantages of this purchase, describing them in the order that is likely to be most convincing to the readers. However, this investment might also have drawbacks, such as the problems involved in converting from the old system to the new one. For your report to appear well researched and unbiased, you need to include these disadvantages in your discussion. You might use the following structure:

I. Introduction, including your recommendation
II. Body
    A. Advantages, beginning with those most appealing to the readers
    B. Disadvantages, including, when possible, ways to minimize or overcome any drawbacks
III. Conclusion

One final word about organization: After you've decided how to arrange your ideas, it's a good idea to write an outline, if you haven't already done so. Having an outline in hand as you draft your paper will help you keep the paper on track. That way, you'll be sure to include all the information you had planned and avoid getting off the subject.

The guidelines for effective writing can now be expanded:

1. **Analyze the purpose of the writing, the accounting issues involved, and the needs and expectations of the readers.**
2. **Organize your ideas so that readers will find them easy to follow.**

WRITING THE DRAFT

The next major step in the writing process is writing the draft. The purpose of this step is to put your ideas in writing. Most writers find that they can write a first draft more easily if they don't try to edit at this stage. Spelling, punctuation, and style are thus not important in the draft. What is important is to write the ideas so that you can later polish and correct what you have written.

If you did your brainstorming at the computer, you may already have parts of your draft if the list of ideas you began with evolved into sentences or paragraphs as you typed.

The outline you have prepared will guide you as you write. However, you may decide to change the outline as you go, omitting some parts that no longer seem to fit or adding other ideas that seem necessary. Feel free to change the outline as you write; when you revise the draft later, you can make sure your thoughts are still well organized.

Although you will use your outline as a guide to the ideas you want to include in your draft, you might find it easier to write the various parts of the document in a different order from the one used in the outline. Some people find introductions hard to write, so they leave them until last. You may also choose to write the easiest sections of your draft first, or you may start writing some parts of the draft while you are still getting the material together for other parts.

One final word of advice on the draft stage: Don't allow yourself to get stuck while you search for the perfect word, phrase, or sentence. Leave a blank space, or write something that is more or less what you mean. You'll probably find the right words later.

REVISING THE DRAFT

The next stage in the writing process is the revision of the draft. In this step, you check your spelling and grammar, polish your style, and make a final check to see that the ideas are effectively and completely presented. As you revise, read the document *from the reader's point of view*.

You'll need to revise most of your writing more than once—perhaps three or four times. The key to revising is to let the writing get cold between revisions; a time lapse between readings enables you to read the draft more objectively and see what you have actually said, instead of what you meant to say. Ideally, revisions should be at least a day apart.

FIGURE 2–4   Examples of Homonyms

See (the verb)	sea (the body of water)
Bear (the animal)	bare (uncovered)
Deer (the animal)	dear (a term of address)
Plane (an airplane)	plain (unadorned)
Break (to divide into parts)	brake (to stop or slow)
Some (a certain amount)	sum (total)
Wood (made from trees)	would (the auxiliary verb)
Eye (what we see with)	I (the pronoun)
Threw (the verb)	through (the preposition)
Know (the verb)	no (negative)
Hour (time)	our (the pronoun)
Write (on paper or a computer)	right (correct)
Their (the pronoun)	there (place)
Which (the pronoun)	witch (the broom rider)
Site (location)	Cite (refer to a source)
Way (direction)	Weigh (determine weight)
So (therefore)	Sew (to stitch with thread)

Another technique is to have a colleague review the draft for both the content and the effectiveness of the writing. Choose a reviewer who is a good writer and evaluate the reviewer's suggestions with an open mind.

Most word processing software has the ability to check the text for grammar problems and certain errors in style, such as sentences that are too long and paragraphs that use the same word too often. The software may also identify some mistakes in punctuation, as well as most misspelled words.

A word of caution about these style analyzers, spell checkers, and grammar checkers—they're not infallible. They can't catch all the weaknesses in your text, and sometimes they flag problems that aren't really there. If you use a computer to analyze your writing, you still must use your own judgment about what changes to make.

Homonyms can cause problems with your writing, for example, but spell checkers and grammar checkers may not find this kind of problem. Homonyms are words that sound the same when spoken aloud, but they have different spellings and meanings. Figure 2–4 shows examples of homonyms that spell checkers or grammar checkers may not recognize.

Another revision technique is to print the document and edit the hard copy by hand. You can then make the revisions in your computer file later. Some writers find that they revise more effectively if they work with a hard copy rather than text on a screen.

The next four chapters of the handbook discuss what to look for when putting your written work in final form.

We now have three guidelines for effective writing:

1. **Analyze the purpose of the writing, the accounting issues involved, and the needs and expectations of the readers.**
2. **Organize your ideas so that readers will find them easy to follow.**
3. **Write the draft and then revise it to make the writing polished and correct.**

THE FINAL DRAFT

After you have polished the style and organization of the paper, you will be ready to put it in final form. Consider questions of document design, such as the use of headings, white space, and other elements of the paper's appearance.

Proofreading is also an important step. Here are some suggestions for effective proofreading:

1. Proofreading is usually more effective if you leave time between typing and looking for errors. You will be able to critique the paper more clearly if you have been away from it for a while.
2. Use your computer's spell check program to eliminate spelling and typographical errors. Remember that the computer program cannot distinguish between homonyms such as *their* and *there* or *affect* and *effect*.
3. In addition to your computer's spell checker, you may also need to use a dictionary to look up any word that could possibly be misspelled, such as words the computer doesn't recognize, or homonyms it may not have flagged. Check also that you've spelled people's names correctly. If you are a poor speller, have someone else read the paper for spelling errors.
4. If you know that you tend to make a certain type of error, read through your paper at least once to check for that error. For example, if you have problems with subject-verb agreement, check every sentence in your paper to be sure the verbs are correct.
5. Read your paper *backwards*, sentence by sentence, as a final proofreading step. This technique isolates each sentence and makes it easier to spot errors you may have overlooked in previous readings.

DEALING WITH WRITER'S BLOCK

Writer's block is a problem everyone faces at some time or another. We stare at blank paper or at a blank screen with no idea of how to get started. The ideas and the words just don't come.

Many of the techniques already discussed in this chapter will help you overcome writer's block. Thinking of writing as a process, rather than a completed product that appears suddenly in its final form, should help make the job less formidable. Any difficult task seems easier if you break it down into manageable steps.

The discussions of the steps in the writing process, especially the section on writing the draft, included suggestions that will help you overcome writer's block. Here is a summary of these techniques:

1. Plan before you write so that you know what you need to say.
2. Write with an outline in view, but write the paper in any order you want. You can rearrange it later.
3. Don't strive for perfection in the draft stage. Leave problems of grammar, spelling, style, and so forth to the revision stage.
4. Begin with the easiest sections to write.
5. Don't get stuck on difficult places. Skip over them and go on to something else. You may find that when you come back to the rough spots later, they are not as hard to write as you thought.

WRITING UNDER PRESSURE

Throughout this chapter, you've seen how writing is easier if you break the project down into steps. It's easy to manage these steps when you have plenty of time to plan, research, draft, revise, and polish.

What about situations in which you don't have the luxury of time? What about writing essay questions on an exam, or on-the-job writing tasks where you have only a little while to produce a letter or memo?

The truth is that any writing project, no matter how hurriedly it must be done, will go more smoothly if you stick with the three basic steps of the writing process: plan, draft, and revise. Even if you have only a few minutes to work on a document, allow yourself some of that time to think about whom you're writing to, what you need to say, and the best way to organize that material. Then draft the paper.

Allow yourself some time to revise as well. Use a spell check program to help locate embarrassing spelling and typographical errors.

WRITING AND ELECTRONIC MEDIA

Some of the writing you will do as a professional accountant will be for electronic transmission, such as email or other documents that are sent over the Internet. Documents sent electronically should be planned, written, and revised with the same care you would use for hard-copy versions. This may be obvious for formal documents, but even email and instant messaging (IM), which we often send in haste and consider to be extremely informal, requires care in order to be effective. Chapter 12 gives guidance on the use of electronic communication, including advice on the use of email.

HELP FROM COLLEAGUES: CRITIQUING

Once you have improved your document as much as you can, you may have another source of help: constructive feedback from one or more colleagues. If you are preparing an assignment for a course, this help may come from other students in the class. In a job situation, you might ask a colleague to review your writing. You will, of course, be willing to return the favor to your colleagues if they ask you to critique their writing.

Here are some tips for giving helpful critiques:

- Reviews of the writing should be both tactful and honest.
- Always point out strengths of the writing, and then make a few suggestions if you see ways the writing could be improved.
- Make suggestions in positive ways, and be as specific as possible. For example, you wouldn't say, "I can't make any sense of this, and your grammar is deplorable!" Rather, you might say, "Can you explain this concept more clearly? Perhaps shorter sentences would help. Also, you might want to check your verbs."
- Ask the writer if you can write your feedback on the paper itself. Then be prepared to discuss what you liked about the paper, as well as ways it could be improved.
- For specific guidelines on what to look for in the papers you critique, use Tips for the Effective Writer found in Figure 1–2.

If a colleague critiques your writing, here are some things to keep in mind:

- Whenever possible, ask people to critique your writing who are themselves good writers.
- Keep an open mind, and resist the natural temptation to be defensive. On the other hand, remember that final responsibility for the document is yours; you'll decide which suggestions to use. Not all advice, however well intended, is helpful.
- Thank the reviewers for their help.

EXERCISES

Exercise 2–1 [General]

Analyze the letter in Figure 2–5. How would you react if you received this letter?

1. Think about these questions and then discuss them with your classmates:
    - What are the strengths of this letter? (It does have some strengths!)
    - What are the weaknesses of the letter? (Hint: Can you find all the typos and spelling errors? In addition to these problems,

FIGURE 2–5   Letter for Exercise 2–1: What Is Wrong with This Letter?

Wright and Wrongh, CPAs
123 Anystreet
Anytown, US 12345

Corner Dress Shop
123 Anyother Street
Anytown, US 12345

Gentleman
We are in receipt of your correspondence and beg to thank you.
    After extensive research we have found what we hope will be
a satisfactory responce to your questions, we hope you will find our
work satisfactory. It is the goal of our firm to alway offer the best,
most expert and reliable service possible to all our clients, all of
whom are value and with whom we hope to have a lont-term working relationship to our mutual advantage.
    There were two possibilities for the resolution of this issue that
we considered after a careful analyses of the applicable IRC sections to your situation. If the first possibility proved relevant, then
you would be subject to a fine of $5500, plus penalties and inter-
est. If athe other possibility was the best solution, then you would
receive a $4400 credit because of a loss carryforard to your current
year returns. As you no doubt know, IRC Sec.341(6)a [paras. 5-9]
stipulate that the regulations we must follow. Thus, to be in compliance with the rules and regs. you must follow the provisions of the
pertinent sections.
    As your CPAs, we are most concerned that we be in complianse
with all standards of professional ethics, and we always keep this in
mind when we advise you on your tax and accounting questions. We
don't want to go to jail, and we're sure you don't either!
    After extensive research, we advise you to file an amended
return immediately because the first possibility enumerated in the
above paragraph proves to be the correct solution to your problem.
    Thanking you in advance, we remain

Yours with highest regards,

M Ostley Wrongh

M. Ostley Wrongh
Wright and Wrongh, CPAs

the letter has a number of less obvious weaknesses. What are
    they?)
2. Revise the letter so that it is more effective. Invent any details you
    may need.

Chapter 9 provides information on letter writing.

Exercise 2–2 [General]

You are a member of Beta Alpha Psi (the accounting honorary society) at a major university. A large local high school has contacted your chapter of the honorary society and asked it to prepare a two-page flyer about opportunities provided by an accounting career and the skills (hard and soft) required to succeed both as an accounting student and as an accounting professional. You have been asked by the president of the honorary society, Sandy West, to write the flyer. She has asked that you prepare it in the form of a memo written to her. Write a memo to Sandy West responding to her request. Chapter 10 provides information on writing memos.

Exercise 2–3 [Managerial]

Jim Kakes, CEO of Kakes Manufacturing Company, needs to hire a new controller as the current controller is retiring. Several other CEOs he knows have suggested he look for someone who is a Certified Management Accountant (CMA). Mr. Kakes is not familiar with this designation and has asked you what it is and whether you believe hiring a CMA would be a good idea, given the extra amount he will have to pay in salary,

Write a memo to Mr. Kakes responding to his request. You may wish to consult Chapter 10 for suggestions on memo organization and format.

Exercise 2–4 [Systems]

You are employed by the consulting division of a large professional services firm. Your expertise is in information systems auditing. You have become interested in gaining professional certification in this area and are aware of an organization, ISACA (formerly known as the Information Systems Audit and Control Association and now known by its acronym only) which offers certification as a CISA (Certified Information Systems Auditor). Write a memo to the head of the consulting division, Mr. Robert Sherrill, requesting that your firm provide the funds for you to attain this certification. You should, of course, explain what this credential is and the benefits to your firm of having a CISA on staff. You have researched the possibility and believe you will need approximately $1,100 to cover the expenses of preparing for and taking the CISA exam.

Chapter 10 provides advice on how to write a memo.

Exercise 2–5 [Managerial/Current Professional Issues]

In 2012, The American Institute of Certified Public Accountants (AICPA) and the Chartered Institute of Management Accountants

(CIMA) entered into a joint venture to offer a new credential, the Chartered Global Management Accountant (CGMA). Write an article for your school's accounting club newsletter discussing this new credential, what its advantages are, and how to obtain it.

Writing for publication is discussed in Chapter 15 of this handbook.

Exercise 2–6 [Auditing]

You are a partner in a medium-size CPA firm and want to convince your partners that the firm should expand the services provided to clients. Specifically, you believe the firm should begin offering *WebTrust* and *SysTrust* services.

Write a memo to your partners to explain what the concepts of *WebTrust* and *SysTrust* services are and why your firm should begin to offer such services. Chapter 10 contains suggestions on memo organization and format.

Exercise 2–7 [Tax]

Your school's accounting honorary society maintains a Web site on which it includes short articles on various accounting topics. The readers of this Web site are primarily other accounting students. The Web master has asked you to write a short article explaining the differences among progressive, proportional, and regressive tax systems, including their relative advantages and disadvantages. Give examples.

Exercise 2–8 [Financial]

For decades, there has been a debate as to whether different GAAP should be established for private companies as opposed to public companies. Often, this has been referred to as the "Big GAAP vs. Little GAAP" controversy. In mid-2012, the Financial Accounting Foundation's board of trustees voted to establish a Private Company Council to determine whether exceptions or modifications to GAAP for privately held companies should be made.

Prepare an outline you can use for a speech to your accounting club on the pros and cons of modifying GAAP for privately held companies. Chapter 16 provides more information on oral presentations.

Exercise 2–9 [International]

For many years, the IFRS (International Financial Reporting Standards) Foundation has worked to develop and promote the adoption of a single set of International Financial Reporting Standards (IFRSs) that are globally accepted. It has done this through its standard-setting body, the International Accounting Standards Board (IASB).

An article in *Accounting Today* entitled "IFRS Foundation Charts IFRS Progress" (http://www.accountingtoday.com/news/IFRS-Foundation-Charts-IFRS-Progress-67016-1.html) reported on the first phase of a study by the IFRS Foundation on progress toward global adoption of IFRSs.

Prepare an outline you can use for a speech to your accounting club on the pros and cons of global adoption of IFRSs, the progress made toward global adoption, and prospects for completion of the effort by the IFRS Foundation. Chapter 16 provides more information on oral presentations.

CHAPTER

The Flow of Thought: Organizing for Coherence

Coherence is one of the seven tips for effective business writing discussed in Chapter 1 (see Figure 1–2 in Chapter 1). Coherent writing is organized so that important ideas stand out. The flow of thought is logical and easy to follow.

Chapter 2 introduced several techniques that will help you make your writing more coherent: analyzing the purpose of the document and the reader's needs, then outlining before you begin to write. This chapter discusses additional ways to ensure coherence in your writing. You'll learn how to write with unity, use summary sentences and transitions, and structure effective paragraphs and essays.

WRITING WITH UNITY

The key to unified writing is to establish the main idea of each document. An office memo or email may contain only one paragraph, but that paragraph has a central idea. A report might be many pages long, but it still has a central idea or purpose, and probably secondary purposes as well. It's important to determine your purpose and main ideas before you begin writing, as discussed in Chapter 2.

You should be able to summarize a main idea in one sentence. In a paragraph, this sentence is called the topic sentence. In longer documents involving more than two or three paragraphs, this sentence is called the thesis statement or statement of purpose.

The main idea is the key to the entire document. Any sentences or details that are unrelated to the main idea, either directly or indirectly, are irrelevant and should be omitted. In longer documents, entire paragraphs may be irrelevant to the main purpose. These irrelevant sentences or paragraphs are called digressions.

When you remove digressions and irrelevant sentences, your writing becomes unified; every sentence is related to the main idea.

The following paragraph is not unified. Which sentences are irrelevant to the topic sentence?

(1) Incorporation offers many advantages for a business and its owners. (2) For example, the owners are not responsible for the business's debts. (3) Investors hope to make money when they buy stock in a corporation. (4) Incorporation also enables a business to obtain professional management skills. (5) Corporations are subject to more government regulation than are other forms of organization.

Sentence 1, the topic sentence, identifies the main idea of the paragraph: the advantages of incorporation. Sentences 3 and 5 are off the subject.

Writing with unity is an important way to make your writing coherent.

USING SUMMARY SENTENCES

In coherent writing, the main ideas stand out. You can emphasize your main ideas by placing them in the document where they will get the reader's attention.

First, as Chapter 2 suggested, it's usually a good idea to summarize your main ideas at the beginning of the document. A long document, especially a report, should have a separate summary section at or near the beginning of the paper. This formal summary may be called an abstract, an executive summary, or simply a summary.

When writing these summary sections, be specific and remember the reader's interests and needs. Let's say you are writing a memo to the management of Turnipseed Importers to explain the advantages of an accounting software package that it will use to manage its inventory. You'll need to summarize those advantages specifically and relate them to Turnipseed. One of these advantages might be stated this way: "This software is particularly easy to use because it provides online help for the type of inventory control issues we often encounter with our seed stores. Competing software companies do not offer this type of online support."

The summary at the beginning of a document can be several sentences, or even several pages long, depending on the length of the document and the complexity of the main ideas or recommendations. Here is an example:

The following procedures will ensure a smooth transition to the new software:

• Management should designate a representative from each department to attend the training workshop provided by the vendor. This workshop will be offered on October 15. (Details will be provided later.)

- Each department should plan a training session for its employees to emphasize the department's use of the system.
- A two-week transition period should be allowed for converting from the old system.
- Troubleshooters should be available to all departments to solve any problems that occur.

Summary sentences are important in other places in a document, especially at the beginning of each section and in the conclusion.

Any paper that is longer than three or four paragraphs probably has more than one main idea or recommendation; each of these ideas is suggested in the introduction or in a separate summary section. Often, the logical way to organize the remainder of the document is to use a separate section of the paper to discuss each idea further. Each section should begin with a summary statement to identify the main idea, or the topic, of that section. The reader will then have a clear idea of what that section is about. It's a good idea to use somewhat different wording from that used in the beginning of the paper.

The principle we've been discussing sounds simple: Begin with your conclusion and then give your support. However, many writers have trouble putting this advice into practice. The difficulty may occur because this order of ideas is the reverse of the process writers go through to reach their conclusions. That is, the typical research process would be to gather information first and then to arrive at the conclusions. A writer might try to take the reader through the same investigative steps as those he or she used to solve the problem or answer the question.

Think about your readers' needs. They're mainly interested in the findings of your research, not in the process you went through to get there. They might want to read about the facts you considered as well as your analytical reasoning; in fact, some readers will carefully evaluate the soundness of your data and methodology. However, their first concern is with the conclusions.

Conclusions can be presented again in a concluding section, especially if the document is very long. Once again, you may need to remind the reader of your main ideas, but be careful not to sound repetitive. The length and complexity of the document determine how much detail to include in your conclusion.

RESPONDING TO READERS' QUESTIONS AND CONCERNS

Earlier chapters discussed planning a document so that it responds to your readers' concerns. That is, you anticipate questions they might have as well as objections they might raise to your recommendations.

As you plan the organization of your document, consider the best places to address these concerns. Questions are simple to handle: Anticipate where the readers are likely to have questions and answer them at that part of your paper.

For responses to objections, again, consider where in the document your readers are likely to raise objections, and if at all possible, respond at that part of your paper. Where you place your responses also depends on how many objections there are and how complicated your responses are. Sometimes responses to readers' concerns are better in a separate section of the paper. For example, suppose you are recommending a certain accounting treatment for a transaction, but you realize that your readers might disagree with you. The first part of the document might explain the reasons for your recommendation, and the final part of the document might explain the disadvantages of other treatments.

TRANSITIONS

Transitions, which are another element of coherent writing, link ideas together. They can be used between sentences, paragraphs, and major divisions of the document. Transitions show the relationship between two ideas: how the second idea flows logically from the first, and how both are related to the main idea of the entire document.

As an example of how transitions work, consider this paragraph. The topic sentence (main idea) is the first sentence; the transitional expressions are in italics:

> (1) Financial statements are important to a variety of users. (2) *First*, investors and potential investors use the statements to determine whether a company is a good investment risk. (3) These users look at such factors as net income, the debt-to-equity ratio, retained earnings, and economic value added (EVA). (4) *Second*, creditors use financial statements to determine whether a firm is a good credit risk. (5) Creditors want to know whether a firm's cash flow is large enough and sufficiently timely to pay its debts. (6) *Third*, government agencies analyze financial statements for a variety of purposes. (7) *For example*, the Internal Revenue Service wants to know whether the company has paid the required amount of taxes on its income. (8) These examples of financial statement users show how diverse their interests can be.

The sentences beginning *first* (2), *second* (4), and *third* (6) give three examples of the paragraph's main idea: the variety of financial statement users. These three sentences relate to one another in a logical, sequential way, which the transitions make clear. These sentences also relate directly to the topic sentence; they illustrate it with specific examples. Sentence 7, which begins with *for example*, relates only indirectly to the main idea of the paragraph, but it relates directly to sentence 6. Sentence 7 identifies one reason why government agencies need access to financial statements.

Transitions can express a number of relationships between ideas. In the sample paragraph, the transitions indicate an enumerated list (2, 4, and 6) and a specific illustration of a general statement (7). Transitions can also imply other relationships between ideas—conclusions, additional information, or contrasts, for example.

To see the importance of transitions within a paragraph, look at the following example, which lacks transitions:

> Incorporation offers several advantages to businesses and their owners. Ownership is easy to transfer. The business is able to maintain a continuous existence even when the original owners are no longer involved. The stockholders of a corporation are not held responsible for the business's debts. If the Dallas Corporation defaults on a $1,000,000 loan, its investors will not be held responsible for paying that liability. Incorporation enables a business to obtain professional managers with centralized authority and responsibility. The business can be run more efficiently. Incorporation gives a business certain legal rights. It can enter into contracts, own property, and borrow money.

Now see how much easier it is to read the paragraph when it has appropriate transitions:

> Incorporation offers several advantages to businesses and their owners. *For one thing*, ownership is easy to transfer, and the business is able to maintain a continuous existence even when the original owners are no longer involved. *In addition*, the stockholders of a corporation are not held responsible for the business's bad debts. If the Dallas Corporation defaults on a $1,000,000 loan, *for example*, its investors will not be held responsible for paying that liability. Incorporation *also* enables a business to obtain professional managers with centralized authority and responsibility; *therefore*, the business can be run more efficiently. *Finally*, incorporation gives a business certain legal rights. *For example*, it can enter into contracts, own property, and borrow money.

Transitional Words and Phrases

Following is a list of commonly used transitional expressions, their meanings, and example sentences showing how some of them work.

- **Adding a point or piece of information:** *and, also, in addition, moreover, furthermore, first/second/third, finally.*

  Example: We appreciate the opportunity to conduct your audit this year and will send you a detailed schedule of our work next week.

- **Making an exception or contrasting point:** *but, however, nevertheless, on the other hand, yet, still, on the contrary, in spite of . . . , nonetheless.*

  Example: Most of our divisions showed a profit his quarter. However, the Houston division was not so successful.

- **Giving specific examples or illustrations:** *for example, for instance, as an illustration, in particular, to illustrate.*

  Example: Financial statements serve a variety of users. For example, investors use them to evaluate potential investments. Other users include . . .

- **Clarifying a point:** *that is, in other words, in effect, put simply, stated briefly.*

  Example: The basic accounting equation is assets equal liabilities plus owners' equity. That is, A = L + OE.

- **Conceding a point to the opposite side:** *granted that, it may be true that, even though, although.*

  Example: Although upgrading our equipment will require a large capital outlay, increased efficiency will more than justify the use of funds.

- **Indicating place, time, or importance:**

  Place: *above, beside, beyond, to the right, below, around.*
  Time: *formerly, hitherto, earlier, in the past, before, at present, now, today, these days, tomorrow, in the future, next, later on, later.*
  Importance: *foremost, most importantly, especially, of less importance, of least importance.*

  Example: In earlier centuries there was no need for elaborate accounting systems. However, the size and complexities of today's businesses make modern accounting a complicated process indeed.

- **Indicating the stages in an argument or process, or the items in a series:** *initially, at the outset, to begin with, first, first of all, up to now, so far, second, thus far, next, after, finally, last.*

  Example: The accounting process works in stages. First, transactions must be analyzed.

- **Giving a result:**   *as a result, consequently, accordingly, as a consequence, therefore, thus, hence, then, for that reason.*

  Example: Generally accepted accounting principles allow flexibility in their application. Therefore, accountants are able to meet the changing needs of the business world.

- **Summing up or restating the central point:**   *in sum, to sum up, to summarize, in summary, to conclude, in brief, in short, as one can see, in conclusion.*

  Example: In conclusion, transitions often make writing much easier to read.

- **Adding emphasis:** *indeed, clearly*

  Example: Indeed, good writing skills are essential for professional success.

Repetition of Key Words and Phrases

Another way to add coherence to your writing is to repeat key words and phrases. Such repetitions are particularly useful for connecting paragraphs and major divisions of documents. These repetitions are typically located at the beginning of a new paragraph or section.

The following outline of a student's essay shows the structure of a discussion on alternatives to the historical cost basis of accounting. Notice how the combination of transitional expressions and repeated key phrases holds the report together. These techniques also tie the parts of the report to the main idea of the paper, which is summarized in the thesis statement. Notice how summary sentences appear throughout the outline.

THE MONETARY UNIT ASSUMPTION

I. Introductory paragraph

    A. Introductory sentences

        One of the basic assumptions made by accountants is that money is an effective common denominator by which the operations of business enterprises can be measured and analyzed. Implicit in this assumption is the acceptance of the stable and unchanging nature of the monetary unit. However, the validity of this assumption has been questioned not only by academicians and theorists, but by practitioners as well.

    B. Thesis statement (main idea of entire paper)

        Several solutions have been proposed by accountants to correct for the changing value of the monetary unit.

II. Body

    A. Nature of the problem

        The unadjusted monetary unit system has been criticized because it distorts financial statements during periods of inflation.

    B. First solution to the problem

        1. One solution to overstating profits solely because of inflation is to adjust figures for changes in the general purchasing power of the monetary unit. (This paragraph describes the solution and its advantages.)

        2. However, the general purchasing power approach has been criticized for several reasons. (This paragraph describes the disadvantages of this approach.)

    C. Second solution to the problem

        1. Instead of the general purchasing power procedure, some favor adjusting for changes in replacement cost. (This paragraph describes this solution.)

        2. One of the major advantages of the replacement cost approach . . . (This paragraph discusses several advantages.)

3. One authority has summarized the criticisms of replacement cost accounting: "Most of the criticisms . . . ." (This paragraph discusses the disadvantages of this approach.)

    D. Third solution to the problem

       1. Still others favor a mark-to-market (fair value) approach in which current exit values are used to value assets when possible.

       2. For certain assets, the FASB now requires the use of this approach. In general the advantages are . . .

       3. Critics of widespread use of this approach argue that . . .

  III. Concluding paragraph

Adjusting for changes in the general purchasing power, adjusting for changes in replacement cost, and the use of the mark-to-market (fair value) approach represent attempts to correct the problems of the stable monetary unit assumption in times of inflation.

Pronouns Used to Achieve Coherence

Another tool you can use to achieve coherent writing is the pronoun. A pronoun stands for a noun or a noun phrase that has previously been identified. The noun that the pronoun refers to is called its *antecedent*. Consider this sentence:

> Investors expect that, over time, their portfolios will increase in value.

In this sentence, the pronoun *their* refers to the noun *investors*. Put another way, *investors* is the antecedent of *their*.

Because pronouns refer to nouns that the writer has already used, pronouns help connect the thoughts of a paragraph. Look at how the pronouns work in this paragraph:

> The audit staff reviewed the financial statements of Western Manufacturing to determine whether the statements had been prepared in accordance with generally accepted accounting principles. *We* found two problems that may require *us* to issue a qualified opinion. First, Western has not been consistent in *its* treatment of accounts receivable. Second, *we* identified several transactions that may violate the matching principle. *We* suggest a meeting with Western's management to discuss these issues.

Pronouns require a word of warning, however. Unless a writer is careful, the reader may not be sure what noun the pronoun refers to. Look at the problem in this sentence:

> The managers told the accountants that they did not understand company policy.

Who didn't understand company policy—the managers or the accountants? This sentence illustrates the problem of ambiguous pronoun reference. Chapter 5 discusses this problem further.

Problems with Transitions

A few problems can occur with transitions other than the failure to use them when they are needed. One problem occurs when a writer uses transitional expressions too often. These expressions are necessary to make the relationship of ideas clear when there might be some confusion. Often this logical relationship is clear without the use of transitional expressions. Consider this paragraph:

> Accountants never finish their education. They work hard for their college degrees; after college they must continue studying to stay current on the latest developments in the profession. They must be thoroughly familiar with changing government regulations and new pronouncements by professional organizations such as the FASB. To improve their professional competence, they participate in a variety of continuing education programs sponsored by such organizations as the AICPA and state accounting societies. Well-qualified accountants are lifetime students, always seeking better ways to serve their clients and the public.

Notice how easy this paragraph is to follow, even though it doesn't use a single transitional expression.

Another problem with transitions occurs when the writer uses the wrong expression, suggesting an illogical connection of ideas. Consider these examples:

FAULTY TRANSITION: GAAP are not established by federal law. For instance, organizations such as the FASB issue these standards, and the FASB is not part of the federal government.

REVISED: GAAP are not established by federal law. Rather, organizations that are not part of the federal government, such as the FASB, issue these standards.

FAULTY TRANSITION: If accountants do not follow GAAP, they may lose their CPA licenses. Therefore, they must follow GAAP to conform to their code of professional ethics.

REVISED: If accountants do not follow GAAP, they may lose their CPA licenses. They must also follow GAAP to conform to their code of professional ethics.

Transitions, when used correctly, are valuable tools for clarifying the relationship between ideas. If you use transitions carefully, along with summary sentences and a logical organization, your writing will be easy to follow.

The next sections of this chapter show how to use these techniques to write coherent paragraphs, discussion questions, essays, and other longer forms of writing.

PARAGRAPHS

This section of the chapter is devoted to techniques of paragraphing: how to plan length, structure, and development so that your paragraphs are coherent.

Length

You might not be sure how long paragraphs should be. Are one-sentence paragraphs acceptable? What about paragraphs that run on for nearly an entire typed page?

One rule is that a paragraph should be limited to the development of one idea. Thus, the length of most paragraphs is somewhere between one sentence and an entire page. However, an occasional short paragraph, even of only one sentence, can be effective to emphasize an idea or to provide a transition between two major divisions of the writing.

Be wary of long paragraphs, which look intimidating and are often hard to follow. You may need to divide a long paragraph into two or more shorter ones. Appropriate transitions can tie the new paragraphs together and maintain a smooth flow of thought.

A good guideline is to limit most of your paragraphs to four or five sentences.

Structure

Another feature of well-written paragraphs is an appropriate structure. We have already suggested that a strong topic sentence can contribute to a unified, coherent paragraph. A topic sentence states the main idea of the paragraph. It is usually the first sentence in the paragraph, and sometimes contains a transition tying the new paragraph to the previous one. All other sentences in the paragraph should develop the idea expressed in the topic sentence.

Two patterns of paragraph organization are useful for most writing tasks that accountants will tackle: the simple deductive paragraph and the complex deductive paragraph. The simple deductive arrangement states the main idea in the first sentence (topic sentence); all other sentences *directly* develop that idea by adding details. A concluding sentence is sometimes helpful. Look again at this paragraph, which illustrates a simple deductive organization:

(1) Accountants never finish their education. (2) They work hard for their college degrees, but after college they must continue studying to stay current on the latest developments in the profession. (3) They must be thoroughly familiar with changing government regulations and new pronouncements by professional organizations such as the FASB. (4) To improve their professional competence, they participate in a variety

of continuing education programs sponsored by such organizations as the AICPA and state accounting societies. (5) Well-qualified accountants are lifetime students, always seeking better ways to serve their clients and the public.

In this paragraph, sentence 1 is the topic sentence, sentences 2 through 4 develop the main idea, and sentence 5 is the conclusion. A simple deductive paragraph has a simple structure such as this one:

1. Topic sentence—main idea
   2. Supporting sentence
   3. Supporting sentence
   4. Supporting sentence
5. Concluding sentence (optional)

A complex deductive paragraph has a more elaborate structure. This paragraph is complex deductive:

(1) Financial statements are important to a variety of users. (2) First, investors and potential investors use the statements to determine whether a company is a good investment risk. (3) These users look at such factors as net income, the debt-to-equity ratio, retained earnings, and economic value added (EVA). (4) Second, creditors use financial statements to determine whether a firm is a good credit risk. (5) Creditors want to know whether a firm has a timely and large enough cash flow to pay its debts. (6) Third, government agencies analyze financial statements for a variety of purposes. (7) For example, the Internal Revenue Service wants to know whether the company has paid the required amount of taxes on its income. (8) These examples of financial statement users show how diverse their interests can be.

In this paragraph, sentence 1 (the topic sentence) states the main idea. Sentence 2 directly supports the main idea by giving an example, but sentence 3 explains sentence 2. Thus, sentence 3 directly supports sentence 2, but only indirectly supports sentence 1. Complex deductive paragraphs have a structure similar to this one:

1. Topic sentence—main idea
   2. Direct support
      3. Indirect support
   4. Direct support
      5. Indirect support
   6. Direct support
      7. Indirect support
8. Conclusion (optional)

Complex deductive paragraphs can have numerous variations. The number of direct supporting sentences can vary, as can the number of indirect supports. Sometime direct supports do not require any indirect supports.

Consider another example of a complex deductive paragraph:

(1) Two of the most popular inventory flow assumptions used by busi-nesses today are FIFO (first-in, first-out) and LIFO (last-in, first-out). (2) FIFO assumes that the first goods purchased for inventory are the first goods sold. (3) Therefore, ending inventory under FIFO consists of the most recent purchases. (4) Because older, usually lower costs are matched with sales revenues, FIFO results in a higher net income and thus higher income tax liabilities. (5) The LIFO flow assumption, on the other hand, assumes that the most recent purchases are the first goods sold. (6) Cost of goods sold, however, is based on more recent and higher prices. (7) Thus, LIFO usually results in lower net income and lower income tax liabilities. (8) This advantage makes LIFO very popular with many businesses.

This paragraph can be outlined to reveal the following structure:

I. Topic sentence (1): Two popular inventory flow assumptions
  A. FIFO (2–4)
    1. Description (2)
    2. Effect on inventory (3)
    3. Effect on net income and taxes (4)
  B. LIFO (5-8)
    1. Description (5)
    2. Effect on inventory (6)
    3. Effect on net income and taxes (7)
    4. Popularity (8)

The descriptions of FIFO and LIFO in this paragraph are very condensed, probably too condensed for most purposes. Moreover, the paragraph is really too long. It would probably be better to divide it between sentences 4 and 5, resulting in two shorter but closely related paragraphs:

(1) Two of the most popular inventory flow assumptions used by busi-nesses today are FIFO (first-in, first-out) and LIFO (last-in, first-out). (2) FIFO assumes that the first goods purchased for inventory are the first goods sold. (3) Therefore, ending inventory under FIFO consists of the most recent purchases. (4) Because older, usually lower costs are matched with sales revenues, FIFO results in a higher net income and thus higher income tax liabilities.

(5) The LIFO flow assumption, on the other hand, assumes that the most recent purchases are the first goods sold. (6) Cost of goods sold, however, is based on more recent and higher prices. (7) Thus, LIFO usually results in lower net income and lower income tax liabilities. (8) This advantage makes LIFO very popular with many businesses.

Both paragraphs now have simple deductive structures. However, the first paragraph is a modified version of a simple deductive structure because the main idea of this paragraph is in the second sentence.

The important idea about both simple and complex deductive paragraphs is their unity: All sentences, either directly or indirectly, develop the main idea of the paragraph as expressed in the topic sentence.

One advantage of deductive paragraphs is that they enable a reader to skim the document quickly and locate main ideas. A busy CEO, for example, may scan a document, reading only the first sentence of each paragraph.

Some writers might wonder about a third type of paragraph organization: paragraphs with an inductive structure. Inductive paragraphs put the main idea last. Supporting sentences lead up to the topic sentence, which is the last sentence in the paragraph. For most business writing, inductive paragraphs are not as effective as simple or complex deductive paragraphs. Business readers like to identify main ideas from the start. They don't like to be kept in suspense, wondering, "What's all this leading up to? What's the point?" Thus, it's a good idea to stick with deductive organization for most, if not all, of your paragraphs.

Paragraph Development

An effective paragraph not only is well organized, but also is well developed. That is, the idea expressed in the topic sentence is adequately explained and illustrated so that the reader has a clear understanding of what the writer is saying.

Several techniques are useful for paragraph development: descriptive and factual details, illustrations or examples, definitions, and appeals to authority.

Descriptive and factual details give a more thorough, concrete explanation of the idea that is expressed in a general way in the topic sentence. Factual details give measurable, observable, or historical information that can be objectively verified. Descriptive details are similar to factual details. They give specific characteristics of the subject being discussed.

When you use details with which your readers are familiar, they can better understand your observations and conclusions. In the following paragraph, the main idea is stated in the first sentence. The paragraph is then developed with factual details:

> Our net income for next year should increase because we've signed a contract with an important new customer. Flip's Frog Ponds, Inc., which last year had more than $4 billion in revenue, has ordered a million lily pads from our horticultural division. This new business should increase our revenues by at least 15%.

Another useful paragraph development technique is using illustrations or examples—typical cases or specific instances of the idea being discussed. Illustrations can take a variety of forms. A paragraph might combine several brief examples, or use one long, extended illustration. The examples can be factually true, or they may be hypothetical, invented for the purpose of illustration.

Definitions are useful to explain concepts or terms that might be unfamiliar to the reader. A definition can be formal, such as the meaning given in a dictionary or an accounting standard, or it can be a more informal explanation of a term. Often a definition is more effective when combined with an illustration.

The following paragraph is developed by definition and illustration:

> *Assets* can be defined as things of value (economic resources) owned by a business. For example, cash is an asset; so are the land, buildings, and equipment owned by a business. Sometimes assets are resources owned by a business, though not tangible. An example of this kind of asset is an account receivable.

Finally, some paragraphs are developed by appeals to authority—facts, illustrations, or ideas obtained from a reputable source such as a book, article, interview, or official pronouncement. Appeals to authority can be paraphrases—someone else's idea expressed in your own words—or direct quotations from the source being used. Chapter 8 gives more information on the correct use of quotations and paraphrases.

By using a variety of techniques, you can fully develop the ideas expressed in the topic sentences of your paragraphs. Factual and descriptive detail, illustration, definition, and authority all give the reader a clear understanding of what you want to explain.

However you decide to develop your paragraphs, remember the importance of your reader's interests and needs. It's better to select supporting details and examples with which the reader is already familiar.

ORGANIZING ANSWERS TO DISCUSSION QUESTIONS AND ESSAYS

A section about the organization of answers to discussion questions and essays might seem too academic for a writing handbook for accountants, but many accounting students take exams with discussion questions. In addition, many of the principles of organizing and developing an essay are applicable to memos, reports, and other types of writing used by accountants in practice.

Responding to essay or discussion questions contained on professional exams such as the CPA exam or the CMA exam is covered more fully in Chapter 13.

Discussion Questions

The key to answering a short discussion question (usually one to three paragraphs) is to write well-organized deductive paragraphs with strong topic sentences. Usually, the question suggests the first sentence of the answer. Consider this example:

> Discuss the sources of authoritative accounting principles.

The answer to this discussion question might begin with the following sentence, which gives the main idea of the answer:

> Authoritative accounting principles derive from many sources.

The answer might then go on to discuss accounting principles promulgated by the FASB and its predecessor organizations. A second paragraph might then discuss accounting principles promulgated by the SEC and other governmental agencies. Finally, a third paragraph might discuss other less authoritative sources such as textbooks and articles in professional accounting publications. The third paragraph might begin with this topic sentence:

> Although less authoritative, textbooks and articles in professional accounting publications can also be important.

Short paragraphs with strong topic sentences, as in the answer outlined in the preceding paragraphs, will help the exam grader identify your main ideas and give you credit for what you know.

Essays

Before you read this section, review the discussion of paragraph structure on pages 44–47. Pay particular attention to the complex deductive pattern of organization.

Complex deductive paragraphs have a main idea (topic sentence) supported by major and minor supports.

Answers to essay questions—which usually are composed of four or more paragraphs—are similar to answers to discussion questions in their use of a deductive structure, with a few modifications. One difference is that the organization of an essay is complex deductive, in that it uses both major and minor supports of the essay's main idea (thesis statement). That is, the essay's paragraphs offer direct support of the thesis. The sentences within each paragraph develop the topic sentence of the paragraph and thereby indirectly support the thesis.

Another difference between an essay and a response to a discussion question is that the thesis statement (main idea of the essay) may come at the end of the first paragraph, in which case it may be preceded by sentences that give background on the topic or otherwise interest the reader in what is being discussed. Finally, the conclusion of an essay may be longer and more complex than the conclusion of a discussion question response.

Below is the outline of a six-paragraph essay.

I. Introduction—first paragraph
    A. Attention-getting sentences (optional)
    B. Thesis statement—main idea of the essay, usually expressed in one sentence

II. Body of the essay—develops the thesis through analysis, explanation, examples, proofs, or steps.
    A. Major support—second paragraph
        1.
        2.   Minor supports—sentences that develop the paragraph in a simple or complex deductive organization
        3.
    B. Major support—third paragraph
        1.
        2.   Minor supports
        3.
    C. Major support—fourth paragraph
        1.
        2.   Minor supports
        3.
    D. Major support—fifth paragraph
        1.
        2.   Minor supports
        3.

III. Conclusion—sixth paragraph
    A. Repeats the essay's main idea (a variation of the thesis statement) or otherwise provides closure
    B. Forceful ending (optional)

Some of the parts of this outline need more discussion.

Attention-Getting Sentences
Some essays begin with attention-getting sentences, which are intended to get the reader interested in the subject. Several techniques can be used:

- Give background information about the topic. Why is the topic of current interest?
- Pose a problem or raise a question (to be answered in the essay).
- Define key terms, perhaps the topic itself.
- Show the relevance of the topic to the reader.
- Begin with an interesting direct quotation.
- Relate a brief anecdote relevant to the topic.
- Relate the specific topic to a wider area of interest.

The following essay introduction uses two of these techniques. It poses a question and then suggests the relevance of the topic to the reader, assuming that the essay was written for accountants. The final sentence of the paragraph is the thesis statement.

> Do accountants need to be good writers? Some people would answer "No" to this question. They believe an accountant's job is limited to arithmetical calculations and computer applications with very little need to use words or sentences. But this picture of an accountant's responsibilities is a misconception. In fact, good writing skills are essential to the successful practice of accounting.

Sometimes you might choose not to use attention-getting sentences, but decide instead to begin your essay with the thesis statement. This is a particularly good strategy to use for exam questions.

Thesis Statement

The thesis statement summarizes the main idea of the essay, usually in one sentence. It can be a *simple* thesis statement, such as the following:

> Good writing skills are essential to the successful practice of accounting.

Alternatively, the thesis statement can be expanded. That is, it can summarize the main supports of the discussion. Here is an example of an expanded thesis statement:

> In fact, successful accountants must have good writing skills to communicate with clients, managers, agencies, and colleagues.

Sometimes, to avoid a long or awkward sentence, you might want to use two sentences for the thesis statement:

> In fact, good writing skills are essential to the successful practice of accounting. During a typical business day, an accountant may write to clients, managers, agencies, or colleagues.

Conclusion

The conclusion should provide the reader with a sense of closure—a feeling that the essay is complete, and that the train of thought has come to a logical end. You can give your essays closure by repeating the main idea, usually in some variation of the thesis statement. You may also want to end with a forceful statement that will stay in the reader's mind, thus giving the discussion a more lasting impact. For a strong ending, you can use several techniques, many of which resemble those used in the introduction:

- Show a broad application of the ideas suggested in the discussion.
- End with an authoritative direct quotation that reinforces your position.
- Challenge the reader.
- Echo the attention-getting sentences. For example, if you began by posing a question in the introduction, you can answer it explicitly in the conclusion.

If you're writing an essay on an exam, a concluding paragraph might not be necessary, but it's important that the essay seem finished. The essay will seem complete if you've developed your thesis statement fully.

Applying Essay Techniques to Other Kinds of Writing

If you are answering an essay question on an exam, you can use the techniques just discussed to organize and develop an effective discussion. Chapter 13, which discusses essay exams more fully, provides additional suggestions. But how do the techniques you use for essays work with the writing formats more typically used by accountants (letters, memos, and reports)?

Everything you write should have a main idea. In an essay, this idea is called the thesis statement; in a memo or report, the main idea might be included in the statement of purpose or recommendations. Whatever you're writing, you should identify the main idea before you even begin your outline. Unless this idea is clear in your mind—or clearly written in your notes—your writing may be rambling and confusing. Your reader might then wonder, "What's this person trying to say? What's the point?"

Whatever you write should be organized around a central idea, just as an essay is organized. Letters, reports, and memos share other features of an essay as well: a basic three-part structure (introduction, body, conclusion), complex deductive organization, and the need for adequate transitions and concrete support.

If you understand the principles discussed in this chapter, you will find it easier to plan and organize the writing tasks that are part of your professional responsibilities.

Sample Essay

The following is an assignment for an essay given in an accounting class. The answer in Figure 3–1 illustrates some of the principles of good organization and development.

Assignment. The International Accounting Standards Board (IASB) is responsible for the development of a set of international accounting standards. Explain in 300-500 words why the development of international accounting standards may be important.

This chapter has added four guidelines to our list of ways to make your writing more effective. We now have seven guidelines:

1. Analyze the purpose of the writing, the accounting issues involved, and the needs and expectations of the readers.
2. Organize your ideas so that readers will find them easy to follow.
3. Write the draft and then revise it to make the writing polished and correct.

FIGURE 3–1   Example of an Essay

The Importance of International Accounting Standards

The need for international accounting standards has received great attention since the late 1980s. This attention is due to the expanding globalization of business and capital markets. When different countries have different business regulations and use different accounting methods, the increased complexity of conducting business and raising capital across national borders presents major challenges. By analogy, consider how difficult the reporting process in our own country would be if each of the 50 states employed different business regulations and a different set of accounting standards. Clearly, in such a case our capital markets as reflected by the activities of the New York Stock Exchange (NYSE) and NASDAQ could not operate as efficiently or robustly as they now do. Indeed, the need for international accounting standards has become more important in recent years.

If investors in international capital markets must make investment choices among corporations that use different accounting standards, competing investment opportunities become less comparable and much more risky. The result is likely to be that fewer investors will undertake the effort or assume the risk of investing in foreign corporations or in corporations that have a lot of foreign holdings. Consequently, fewer corporations may list their securities on a foreign exchange. Ultimately, such difficulties could seriously impede the expansion of international capital markets and the development of more healthy international economies.

The International Accounting Standards Board (IASB) has been responsible for setting international standards since 2001. Together with its predecessor, the International Accounting Standards Committee (IASC), these two organizations have issued numerous International Accounting Standards (IASs) and International Financial Reporting Standards (IFRSs). Through its efforts the IASB hopes to achieve convergence of international financial reporting standards.

Most international accounting organizations, securities exchanges, and governments support this effort to harmonize standards. Several of the world's securities exchanges either permit or require compliance with IASs and IFRSs by their registrants. The International Organization of Securities Commissions (IOSCO) and the Organization for Economic Cooperation and Development (OECD) cooperate with the IASB in its development of international financial reporting standards. The European Union has accepted the international standards issued by the IASC and the IASB for its member countries.

Although the prospect for uniform financial reporting standards among all countries is not realistic, reducing differences through the concept of harmonization is clearly a worthwhile goal.

4. Make the writing unified. All sentences should relate to the main idea, either directly or indirectly. Eliminate digressions and irrelevant detail.

5. Use summary sentences and transitions to make your writing coherent.

6. Write in short paragraphs that begin with clear topic sentences.

7. Develop paragraphs by illustration, definition, detail, and appeals to authority.

TEST YOURSELF

Is the following paragraph coherent? If not, revise it to improve its organization, using some of these techniques:

- Write a strong topic sentence stating the paragraph's main idea.
- Use transitional devices to show the relation between sentences.
- Eliminate sentences that don't fit.
- Divide long, disunified paragraphs into shorter, unified ones.
- Rearrange sentences by grouping ideas together (add sentences if necessary).

> Accountants used to enter data into spreadsheets by hand. Accountants performed calculations by hand, and they had adding machines. Much of the work accountants did in the past was tedious and time consuming. Computers have drastically changed the practice of accounting. If accountants made errors, accountants would have to erase the mistakes with chemicals that would dissolve the ink. These chemicals could stain their clothes and sometimes irritate their skin and make their desks messy.

TEST YOURSELF: ANSWER

This paragraph needs revision. Here is one possibility:

> Computers have drastically changed the practice of accounting in the past few decades. In the past, accountants performed calculations by hand, or perhaps with the help of adding machines. They entered data into spreadsheets by hand; if they made errors in their entries, they would have to erase the mistakes with chemicals that dissolved the ink, or they would have to enter the data again from the beginning. These examples suggest that much of the work accountants did in the past was tedious and time consuming.

EXERCISES

Exercise 3–1 [General]

Some of the following paragraphs are effectively organized, but some lack unity and/or coherence. Analyze the paragraphs to decide which ones need revision. Then revise the faulty paragraphs, using some of these techniques.

- Write a strong topic sentence stating the paragraph's main idea.
- Use transitional devices to show the relation between sentences.
- Eliminate sentences that don't fit.
- Divide long, disunified paragraphs into shorter, unified ones.
- Rearrange sentences by grouping ideas together (add sentences if necessary).

1. Government accountants help national, state, and local governments control spending and budgeting. Government spending could run rampant. Governmental accounting is similar to industrial accounting in many of its functions. Government accountants help prevent the government from wasting taxpayers' money.

2. One service that public accountants perform is auditing. Accountants examine clients' financial statements to see if they are in conformity with generally accepted accounting principles. Accountants give credibility to financial statements. Public accountants offer management consulting services. Management consultants suggest ways firms can improve such functions as information processing, budgeting, and accounting systems. Taxes are an increasingly complex area. Accountants prepare and file returns and advise clients how to incur the smallest tax liability on a transaction.

3. Many corporations can benefit from convertible debt. Firms should be aware of the hardships that may arise from conversion or non-conversion. Firms should be aware that accounting requirements may impose potentially unfavorable effects on earnings per share. Corporations want to obtain low-cost funds now and desire also to increase their equity in the future.

4. Although the purchase of our supplier's stock may offer us several advantages, there are also some potential problems we should consider. For one thing, we may not always need the supplier's raw material, because we may not always manufacture the product that requires this material. And even if we continue to manufacture our product, our research and development staff may discover a cheaper, synthetic raw material. Finally, if we do purchase the stock but later need to resell it, we cannot be assured that the stock will be marketable at that time.

Exercise 3–2 [General]

Write a sentence outline for one of the following topics. Assume the outline is for a report that you are preparing for your client, Eleanor Johnson. Eleanor is the owner/manager of a small jewelry store with 10 employees. She is astute about business matters, but she has little training in accounting.

Include in your outline a sentence stating the main idea or purpose of the report. Divide your subject into logical subtopics, stating in a sentence the main idea of each division. Finally, show the transitional devices you would use to tie the report together. (For a model outline, see page 50 of this chapter.)

Topics:

1. How to reconcile a bank statement.
2. Internal control for cash in Eleanor Johnson's store.
3. Possible causes for low inventory turnover in the store's china department. (Invent some possible causes for this hypothetical situation.)

Exercise 3–3 [Financial]

Write about the following topics using the techniques covered in this and earlier chapters. Your answers might range from one to six paragraphs or more, depending on the topic.

1. Discuss how to test for impairment of intangible assets with indefinite lives under FASB standards.
2. Discuss the role of the International Integrated Reporting Council (IIRC) in the future development of corporate reporting.
3. Define *fair value accounting* and discuss the pros and cons of its use.
4. Explain the difference between revenues and gains.
5. Explain the differences between depreciation, amortization, and depletion.
6. Discuss the importance of convergence in the context of establishing International Financial Reporting Standards (IFRSs) as well as the pros and cons of adopting IFRSs in the United States.

Exercise 3–4 [Systems]

Write about the following topics using the techniques covered in this and earlier chapters. Your answers might range from one to six paragraphs or more, depending on the topic.

1. Explain the two approaches to database design, normalization and semantic data modeling.
2. A database can view data in either a physical view or a logical view. Explain each of these views and when each may be useful.
3. Explain what COBIT is and the benefits of its use.
4. Explain the Systems Development Life Cycle, which describes the design and implementation of an information system. What role do accountants play in this cycle?
5. Explain and discuss the use of cloud computing to improve systems efficiency.

Exercise 3–5 [Managerial]

Write about the following topics using the techniques covered in this and earlier chapters. Your answers might range from one to six paragraphs or more, depending on the topic.

1. Discuss the purpose of the IMA (the Association of Accountants and Financial Professionals in Business), which was formerly known as the Institute of Management Accountants.
2. Discuss why ethics is important in managerial accounting.
3. Discuss the function of Financial Executives International (FEI).
4. Discuss the Certified Management Accountant (CMA) certification process including what the CMA is, how it differs from the CPA, and what the benefits of acquiring the designation may be.
5. Define internal control and discuss its importance.

Exercise 3–6 [Auditing/Current Professional Issues]

Write about the following topics using the techniques covered in this and earlier chapters. Your answers might range from one to six paragraphs or more, depending on the topic.

1. Discuss the pros and cons of requiring audit firm rotation and shareholder ratification of audit firms.
2. Discuss the role of the National Peer Review Committee (NPRC), which was formally known as the Center for Public Company Audit Firms Peer Review Program (CPCAFPRP).
3. Discuss what the consequences may be if the Public Company Accounting Oversight Board (PCAOB) finds significant performance deficiencies during its inspection of an audit firm.
4. Discuss the controversy of whether to allow major auditing firms to also operate a consulting practice.

Exercise 3–7 [Tax]

Write about the following topics using the techniques covered in this and earlier chapters. Your purpose is to provide a very general explanation to readers who have never heard of these terms or topics. Your answers might range from one to six paragraphs or more, depending on the topic.

1. Discuss the concepts of *dependency exemption* and *personal exemption* as they apply to the income tax of individuals.
2. Discuss the concept of *constructive receipt* as it applies to the income tax of individuals.
3. Discuss the American Opportunity Tax Credit and the Lifetime Learning Credit, including the requirements of these credits.

4. For individual tax purposes, why is the distinction between deductions *for* adjusted gross income and deductions *from* adjusted gross income important?

5. Discuss the Foreign Account Tax Compliance Act (FATCA). Include an explanation of its requirements and a discussion of its objectives.

CHAPTER

A Sense of Style: Writing with Conciseness and Clarity

So far we've looked at writing mainly as an organizational task: planning the structure and contents of the paper so that it achieves its purpose in a way readers will find meaningful. We have stressed the quality of coherence: writing that is easy to follow, with main ideas that stand out. Chapters 2 and 3 looked at writing in terms of large units—the document as a whole as well as sections and paragraphs.

We turn now to a more detailed level of effective writing. This chapter looks at word choices and sentence structures that contribute to a vigorous and readable writing style. In this discussion of style, we emphasize two other important qualities of effective writing: conciseness and clarity (two of the writing tips listed in Figure 1–2 in Chapter 1).

CONCISENESS

Readers prefer concise writing so they can find the information they need quickly and easily. Chapter 3 showed how to make your writing more concise by eliminating digressions and irrelevant detail. In general, concise writing contains no unnecessary elements—no extra words, phrases, sentences, or paragraphs. This makes up the eighth rule of effective writing:

Be concise—make every word count.

Unnecessary Words

The easiest way to make every word count is to see how many words you can cross out of your writing, often with only a simple revision of the sentence. These examples show how sentences can be revised to eliminate unnecessary words:

WORDY: Participants in the audit of XYZ Company found a large number of weaknesses in the system of internal control of the company. [22 words]

CONCISE: The auditors found many weaknesses in XYZ's internal controls. [9 words]

WORDY: It is my understanding that a good number of our new employees are using their company email accounts for communicating with their friends and family. [25 words]

CONCISE: Many of our new employees are using company email accounts for personal communication. [13 words]

WORDY: We hope the entire staff will help us in our attempts to use less energy. [15 words]

CONCISE: We hope the entire staff will help us use less energy. [11 words]

WORDY: Forecasts for profits for the coming year range all the way from $300,000 to upwards of $500,000. [17 words]

CONCISE: Next year's profit forecasts range from $300,000 to $500,000. [9 words]

WORDY: To stay informed on the latest information, accountants must read a great number of published materials about accounting. [18 words]

CONCISE: To stay current, accountants must read many accounting publications. [9 words]

WORDY: In order to reach our tax liability reduction goals, we changed the way we accounted for the purchase. [18 words]

CONCISE: To reduce our tax liability, we changed the way we accounted for the purchase. [14 words]

Watch out for *there is* and *there are*. They can usually be eliminated. *The fact that*, *which is*, *who is*, and *which are* can sometimes be left out as well:

WORDY: His partner, who is an engineer, reviewed the plans. [9 words]

CONCISE: His partner, an engineer, reviewed the plans. [7 words]

WORDY: There are several strategic planning strategies that we can use to reduce our income taxes. [15 words]

CONCISE: We can reduce our income taxes through strategic planning. [9 words]

WORDY: I would like to call your attention to the fact that we have a staff meeting scheduled for next Wednesday. [20 words]

CONCISE: Remember our staff meeting scheduled for next Wednesday. [8 words]

or (even better)

Remember next Wednesday's staff meeting. [5 words]

WORDY: In spite of the fact that our costs rose by 10%, we still were able to keep our prices stable. [20 words]

CONCISE: Although costs rose by 10%, our prices remained stable. [9 words]

Simplicity

Another way to make your writing concise is to write as simply as possible. Sometimes writers get into the habit of using big words and long, complicated sentences. Such writing is hard to read.

SEC Commissioner Cynthia A. Glassman has offered this example of a footnote disclosure that is almost impossible to understand[1]:

> Any interest collections on the loans remaining after payments of interest on the notes and the company's expenses will be available to cover any losses on the loans that are not covered by the insurance policies.

Glassman has suggested this translation into plain English:

> After we pay our expenses and interest on the notes, we will use any remaining funds to cover uninsured losses.

For an example of simple, clear writing, review the narrative description of a payroll processing system shown in Figure 1–3 (page 7). Notice how the choice of familiar, simple words makes the narrative easy to understand. The narrative's sentences, which are mostly short and always clear, also contribute to the document's effectiveness.

The ninth technique for effective writing style is simplicity.

Keep it simple—simple vocabulary and short sentences.

Good writers use short, everyday words as much as possible. For example, they may write *use* instead of *utilize* and *help* instead of *assistance*. Shorter, familiar words are easier to read and make writing more forceful.

Table 4–1 shows two columns of words. Column B lists short, familiar words; Column A lists longer, more difficult words that are often substituted for the everyday words in Column B. The table also shows how single words (*because*) can often replace phrases (*for the reason that*). As a general rule, use the words and phrases in Column B rather than those in Column A. Some of the terms in Column A can be omitted (such as *it should be noted that*).

Another way to achieve a simple, readable style is to use short sentences. Short sentences are particularly important when you are explaining complicated ideas.

The average sentence should be about 15 words long.

TABLE 4–1 Simplifying Word Choices

As a rule, use the words and phrases in Column B rather than those in Column A.

Column A	Column B
above-mentioned firms	these firms
absolutely essential	essential
activate	begin
advise	tell
aggregate	total
along the lines of	like
anticipate	expect
as per your request	as you requested
assist	help
at all times	always
at this point in time	now
at this time	now
attempt	try
commence	begin
communicate	write, tell
completely eliminated	eliminated
comprise	include
consider	think
constitute	are, is
discontinue	stop
disutility	uselessness
due to the fact that	because
during the time that	while
earliest convenience	promptly, soon
effort	work
enclosed herewith	enclosed
enclosed please find	enclosed is
endeavor	try
exercise care	be careful
facilitate	ease, simplify
failed to	didn't
few in number	few
for the purpose of	for
for the reason that	since, because
from the point of view that	for
furnish	send, give
i.e.	that is
implement	carry out
in advance of	before
in all cases	always
in many cases	often
in most cases	usually
in behalf of	for
in connection with	about
in terms of	in
in the amount of	of, for
in the case of	if
in the event that (of)	if
in the nature of	like

(cont.)

TABLE 4–1   *(cont.)*

Column A	Column B
in the neighborhood of	about
in this case	here
indicate	show, point out
initiate	begin
in view of the fact that	because
inasmuch as	since
investigate	study
it has come to my attention	Ms. Jones has just told me; I have just learned
it is felt	I feel; wc feel
it is our understanding that	we understand that
it should be noted that	(omit)
maintain	keep
maintain cost control	control cost
make a purchase	buy
make application to	apply to
make contact with	scc, meet
maximum	most, largest
minimum	least, smallest
modification	change
obtain	get
on the order of	about
on the part of	by
optimum	best
past history	history
per annum	annually, per year
period of time	time, period
pertaining to	about, for
philosophy	plan, idea
please be advised that	(omit)
prepare an analysis	analyze
presently	now
prior to	before
procure	get, buy
provide	give
provide continuous indication	indicate continuously
pursuant to your inquiry	as you requested
range all the way from	range from
regarding	about
relative to	about
represent	be, is, are
require	need
so as to	to
subsequent to	after, later
substantial	large, big
sufficient	enough
terminate	end, stop
the major part of	most of
the manner in which	how
the undersigned; the writer	I, me
thereon, thereof, thereto, therefrom	(omit)

(cont.)

TABLE 4–1 (*cont.*)	
Column A	**Column B**
this is to acknowledge	thank you for; I have received
this is to inform you that we shall send	we'll send
through the use of	by, with
transpire	happen
true facts	facts
under separate cover	by June 1, tomorrow, separately, by parcel post
until such time as	until
utilize	use
vital	important
with a view to	to
with reference to	about
with regard to	about
with respect to	on, for, of, about
with the object to	to
with the result that	so that

Note that 15 words is an *average*. Some sentences are longer, some shorter. In fact, it's a good idea to vary sentence lengths so that the writing doesn't become monotonous. Sentence variation will be discussed again later in this chapter.

Verbs and Nouns

Another way to make your writing more concise is to use active verbs and descriptive nouns, rather than lots of adverbs and adjectives. The tenth rule of effective writing is

> ***Write with active verbs and descriptive nouns.***

See how this sentence can be improved:

WORDY: There are many positive advantages to making investments in the latest state-of-the-art technology. [16 words]

CONCISE: State-of-the-art technology offers many advantages. [8 words]

One common cause of wordy writing is hidden verbs. For example,

> *came to a conclusion that* instead of *concluded*
> *causes a misstatement of* instead of *misstates*
> *makes an analysis of* instead of *analyzes*
> *will serve as an explanation of* instead of *will explain*

What are the hidden verbs in the following sentences?

> The auditors came to the conclusion that the financial statements were not complete.
> Johnson made reference to the new tax laws to support his recommendation.

In the first sentence, the hidden verb is *concluded*; in the second sentence, it is *referred*. The revised sentences are a little less wordy, a little more forceful:

> The auditors concluded that the company's financial statements were incomplete.
> Johnson referred to the new tax laws to support his recommendation.
> *or*
> Johnson supported his recommendation by referring to the new tax law.

Here are some other sentences with hidden verbs, followed by revisions to make them more concise:

HIDDEN VERB: After we study the department's needs, we will be able to make a recommendation of the best system to put in place. [22 words]

REVISED: After we study the department's needs, we can recommend the best system to put in place. [16 words]

HIDDEN VERB: The partners have made a decision that the firm should broaden its client base. [14 words]

REVISED: The partners have decided that the firm should broaden its client base. [12 words]
> *or (even better)*
The partners have decided to broaden the firm's client base. [10 words]

HIDDEN VERB: The IT specialist made an analysis of the department's computer problems. [11 words]

REVISED: The IT specialist analyzed the department's computer problems. [8 words]

HIDDEN VERB: This method will result in a distribution of the costs between the balance sheet and the income statement. [18 words]

REVISED: This method will distribute the costs between the balance sheet and the income statement. [14 words]

HIDDEN VERB: We are able to make the determination of the historical cost of this equipment due to the fact that we have records of its purchase. [25 words]

REVISED: We can determine this equipment's historical cost because we have records of its purchase. [14 words]

Finally, avoid sentence introductions that weaken the sentence idea. Don't apologize for or hedge about what you're saying:

WORDY: It has come to my attention that we need additional staff for this audit. [14 words]

CONCISE: We need additional staff for this audit. [7 words]

WORDY: I am writing this letter in an attempt to explain how to improve your tax planning. [16 words]

CONCISE: This letter will explain how to improve your tax planning. [10 words]

WORDY: Enclosed please find our invoice for $400. [7 words]
CONCISE: Our invoice for $400 is enclosed. [6 words]

WORDY: This is to acknowledge receipt of your letter of June 1. [11 words]
CONCISE: Thank you for your letter of June 1. [8 words]

WORDY: This is to inform you that we are sending a check in the amount of $798.14. [16 words]
CONCISE: We're sending a check for $798.14. [6 words]

In summary, clear, readable writing contains no unnecessary words. Be concise—your writing will be more forceful.

CLARITY

Unless you write clearly, your readers will not understand what you meant to say. One way to write with clarity is to be concise, so that important ideas are not buried in unnecessary words and details. Writing as simply as possible will also help you achieve clarity because you'll be using words the reader knows and feels comfortable with.

Other techniques for improving the clarity of your writing include the careful use of jargon and precise, concrete word choices.

Jargon

Jargon is "the technical terminology or characteristic idiom of a special activity or group."[2] We all recognize accounting jargon: words and phrases such as *amortization*, *accrual*, *debit*, *GAAP*, and *deferred income taxes*.

One kind of jargon is acronyms: words composed of the first letter of a group of words, such as *FASB*, *ASR*, *GAAP*, and *LIFO*. To introduce an acronym, write out the words of the acronym, with the acronym in parentheses:

Some companies account for inventory using the Last-In-First-Out (LIFO) method.

One of the earliest groups to set accounting standards was the Committee on Accounting Procedure (CAP).

After you have identified the acronym, you can use the acronym alone throughout the rest of the document. If you're sure that the readers will be familiar with an acronym, and if you're writing an informal document, it's usually acceptable to use the acronym without writing it out.

Unless you use acronyms and other forms of jargon carefully, they will detract from the clarity of your writing. Two guidelines can help you decide when to use jargon and when to look for other words. The first is to remember the readers' needs and to use language they will understand. Another accountant will probably understand what you mean by *straight-line depreciation*, but managers or clients who have not studied accounting may not. Be careful when using jargon even with your accounting colleagues. Would everyone with a degree in accounting know what you mean by *back-flush costing*?

The second guideline for the use of jargon is to keep your word choices as simple as possible. Avoid jargon when ordinary language will say what you mean. For example, why say "the bottom line" if you mean net income or loss?

Jargon may be unavoidable when you need to communicate technical information as efficiently as possible, but remember the needs of your readers. Define or explain any technical terminology with which they may not be familiar, as stated in the next rule of effective writing:

Use jargon only when your readers understand it.

Define technical terms when necessary.

Precise Meaning

Precision is one of the most important elements of clear writing. Word choices must be accurate and sentences must be constructed so that their meaning is clear. Precision is particularly important in accountants' writing because accountants are often legally responsible for the accuracy of what they write. Moreover, the technical nature of accounting makes precise writing a necessity. Consider this sentence:

UNCLEAR: The major drawback of the current value method is verifiability.

REVISED: The major drawback of the current value method is *the lack of* verifiability.

The revision certainly improves the precision and intelligibility of the sentence! The next rule for an effective writing style is precision.

Be precise—avoid ambiguous and unclear writing.

Word Choices

Imprecise writing has several causes. One culprit is poor diction, or the inaccurate use of words:

The major *setback* of the old system is that it is inefficient. [Poor diction. The writer meant *drawback*.]

The advantage of measurements in terms of market values is that the values reflect *what the item is worth*. [What is the precise meaning of the italicized phrase? *Worth* is vague.]

In these examples, the diction problems are italicized:

POOR DICTION: The users of our financial statements may see the decline in our revenues and become *worrisome.*

REVISED: The users of our financial statements may see the decline in our revenues and become worried.

POOR DICTION: Our advertising expense, which is 1% of total sales, is a *negligent* amount.

REVISED: Our advertising expense, which is 1% of total sales, is a negligible amount.

POOR DICTION: The reason for this purchase was to *help from* liquidating LIFO layers.

REVISED: The reason for this purchase was to prevent the liquidation of LIFO layers.

Unclear, awkward writing can also result from the misuse of words ending in *-ing*:

AWKWARD AND UNCLEAR: We do not have all the data, therefore failing to complete the analysis.

REVISED: We do not have all the data, so we can't complete the analysis.

AWKWARD AND UNCLEAR: In finding out this information, we will have to be thorough in our asking of questions of the concerned parties.

REVISED: To find out this information, we must thoroughly question the concerned parties.

AWKWARD AND UNCLEAR: When purchasing bonds at a discount, the investment cost is less than the face value of the investment.

REVISED: When bonds sell at a discount, the investment cost is less than the face value of the investment.

Faulty Modifiers

Another type of imprecise writing is misplaced and dangling modifiers. With a misplaced modifier, the modifying word or phrase is not placed next to the sentence element it modifies. The result is a confusing sentence:

Process cost systems are often used by businesses that produce goods for general distribution *such as oil refineries and dairies*. [The italicized phrase appears to modify *goods*, but it really modifies *businesses*.]

Process cost systems are often used by businesses such as oil refineries and dairies, which produce goods for general distribution.

Consider another sentence with a misplaced modifier:

This technique identifies tax returns for audits with a high probability of error.

Revised:

To identify tax returns for audit, this technique flags returns that have a high probability of error.

Dangling modifiers, which usually come at the beginning of a sentence, do not actually modify any word in the sentence. Usually the word modified is implied rather than stated directly. Look at this sentence:

After buying the bonds, the market price will fluctuate.

This sentence illogically suggests that the buyer of the bonds is "the market price." The writer probably meant something like this:

After we buy the bonds, the market price will fluctuate.

Here's another example:

As a successful company, disclosure of quarterly profits will attract investors.

One possible revision:

Because we are a successful company, disclosure of our quarterly profits will attract investors.

Pronoun Reference

Faulty pronoun reference can also cause writing to be ambiguous and confusing:

Capitalization of interest is adding interest to the cost of an asset under construction which increases its book value.

The meaning of this sentence is unclear. What increases book value? *Which* and *its* are confusing; their references are vague. Here is one possible revision:

Capitalization of interest is adding interest to the cost of an asset under construction. The added interest increases the asset's book value.

Faulty pronoun reference can be labeled *vague*, *ambiguous*, or *broad*. These terms all mean that the writer doesn't make clear what the pronoun refers to. The pronoun *this* is particularly troublesome:

FAULTY REFERENCE: Last year the company changed from FIFO to LIFO and created a LIFO reserve. Because of *this*, the company decided to reduce inventories.

REVISED: Last year the company changed from FIFO to LIFO and created a LIFO reserve. Because of this change, the company decided to reduce inventories.

FAULTY REFERENCE: The use of generally accepted accounting principles does not always produce the true financial position of a company. *This* is a problem for the FASB.

REVISED: The use of generally accepted accounting principles does not always produce the true financial position of a company. This weakness in the principles is a problem for the FASB.

A good rule is to never use *this* by itself. Add a noun or phrase to define what *this* is.

Another pronoun that can cause reference problems is *it*:

FAULTY REFERENCE: The inventory valuation method can correspond to the physical flow of goods, but *it* is not necessary.

REVISED: The inventory valuation method can correspond to the physical flow of goods, but this correspondence is not necessary.

FAULTY REFERENCE: Many people prefer to itemize deductions for their income tax to decrease their tax liability, but *it* is not always done.

REVISED: Many people prefer to itemize deductions for their income tax, but not everyone chooses to itemize.

Misplaced and dangling modifiers and faulty pronoun reference are grammatical errors, which are discussed further in Chapter 5. However, writing can be grammatically correct and still be imprecise. Consider this sentence:

UNCLEAR: Your writing is not clear because your readers can't understand it.

REVISED: Readers can't understand what you write because your writing isn't clear.

The revision certainly makes a difference in our ability to understand the sentence.

The ability to write precisely is often a function of careful reading and critical thinking. For example, an accounting professor assigned his Accounting Theory students two papers for the quarter. He then wrote the following statement on the board:

An Accounting Theory student who completes the course requirements for this class will write a total of two papers this semester. True or false?

The careful thinkers in the class realized that the statement might not be true. The students could write papers for other classes as well. Therefore, some students could write more than two papers for the semester.

Learn to analyze carefully what you read and what you write. Then write so that your meanings are clear and precise.

Concrete, Specific Wording

Chapter 3 discussed using concrete facts, details, and examples to develop paragraphs. Concrete, specific writing adds clarity to your documents and makes them much more interesting.

Concrete writing can be best explained by defining its opposite: abstract writing. Abstract writing is vague, general, or theoretical. Abstract writing is hard to understand because it's not illustrated by particular, material objects. Concrete writing, on the other hand, is vivid and specific; it brings a picture into the reader's mind.

Illustrations of abstract and concrete writing styles make them easier to understand:

ABSTRACT: Historical cost is important in accounting. It is easy for accountants to use, and it is often seen in the financial statements. Historical cost has some disadvantages, but it has its good points, too.

CONCRETE: Historical cost is the amount of money paid for an object when it was purchased. For example, if a truck was purchased in 2014 for $60,000, then $60,000 is the truck's historical cost. An argument in favor of the use of historical cost to value assets is that such values are usually easy to determine from invoices and other records of the original purchase.

However, in times of inflation the historical cost of an asset may not indicate its true value. For example, an acre of land bought in 1980 for $20,000 might be worth several times that amount today, but it would still be recorded in the owner's books and on the balance sheet at its historical cost. Thus, one disadvantage of historical cost accounting is that it often undervalues assets.

By giving more detailed information and specific, concrete examples of historical cost, the second example makes this concept easier to understand and more interesting to read.

In the following examples, vague, abstract sentences are replaced by more concrete writing:

VAGUE: Accountants should write well.

REVISED: Accountants need to write clear, concise letters to their clients and other business associates. [This sentence replaces the vague *well* with two characteristics of effective writing: *clear* and *concise*. The revision also gives an example of one type of accountants' writing: letters to clients and associates.]

VAGUE: Action on today's stock market was interesting.

REVISED: The Dow Jones Industrial Average dropped 223 points today.

The example just given illustrates a particularly effective technique you can use to make your writing concrete: Illustrate your ideas with specific details about the situation you're discussing. That is, if you're writing about action on the stock market, as in the foregoing example, add relevant details about what happened to clarify what you mean.

By adding specific, concrete details, you will avoid vague sentences like this one:

We should disclose this expense because of comparability.

If we revise the sentence to be more specific and concrete, the meaning becomes much clearer:

We should disclose the advertising expense so that this year's statements will be comparable to those of prior years.

See how specific wording improves the clarity of this sentence:

VAGUE: The financial statements are alarming.
CLEAR: Smith Company's financial statements for 2014 show a net loss of $8,943,617.

VAGUE: This liability should appear on the income statement because of materiality.
CLEAR: This liability should appear on the income statement because the amount, which is $55,000, is material.

Finally, remember the readers' interests when you select the details to include in your writing; choose the details they will find meaningful and relevant. Which of the following two sentences would you prefer to read in a letter from your tax accountant?

Your tax situation this year poses some interesting possibilities.

If you can document your business expenses this year with the necessary receipts, you may be eligible for a refund of at least $5,500.

Concrete writing is next on the list of effective writing techniques:

Be concrete and specific—use facts, details, and examples.

READABLE WRITING

If your writing is interesting to read, it will almost always be clear. Lively, natural sentences hold readers' attention and keep them involved in what you are saying, so they have an easier time understanding your ideas.

This section of the chapter is devoted to several techniques that will make your sentences readable and clear: using active voice, writing with variety and rhythm, and using the appropriate tone.

Passive and Active Voice

This technique for achieving a good writing style might seem technical, but it will become clear after a few definitions and examples.

Use active voice for most sentences.

In the active voice, the subject of the sentence performs the action described by the verb.

ACTIVE: Most corporations issue financial statements at least once a year.

Passive voice, on the other hand, describes an action done to somebody or something by another agent. The agent is not always named in the sentence.

PASSIVE: Financial statements are issued (by most corporations) at least once a year.

This formula will help you identify passive voice verbs:

Passive voice   = | a form of the verb *to be* | + | the past participle of another verb (usually ending in *-ed*) |

Forms of the verb *to be*:
is, are, were, was, been, being, be, am

Typical past participles:
accrued, received, used, computed, given, kept

Sometimes passive verb phrases also contain a form of *to have* (*has, have, had, having*) or an auxiliary (*will, should, would, must,* and so on), but passive voice always contains a *to be* form plus a past participle.

Active voice sentences are often clearer than passive voice sentences. Consider these examples:

PASSIVE: The gasoline tax was raised by 50%.
ACTIVE: The state legislature raised the gasoline tax by 50%.

PASSIVE: It is predicted that the stock's price will double. [In this example, most readers would want to know who made the prediction.]
ACTIVE: The controller predicted that the stock's price will double.

PASSIVE: It was decided that employees would be required to work on Saturday.
ACTIVE: The company president decided to require employees to work on Saturday.

Unfortunately, writers of "officialese," especially in government, business, and research, have so badly overused passive voice that we tend to accept it as standard style. Passive voice is seldom effective— it lacks the forcefulness and clarity of active voice. Compare the following pairs of sentences:

PASSIVE: In many college accounting courses, effective writing skills are emphasized.

ACTIVE: Many college accounting courses emphasize effective writing skills.

PASSIVE: A determination has been made that the statements are in violation of GAAP.

ACTIVE: The auditors have determined that the statements are in violation of GAAP.

PASSIVE: Further research should be conducted before an opinion can be issued.

ACTIVE: The auditors should conduct further research before they issue an opinion.

PASSIVE: In SAS No. 1, responsibilities and functions of the independent auditor are described.

ACTIVE: SAS No. 1 describes responsibilities and functions of the independent auditor.

Good writers avoid using passive voice in most situations. They ask themselves two questions: What is the action (verb)? Who or what is doing it (subject)?

One word of warning: Avoid substituting a weak active verb for passive voice. Be particularly careful of colorless verbs such as *to exist* and *to occur*. The following sentences are written in active voice, but the sentences are weak:

Capitalization of option costs on land subsequently purchased should occur.

FIFO bases itself on the assumption that the first inventory acquired is the first inventory sold.

Use descriptive, vigorous verbs to substitute for weak verbs:

We must capitalize option costs on land that we subsequently purchased.

The assumption that underlies FIFO is that the first inventory acquired is the first inventory sold.

When to Use Passive Voice

Although it's usually better to write in active voice, passive voice is sometimes preferable. For example, the two sentences in the preceding example could be effectively written in passive voice:

Option costs on land that we subsequently purchased should be capitalized.

FIFO is based on the assumption that the first inventory acquired is the first inventory sold.

Passive voice may also be necessary to avoid an awkward repetition of sentence subjects, especially in paragraphs where the same agent is performing all the action or the agent is obvious or irrelevant:

The property was appraised in 2014 at $400,000.

In this sentence, it would probably not be necessary to identify who did the appraisal.

Another consideration about active and passive voice is that sometimes you may want to emphasize the passive subject. For example, you would say:

Our system has been hacked.

rather than:

Some person or persons unknown have hacked our system.

Finally, passive voice may enable you to be tactful when you must write bad news or some sort of criticism:

These figures were not calculated correctly.

This sentence doesn't say who is at fault for the erroneous calculation; here, passive voice may be the most diplomatic way to identify the problem without assigning blame.

We talk more about writing tactfully later in the chapter.

Variety and Rhythm

Another way to make your writing natural and more readable is to add variety, which is the next technique on the list.

Vary vocabulary, sentence lengths, and sentence structures.

Read the writing aloud to hear how it sounds.

The purpose of sentence variety is to avoid monotony—a singsong, awkward repetition of the same sentence rhythms or overuse of a word or phrase. Read the following paragraph aloud:

Financial analysts use ratios to analyze financial statements. Ratios show a company's liquidity. The current ratio shows the ratio of current assets to current liabilities. Ratios also show a company's solvency. The equity ratio is an example of a solvency ratio. It shows the ratio of owners' equity to total assets. Ratios also show profitability. The return-on-investment ratio is an example. It shows the ratio of net earnings to owners' equity.

This paragraph does not sound pleasing. In fact, it could easily lull the reader to sleep. The sentences are too similar in length and structure and the word *ratio* is repeated too often. Let's try again:

Ratios based on financial statements can reveal valuable information about a company to investors, creditors, and other interested parties. Liquidity ratios show whether a company can pay its debts. The quick ratio, for example, is a good indication of debt-paying ability for companies with slow inventory turnover. Ratios can also indicate a company's solvency; the equity ratio, for instance, shows the percentage of owners' equity to total assets. Investors in bonds use this figure to evaluate the safety of a potential investment. Finally, ratios can give a measure of a company's profitability, which is of special interest to potential investors. The earnings-per-share ratio is probably the most popular of the profitability ratios.

Another cause of monotonous sentences is too many prepositional phrases, particularly when several are linked together. Look at the following sentence. Prepositions are in bold type; the rest of the phrase is underlined:

The communication **of** <u>information</u> **about** <u>the income</u> **of** <u>a corporation</u> will provide **to** <u>potential investors</u> **in** <u>the corporation</u> help **in** <u>the making</u> **of** <u>their investment decision</u>.

This sentence contains seven prepositional phrases, several of which are linked together. A good rule is to avoid more than two or three prepositional phrases in a sentence. The sentence can be revised as follows:

Information about a corporation's income will help investors make sound decisions.

Here is a partial list of prepositions:

about	by	like	together with
after	during	near	under
as	for	of	until
at	from	on	up
because of	in	over	with
before	in front of	through	
between	in regard to	to	

Variety is an important element of readable writing because it gives sentences and paragraphs a pleasing rhythm. Read your paragraphs aloud. If you notice a word or phrase repeated too often, look for a synonym. If the sentences sound choppy and monotonous, vary their structures and lengths. Often a change in the way sentences begin improves the rhythm of the paragraph. Add an occasional short sentence and an occasional longer one (but be sure longer sentences are still easy to understand). Avoid using too many prepositional phrases. You don't want to bore your readers, and varied sentences are one way to keep your writing lively.

Tone

The tone of a document reflects the writer's attitude toward the topic or the readers. Tone might also be described as the effect the writing has on the reader or the impression the document makes. A letter can have a formal or informal tone; it can be personal or impersonal. It can be apologetic, cold, humorous, threatening, arrogant, respectful, or friendly.

Choosing the best tone for a document depends, in part, on who the reader will be. If you are writing to a colleague who is also a good friend, you can be much more informal than if you are writing to someone you don't know well. Be particularly careful to show respect to those who are much older than you are or those in higher positions of authority.

One way to decide on the proper tone of a document you are writing is to imagine that you are in a conversation with your reader. How formal would you be? How would you show that you were interested in your reader's point of view and concerns? No matter how formal (or casual) you decide to make your tone, always be courteous. Treat your correspondent with tact, politeness, and respect. Avoid abruptness, arrogance, condescension, or any other form of rudeness. Remember that the choice of tone may involve ethical considerations: Treat others as you wish to be treated.

Here are some examples of poor tone:

Tax planning is a complicated subject, so I have tried to simplify it for you. [This sentence is condescending; it implies that the reader is not very bright.]

I acknowledge receipt of your letter and beg to thank you. [Too formal and artificial.]

Send me that report immediately. I can't understand why it has taken you so long to prepare it. [In certain situations you might *think* this way, but it's better to write with tact and courtesy.]

For all but the most formal documents, such as some contracts, the use of personal pronouns (*you*, *I*, *we*) contributes to a warm, personal tone. Keep the first person singular pronouns (*I*, *me*, *my*, *mine*) to a minimum; focus instead on the reader with second person (*you*, *your*, *yours*) or, in some cases, first person plural (*we*, *us*, *our*, *ours*).

A personal tone, including personal pronouns, is especially effective when the message you are conveying is good news or neutral information. When you must write bad news or criticize someone, it's better to be impersonal in order to be tactful. Passive voice can also make a sentence more tactful:

TACTLESS: You failed to sign your income tax return.
  BETTER: Please sign your return on the line indicated.

Another guideline for an effective tone is to stress the positive. Emphasize what can be done rather than what cannot:

NEGATIVE: Because you were late in sending us your tax information, we cannot complete your tax return by April 15.

POSITIVE: Now that we have the information on your taxes, we can complete your tax return. We will request an extension of the deadline so that you will not be fined for a late filing.

Finally, be honest and sincere; avoid exaggeration and flattery. This sentence doesn't sound credible:

Working with you on this audit has shown me what a superb accountant you are.

In the final analysis, the guidelines for an effective writing tone are the same as those for good relationships. Learn to view a situation from the other person's point of view and communicate in a way that shows empathy and respect.

Here, then, is another guideline for an effective writing style.

> ***Write from the reader's point of view.***
> ***Use tone to show courtesy and respect.***

This chapter on style has discussed nine guidelines for effective writing, making a total of sixteen.

1. Analyze the purpose of the writing, the accounting issues involved, and the needs and expectations of the readers.
2. Organize your ideas so that readers will find them easy to follow.
3. Write the draft and then revise it to make the writing polished and correct.
4. Make the writing unified. All sentences should relate to the main idea, either directly or indirectly. Eliminate digressions and irrelevant detail.
5. Use summary sentences and transitions to make your writing coherent.
6. Write in short paragraphs that begin with clear topic sentences.
7. Develop paragraphs by illustration, definition, detail, and appeals to authority.
8. Be concise—make every word count.
9. Keep it simple—simple vocabulary and short sentences.
10. Write with active verbs and descriptive nouns.
11. Use jargon only when your readers understand it. Define technical terms when necessary.
12. Be precise—avoid ambiguous and unclear writing.
13. Be concrete and specific. Use facts, details, and examples.
14. Use active voice for most sentences.
15. Vary vocabulary, sentence lengths, and sentence structures. Read the writing aloud to hear how it sounds.
16. Write from the reader's point of view. Use tone to show courtesy and respect.

TEST YOURSELF

Revise the following sentences so that they are written in a more effective style, using the techniques covered in this chapter. Answers are provided on pages 79–80.

1. Marie Ortega made reference to recent research in her report.
2. At the seminar information was provided on recent developments in the profession.
3. After reading the following paragraphs, a recommendation will suggest a way we can reduce the cost of the purchase.
4. Complete information was wanted by management on the new project that had been proposed by the engineers.
5. The important issue to address in this company's situation is that of the expression of an opinion of the going concern.
6. To determine what information to include in our report for 2014, we will make an analysis of the users' needs.
7. This recommendation can easily be implemented by our clients.
8. The main problem of this company is to minimize the amount of taxes for 2014.
9. It is our recommendation that Byron Corporation choose to value the property at $95,000.
10. The letter discussed the alternative ways to finance the purchase of the new equipment. Its purpose was. . . .

TEST YOURSELF: ANSWERS

(Note: Some of the errors in the previous sentences can be corrected in more than one way; this key shows only one possible correction. If you recognize the error, you probably understand how to correct it.)

1. Maria Ortega referred to recent research in her report.
2. The seminar provided information on recent developments in the profession.
3. The following paragraphs will explain how we can reduce the cost of the purchase.
4. Management wanted complete information on the new project that the engineers had proposed.
5. We must determine whether this company is a going concern.
6. To determine what to include in our 2014 report, we will analyze users' needs.
7. Our clients can easily implement this recommendation.
8. This company's main problem is to minimize taxes for 2014.

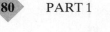

9. We recommend that Byron Corporation value the property at $95,000.
10. The letter discussed the alternative ways to finance the purchase of the new equipment. The purpose of the letter was. . . .

EXERCISES

Exercise 4–1 [General]

Revise the following sentences so that they are written as simply and concisely as possible. Be alert for hidden verbs.

1. We should not make reference to projections that are unrealistic in our plan.
2. These techniques will provide for an improved control of inventory.
3. This is to acknowledge receipt of your letter of April 30.
4. We will endeavor to complete your returns prior to April 15.
5. I am in need of improved writing skills.
6. In conclusion, I would like to state that I feel this seminar is an excellent opportunity.
7. There are several benefits that can come from attending the seminar.
8. Per the discussion held with you during our recent visit, there are several control objectives within the above-mentioned cycles that need to have techniques established or refined to assure that these objectives are met.
9. Utilization of linear models alone may lead to unnecessary limitations as to the inferences that one may be able to draw from the data.
10. This method provides proper allocation of costs.

Exercise 4–2 [General]

Review the lists of simplified word choices in Table 4–1. Then, without looking at the list again, write a shorter and/or simpler version of the following words and phrases.

Example:

Original: **Simplify to:**
in all cases always

1. i.e.
2. enclosed please find
3. facilitate
4. initiate
5. prior to
6. so as to

7. the major part of
8. make a purchase
9. make an analysis of
10. for the purpose of
11. in the amount of
12. optimum
13. maintain cost control
14. the writer
15. this is to acknowledge

Exercise 4–3 [General]

Identify the jargon in the following sentences.

1. We'll have to research the regs and rules that apply to this problem.
2. Negative cash flows may affect our position with our creditors.
3. SOX requirements have created additional work for our department.
4. The FASB and the SEC, as well as the AICPA, are organizations that concern the profession of accounting.
5. GAAP requires a different treatment of inventory costs.
6. The project's NPV was negative, so it was rejected.
7. My CPA advised me to file a Schedule C with my return.
8. Because of her income this year, she will be able to recapture.
9. Our auditors must follow all requirements of the PCAOB.
10. Credit Cash for $200.

Exercise 4–4 [General]

The meaning of the following sentences is not clear. Revise the sentences so that they are unambiguous and precise.

1. The unexpected retirement of six auditors created a heavier workload for the remaining staff, causing them to miss several deadlines. This is a problem.
2. The branch office will be located at a new cite.
3. The stock's price dropped by a negligent amount.
4. This product is unique. Only two manufacturers produce it.
5. The HB Transportation Company's improved position is due to decreasing fuel prices and the company's response in increasing prices.
6. Expense recognition states that once a cost expires, we should recognize expense.
7. After calculating the tax effects, the selling price of the property seemed more reasonable.
8. This policy is based on a logical rational.
9. The FASB has not officially written a pronouncement on the handling of requisition costs.
10. These financial statements upset two accounting standards.

Exercise 4–5 [General]

The following sentences are abstract or vague. Revise them, using facts, details, or examples to make them more concrete. You may need to replace one vague sentence with several concrete sentences, or even a short paragraph. Alternatively, you could introduce a short paragraph with an abstraction and then develop the idea with more concrete, specific sentences. Feel free to invent details that make the ideas more specific.

1. This will be difficult to implement.
2. The financial statements surprised investors.
3. The new legal action is encouraging.
4. Accounting for leases is tricky.
5. Investors were interested in the president's report.
6. The firm sold the asset for its cost. [Hint: What cost?]
7. Morale is a problem.
8. The audit did not satisfy me.
9. I've discovered a shocking thing about our pension plan.
10. Communication is important.

Exercise 4–6 [General]

Identify the passive-voice constructions in the following sentences and revise them to active voice. Be careful not to substitute weak active verbs for passive voice. For some sentences you may need to invent a subject for the active verb.

Example:

PASSIVE: That alternative could have been followed.
ACTIVE: We (or the firm, our client, McDonough Corporation, etc.) could have followed that alternative.

1. This information was prepared by our research department.
2. No audit work on XYZ's internal control was performed by our firm.
3. Our opinion on the financial statements may have to be modified.
4. These disclosures are required for external reporting,
5. This procedure can easily be implemented.
6. It is recommended that finished parts inventories be physically controlled.
7. Although our computer was purchased last year, it is already obsolete.
8. At the seminar guidelines will be provided for lease accounting.
9. In many college accounting courses effective writing skills are emphasized.
10. The prior years' working papers were reviewed.

Exercise 4–7 [General]

Identify the prepositional phrases in the following sentences. Where too many phrases are linked together, revise the sentence.

Example:

The problem of our client will be solved through the selection of one of the accounting methods presented.

Prepositional phrases identified:

The problem **of** <u>our client</u> will be solved **through** <u>the selection</u> **of** <u>one</u> **of** <u>the accounting methods presented</u>.

Revised:

One of the accounting methods should solve our client's problem.

1. The effects of the ruling by the IRS will affect the reported income of XYZ Corporation.
2. The controller of the company called a meeting for 9:00 a.m. to discuss problems with the quarterly financial statements of the company.
3. An accrual of expenses reports a more accurate picture of the operations of the current business period of the company.
4. Improvements of the efficiency of production will change the forecast for income in the year to come.
5. The main problem of the staff is the determination of the cost at which to record the purchase.
6. The effect on our audit report of the sale of the bonds is twofold.
7. The income tax return for Steve Warren was filed on April 10.
8. The calculation of the present values of the principal of the bonds and their cash flows will reveal our risk.
9. The amortization of the discount of the bond will allow us to realize the cash flows of the bond at an even rate throughout the life of the bond.
10. The determination of the net income of the company will pose no problems for the accountants in our department.

Exercise 4–8 [General]

Read this paragraph aloud and notice how monotonous it sounds. Then revise it so that sentence lengths and structures are more varied. Note also when a word or phrase is repeated too often.

Regional Coach Lines (RCL) runs bus service between several cities in three states. RCL also carries freight for several regional businesses. RCL's financial statements have reported poor profits for several years. Poor profits were caused by increased costs of operations including fuel costs, labor costs, and other costs. Increased costs caused RCL to increase passenger fares and freight prices. These increases caused passenger and freight volume to decrease drastically. Therefore, 2014 was a disastrous year for RCL. Preliminary information shows RCL is on the verge of bankruptcy.

Exercise 4–9 [General]

Revise the following sentences so that they are more effective, based on the guidelines discussed in this chapter.

1. The CEO made reference to the pension plan in his address.
2. A qualified opinion was issued on the 2014 financial statements.
3. Two weeks of vacation will be taken by new employees.
4. The completion of the project by the due date of next week will challenge the accountants in the department.
5. Wordiness is the problem that makes my writing less effective than it ought to be.
6. This memo provides an explanation of our policies on the use of company email.
7. The auditors came to the conclusion that additional procedures should be performed by them on inventory.
8. There are several benefits that can come from investing in new equipment.
9. Expense recognition states that once a cost expires, we should recognize expense.
10. The option kept the land available until a decision was reached about whether to buy it.

Exercise 4–10 [General]

Revise the following paragraph, using the techniques covered in the chapter, as necessary.

> The purpose of this memo is an attempt to explain the three alternatives that have been proposed for recording the cost of the land that has been purchased by our company. The reasons for the recommendation I decided upon are discussed below along with the strong and weak points of the other proposed alternatives that I do not recommend. If one of these alternatives had been more consistent with GAAP, that alternative could have been followed.

NOTES

1. Cynthia A. Glassman, "Speech by SEC Commissioner: Remarks at the Plain Language Association International's Fifth International Conference," Securities and Exchange Commission, 2005.

   http://www.sec.gov/news/speech/spch110405cag.htm (24 January 2013).
2. *Merriam-Webster's Collegiate Dictionary*, 11th ed. (Springfield, Mass: Merriam-Webster, Incorporated, 2004), 670.

CHAPTER

Standard English: Grammar, Punctuation, and Spelling

O ne way to improve the clarity of your writing is to use Standard English, the language used by business, government, and professionals for daily business purposes. Standard English is defined as "the English that with respect to spelling, grammar, pronunciation, and vocabulary is substantially uniform though not devoid of regional differences, that is well established by usage in the formal and informal speech and writing of the educated, and that is widely recognized as acceptable wherever English is spoken and understood."[1]

In addition to improving the clarity of what you write, using Standard English will help you produce professional, polished documents, which is the final tip for writers given in Figure 1–2 in Chapter 1. A mastery of Standard English tells the reader much about you as a person and as a professional. Your use of correct grammar says that you are an educated person who understands and appreciates the proper use of language.

A grammatically correct document, free of mechanical and typographical errors, also shows that you know the importance of detail and are willing to spend the time necessary to prepare an accurate, precise document. Careful attention to detail is an important skill for an accountant, whether the detail is verbal or quantitative.

This chapter presents some of the most common errors in grammar, punctuation, and spelling. Because only a few principles can be covered in this short space, you should consult an English handbook for more complete coverage. This discussion focuses on areas that typically give accountants the most trouble.

MAJOR SENTENCE ERRORS

Major sentence errors include three kinds of problems: fragments, comma splices, and fused (or run-on) sentences. These errors are very distracting to readers and often seriously interfere with their ability to understand the meaning of a sentence.

Fragments

A sentence fragment is just what its name suggests: part of a sentence. Recall that every sentence needs two essential elements, a subject and a verb (or predicate). In sentence fragments, at least one of these elements may be missing. A sentence fragment may also be recognized because it expresses an incomplete thought. Here are some examples:

> To attract a wider client base.

> For example, all the employees who are eligible for retirement. [The subject is *employees*. In the phrase that modifies the subject, the verb *are* is related to the pronoun *who*, but the predicate for the sentence is missing.]

> The reason being that we must find ways to cut overhead. [*Being* is a present participle*; it cannot be substituted for a complete verb such as *is* or *was*.]

> Although our new system makes billing much faster. [This dependent clause has a subject and verb, but it cannot stand alone as a sentence because it is introduced by a subordinate conjunction, *although*.]

Comma Splices

The second major sentence error is comma splices, which occur when independent clauses are linked by a comma alone. An independent clause is a group of words with a subject and a verb; it can stand alone as a sentence. These two independent clauses are punctuated as separate sentences:

> Increases in assets are recorded as debits on the left side of a T-account. Decreases are recorded as credits on the right side.

Sometimes writers want to combine two independent clauses into one sentence. This can be done correctly in several ways:

1. Put a semicolon (;) between the clauses.

> Increases in assets are recorded as debits on the left side of a T-account; decreases are recorded as credits on the right side.

2. Combine the clauses with a coordinating conjunction (*and*, *but*, *for*, *or*, *nor*, *yet*, *so*).

> Increases in assets are recorded as debits on the left side of a T-account, and decreases are recorded as credits on the right side.

3. Combine the clauses with a semicolon, a conjunctive adverb, and a comma. (Conjunctive adverbs include *however*, *therefore*, *thus*, *consequently*, *that is*, *for example*, *nevertheless*, *also*, *furthermore*, *indeed*, *instead*, *still*.)

> Increases in assets are recorded as debits on the left side of a T-account; however, decreases are recorded as credits on the right side.

---

*Consult a grammar handbook for explanations of technical grammatical terms such as this.

Study the following comma splices. The independent clauses are joined by a comma alone:

COMMA SPLICE: Accounting firms realize the importance of effective writing, they may offer training to improve employees' skills.

REVISED: Accounting firms realize the importance of effective writing, so they may offer training to improve employees' skills.

or

Because accounting firms realize the importance of effective writing, they may offer training to improve employees' skills. [This revision changes the first independent clause into a dependent clause.]

COMMA SPLICE: We have expanded the service offered to our clients, we need to hire additional staff accountants.

REVISED: Because we have expanded the service offered to our clients, we need to hire additional staff accountants.

COMMA SPLICE: These transactions were not recorded correctly, they were not recorded in the proper accounts.

REVISED: These transactions were not recorded correctly; they were not recorded in the proper accounts.

or

(to make the sentence more concise)

These transactions were not recorded in the proper accounts.

Fused Sentences

Fused sentences, which are also called run-on sentences, occur when two independent clauses are joined without any punctuation at all:

FUSED SENTENCE: Generally accepted accounting principles are not laws passed by Congress however, the AICPA's code of professional ethics requires accountants to follow GAAP.

REVISED: Generally accepted accounting principles are not laws passed by Congress. However, the AICPA's code of professional ethics requires accountants to follow GAAP.

FUSED SENTENCE: The Director of Human Resources emailed all employees about the new vacation policy he wanted them to have time to plan their vacations.

REVISED: The Director of Human Resources emailed all employees about the new vacation policy so they would have time to plan their vacations.

PROBLEMS WITH VERBS

The correct use of verbs is a complicated matter in any language, as you will appreciate if you have ever studied a language other than English. For writers whose first language is English, the correct use of verbs usually presents few problems.

Verb problems do sometimes occur, however, even in the writing of fluent speakers of English. We will now look briefly at some of those problems.

Tense and Mood

The *tense* of a verb reflects the time of the action described by the verb:

PAST TENSE: The company *increased* its investment in R&D last year.

PRESENT TENSE: The company *is increasing* its investment in R&D this year.

or

Is the company *increasing* its investment in R&D this year?

or

The company *increases* its investment in R&D every year.

FUTURE TENSE: The company *will increase* its investment in R&D next year.

Usually the choice of tense is logical and gives writers few problems.

The *mood* of a verb, however, is a little more confusing than its tense. Three moods are possible: indicative (states a fact or asks a question), imperative (a command or request), and subjunctive (a condition contrary to fact). The subjunctive mood causes the most trouble, although we often use it without realizing it:

If I *were* you, I would double-check those vouchers. [condition contrary to fact]

The most common use of the subjunctive is to follow certain verbs such as *recommend*, *suggest*, and *require*:

I recommend that we *hire* Jill Edmonds.

I suggest that he *contact* the sales representative immediately to discuss the lost orders.

The IRS requires that our client *include* that income in this year's return.

One common problem is an unnecessary shift in tense or mood:

TENSE SHIFT: The president *approached* the podium and then *announces* the good news. [Shift from past to present tense.]

REVISED: The president *approached* the podium and then *announced* the good news.

MOOD SHIFT: We *must credit* Cash to account for the purchase of the computer paper. Then *debit* Office Supplies. [Shift from indicative to imperative mood.]

REVISED: We *must credit* Cash to account for the computer paper purchase and then *debit* Office Supplies. [This sentence has a single subject, *we*, and compound indicative verb, *must credit . . . and . . . debit.*]

MOOD SHIFT: If we *increase* inventory, we *would service* orders more quickly. [Shift from indicative to subjunctive.]

REVISED: If we *increase* inventory, we *will service* orders more quickly.

or

If we *increased* inventory, we *would service* orders more quickly.

MOOD SHIFT: If we *changed* our credit policy, we *will attract* more customers. [Shift from subjunctive to indicative.]

REVISED: If we *changed* our credit policy, we *would attract* more customers.

or

If we *change* our credit policy, we *will attract* more customers.

Subject-Verb Agreement

Another major problem with verbs is subject-verb agreement. A verb should agree with its subject in number. That is, singular subjects take singular verbs; plural subjects take plural verbs. Note that singular verbs in the present tense usually end in *s*:

The IT specialist checks the system every week.

Two IT specialists check the system every week.

Some irregular verbs (*to be, to have*, etc.) look different, but you will probably recognize the singular and plural forms:

The *manager is* excited about the new product.

The *managers are* excited about the new product.

The Drastic Measures *Corporation has* five frantic accountants on its staff.

Some *corporations have* enough accountants to handle the workload efficiently.

There are a few difficulties with this rule. First, some singular subjects are often thought of as plural. For example, *each, every, either, neither, one, everybody,* and *anyone* take singular verbs:

Each of the divisions *is* responsible for maintaining accounting records.

Second, sometimes phrases coming between the subject and the verb make agreement tricky:

The *effect* on our financial statements for the past two years *was* negligible.

Finally, two or more subjects joined by *and* take a plural verb. When subjects are joined by *or*, the verb agrees with the subject closest to it:

Ellen Atkins and John Simmons are partners.

Either *Ellen Atkins or John Simmons is* the partner-in-charge.

Either *the controller or the managers have called* this meeting.

Either *the managers or the controller has called* this meeting.

PROBLEMS WITH PRONOUNS

Two common problems with pronouns are agreement and reference. Understanding agreement is easy: A pronoun must agree with its antecedent (the word it stands for). Thus, singular antecedents take singular pronouns and plural antecedents take plural pronouns:

Susan took *her* check to the bank.
Each *department* is responsible for servicing *its* own equipment.

This rule usually gives trouble only with particular words. Note that *company*, *corporation*, *firm*, *management*, and *board* are singular; therefore, they take singular pronouns:

The *company* increased *its* profits by fifty percent. (Not *company* . . . *their*.)

The *corporation* hired two new accountants to supervise *its* internal control procedures. [Not *corporation* . . . *their*.]

The *Board* of Directors discussed earnings projections in *its* quarterly meeting. [Not *Board* . . . *their*.]

Management issued *its* quarterly report. [But: The *managers* issued *their* report.]

The second problem with pronouns is vague, ambiguous, or broad reference. The pronouns that give the most trouble are *this*, *that*, *which*, and *it*. This problem was discussed in Chapter 4, but here are some additional examples for you to consider:

FAULTY REFERENCE: Although our bottling machines were purchased last year, this year's revenue depends on them. *This* associates the true cost with this year's revenues.

REVISED (ONE POSSIBILITY): Although our bottling machines were purchased last year, this year's revenue depends on them. To associate the true cost of the machines with this year's revenue, we must apply the matching principle.

FAULTY REFERENCE: Adjusting entries are needed to show that expenses have been incurred, but not paid. *This* is a very important step.

REVISED: Adjusting entries are needed to show that expenses have been incurred, but not paid. Making these adjusting entries is a very important step.

Although agreement and reference cause writers the most problems with pronouns, occasionally other questions arise.

One question is the use of first and second person, which some people have been taught to avoid. In the discussion of tone in Chapter 4 we saw how using these personal pronouns can often contribute to an effective writing style for many informal documents. Personal pronouns are not usually appropriate in formal documents, such as some reports and contracts.

A few other cautions apply in the use of personal pronouns. First, use first person singular pronouns (*I*, *me*, *my*, and *mine*) sparingly to avoid writing that sounds self-centered. The second problem to avoid is using *you* in a broad sense to mean people in general, or as a substitute for another pronoun:

INCORRECT: I don't want to file my income tax return late because the IRS will fine *you*.

REVISED: I don't want to file my income tax return late because the IRS will fine *me*.

Pronouns and Gender

English has no singular personal pronouns that refer to an antecedent that could be either masculine or feminine. Until about a generation ago, the masculine pronouns (*he*, *him*, *his*) were understood to stand for either gender:

Every auditor should submit his reports on time.

Sentences like this one were common even though the pronoun's antecedent (in this case, *auditor*) could be either male or female.

Most people today believe that this older pronoun usage is no longer appropriate. They prefer to use pronouns that are gender neutral, unless, of course, the antecedent is clearly male or female:

The *controller* of Marvelous Corporation was pleased with *his* company's financial statements. [The controller is a man.]

or

The *controller* of Marvelous Corporation was pleased with *her* company's financial statements. [The controller is a woman.]

When the pronoun's antecedent is not clearly male or female, many people write sentences like these:

> Every *auditor* should submit *his or her* reports on time.

> Every *auditor* should submit *his/her* reports on time.

Unfortunately, constructions such as *he or she* and *he/she* can be awkward, especially if several occur in the same sentence:

> Every auditor should submit *his or her* reports on time to fulfill *his or her* professional obligations.

What's the solution? The best approach for most sentences is to use plural nouns and pronouns so that the language will be inclusive:

> Auditors should submit *their* reports on time to fulfill *their* professional obligations.

For some sentences, however, you can't use plurals. In these situations, some writers use gendered pronouns arbitrarily and switch often; sometimes they use a feminine pronoun and sometimes a masculine one. Whatever approach you use to avoid gender bias in your use of pronouns, keep these guidelines in mind:

- Most of today's business publications prefer gender-neutral writing, including a careful use of pronouns. If you use the older style, your writing will seem outdated.
- Some of your readers will be annoyed by a choice of pronouns that seems to be gender-biased.

PROBLEMS WITH MODIFIERS

Chapter 4 discussed the two main problems that can occur with modifiers: misplaced modifiers, which occur when the modifier is not placed next to the word it describes, and dangling modifiers, which do not modify any word in the sentence:

MISPLACED MODIFIER: We only found one problem with the audit. [*Only* is misplaced. It should be next to the word or phrase it modifies.]

REVISED: We found only one problem with the audit.

DANGLING MODIFIER: When preparing financial statements, GAAP must be adhered to.

REVISED: When preparing financial statements, we must adhere to GAAP.

The best guideline for using modifiers correctly is to place them next to the word or phrase they describe. For a further discussion of problems with modifiers and additional examples, see Chapter 4.

PARALLEL STRUCTURE

Parallel sentence elements are those that are grammatically equal (such as verb phrases, noun phrases, dependent clauses, and sentences). When these items appear in a list or a compound structure, they should be balanced, or parallel. Noun phrases should not be matched with clauses, for example, nor should sentences be matched with phrases. One-word nouns and noun phrases are considered parallel, however, and can be combined in a list or compound structure.

These examples illustrate problems with parallel structure:

STRUCTURE NOT PARALLEL: During the meeting management will explain the purpose of the new policy, when it will go into effect, and its advantages. [This sentence combines a noun phrase, a dependent clause, and another noun phrase.]

REVISED: During the meeting management will explain the purpose of the new policy, its implementation date, and its advantages.

STRUCTURE NOT PARALLEL: We recommend the following procedures:

- Hire a consultant to help us determine our needs. [verb phrase]
- Investigate alternative makes and models of equipment. [verb phrase]
- We should then set up a pilot program to assess retraining needs for employees who will use the new equipment. [sentence]

REVISED: We recommend the following procedures:

- Hire a consultant to help us determine our needs. [verb phrase]
- Investigate alternative makes and models of equipment. [verb phrase]
- Set up a pilot program to assess retraining needs for employees who will use the new equipment. [verb phrase]

APOSTROPHES AND PLURALS

The rules for apostrophes and plurals are quite simple, but many people get them confused. Most plurals are formed by adding either *s* or *es* to the end of a word. If you are unsure of a plural spelling, consult a dictionary.

With one exception, apostrophes are never used to form plurals. Apostrophes are used to show possession. For singular words the form is '*s*. For plural words the apostrophe comes after the *s*:

Singular	Plural
client's file	clients' files
statement's format	users' needs
business's budget	businesses' budgets

A common mistake is *stockholder's equity*. When stockholder(s) is plural (it usually is), the apostrophe comes after the *s*: *stockholders' equity*.

The plural-apostrophe rule has one exception. The plurals of letters or acronyms can be formed with '*s*. Either choice in the following sentences is correct:

Most CPAs [or CPA's] are familiar with these regulations.

Cross your *t*'s and dot your *i*'s. [Or: Cross your *ts* and dot your *is*.]

Often a phrase requiring an apostrophe can be rewritten using *of* or its equivalent:

the president's letter [the letter of the president]
June's income [the income for June]
a week's work [the work of a week]
the year's total [the total for the year]

Either of these possessive forms is correct, but remember the caution given in Chapter 4 about using too many prepositional phrases in a sentence. The result can be awkward or wordy.

And note these possessive plurals:

two companies' statements
five months' income
three weeks' work
prior years' statements
ten years' total

Ten years' total might also be written *ten-year total*, but analyze the difference in meaning between *ten-year total* and *ten years' totals*.

Finally, some writers confuse *it's* with *its*. *It's* is a contraction of *it is*; *its* is the possessive pronoun:

It's time to hire new accountants.

The firm was proud of its new hires.

COMMAS

Commas are important because they can make sentences easier to understand. Lack of a comma makes the meaning of this sentence ambiguous:

I wouldn't worry because you appear to have a thriving business.

Adding a comma clears up the confusion:

I wouldn't worry, because you appear to have a thriving business.

Comma Guide Sheet

This guide sheet will help you determine when to use (or not use) commas.

Use Commas:

1. Before *and*, *but*, *or*, *not*, *for*, *so*, and *yet* when these words come between independent clauses:

We sent Mr. Alvarado an invoice for our services, and he mailed a check the next day.

Our competitors increased their advertising, but our customers remained loyal.

2. Following an introductory adverbial clause:

If we purchase this program, we will be able to generate our reports more quickly.

Although we worked all night, we didn't finish the report.

3. Following transitional expressions and long introductory phrases:

In a letter addressed to its corporate clients, the firm explained the changes in the services it would offer.

To improve the service to our Atlanta customers, we are adding three new sales representatives. However, we still need four more representatives.

4. To separate items in a series (including coordinate adjectives):

Accounting students must be intelligent, dedicated, and conscientious.

Jenny Tran, Sam Clark, and Raul Ramirez announced they would retire next year.

5. To set off nonrestrictive clauses and phrases (compare to rule 4 under the heading *DO NOT USE COMMAS*):

The SEC, which is an agency of the federal government, is concerned with the independence of auditors.

The annual report, which was issued in March, contained shocking news for investors.

The main office, located in Boston, employs 350 people.

6. To set off contrasted elements:

Treasury stock is a contra-capital account, not an asset.

We want to lower our prices, not raise them.

7. To set off parenthetical elements:

Changes in accounting methods, however, must be disclosed in financial statements.

"Our goal," he said, "is to dominate the market."

Do Not Use Commas:

1. To separate the subject from the verb or the verb from its complement:

Incorrect:
Some international mutual funds, have shown high returns.

Correct:
Some international mutual funds have shown high returns.

Incorrect:
We must correctly record, these entries.

Correct:
We must correctly record these entries.

2. To separate compound verbs or objects:

Incorrect:
She wrote angry letters to her CPA, and to her attorney.

Correct:
She wrote angry letters to her CPA and to her attorney.

But note this usage:
She wrote angry letters to her CPA, her attorney, and the Chamber of Commerce. [Commas are correct in this sentence because they separate the items in a series. See rule 4 under the heading *USE COMMAS.*]

3. To set off words and short phrases that are not parenthetical:

Incorrect:
Financial transactions are recorded, in journals, in chronological order.

Correct:
Financial transactions are recorded in journals in chronological order.

4. To set off restrictive clauses, phrases, or appositives (compare to rule 5 under the heading *USE COMMAS*):

Incorrect:
An advantage, of computerized tax programs, is the accuracy of the returns.

Correct:
An advantage of computerized tax programs is the accuracy of the returns.

Incorrect:
The person, who discovered this error, deserves a promotion.

Correct:
The person who discovered this error deserves a promotion.

5. Before the first item or after the last item of a series (including coordinate adjectives):

Incorrect:
Some asset accounts are noncurrent, such as, land, buildings, and equipment.
[The faulty comma is the one before *land*.]

Correct:
Some asset accounts are noncurrent, such as land, buildings, and equipment.

COLONS AND SEMICOLONS

The rules for colons (:) are few and easy to master, although sometimes writers use them incorrectly. Used correctly—and sparingly—colons can be effective because they draw the reader's attention to the material that follows the colon.

Colons can be used in the following situations:

1. To introduce a series:

Three people spoke at the meeting: Elaine Brodie, CEO of Halifax Industries; John Mitchell, President of Oxford Inc.; and Billie Martin, CEO of Gigantic Corporation.

2. To introduce a direct quotation, especially a long quotation that is set off from the main body of the text:

The senior partner issued the following instruction: "All audit workpapers should include concise, well-organized memos summarizing any problem revealed by the audit."

Professor David A. Ziebart has this to say about technical accounting research:

. . . [technical accounting] research . . . is a process, and its result is a defensible solution to the problem or issue at hand. By process we mean a systematic routine of identifying the problem or issue, specifying alternative plausible solutions, conducting an inquiry into the propriety of the alternatives, evaluating the authoritative literature found, making a choice among the alternatives, and communicating the results. Since the solution must be defensible, the accounting professional must be certain that the search of the professional literature is exhaustive and the reasoning employed in determining the solution is sound.[2]

3. To emphasize a summary or explanation:

Our study of Sebastian Enterprises has revealed one primary problem: Unless management hires new researchers to develop technical innovations, Sebastian will lose its position of market dominance.

Note: When the summary or explanation following the colon is a complete sentence, as in this example, it is correct to capitalize the first letter of the sentence, or to use a lowercase letter:

Our study of Sebastian Enterprises has revealed one primary problem: unless management hires new researchers to develop technical innovations, Sebastian will lose its position of market dominance.

4. Following the salutation in a business letter:

Dear Ms. Wade:

When a colon introduces a series, an explanation, or a summary, the clause that precedes the colon should be a complete statement:

We have sent engagement letters to the following clients: B and B Conglomerates, Abigail's Catnip Boutique, and Sharkey's Aquarium Supplies.

not

We have sent engagement letters to: B and B Conglomerates, Abigail's Catnip Boutique, and Sharkey's Aquarium Supplies.

Semicolons (;) are used for only two situations: between independent clauses (see the discussion of comma splices on pages 86–87) and between items in a series, if the items themselves have internal commas:

Promotions were announced for Ann Moore, regional vice president; Larry Yeo, sales manager; and John Green, internal control manager.

DIRECT QUOTATIONS

The punctuation of direct quotations depends on their length. Short quotations (fewer than five typed lines) are usually run in with the text and enclosed with quotation marks. Longer quotations are set off from the text—indented 1 inch from the left margin—with no quotation marks. Direct quotations should be formally introduced; a colon may separate the introduction from the quoted material. Study the following examples:

According to a recent publication of the FASB, "*Accounting Standards Codification*™ is the source of authoritative generally accepted accounting principles (GAAP) recognized by the FASB to be applied to nongovernmental entities."[3]

The FASB has issued the following statement about codification:

The FASB *Accounting Standards Codification*™ is the source of authoritative generally accepted accounting principles (GAAP) recognized by the FASB to be applied to nongovernmental entities. The

Codification is effective for interim and annual periods ending after September 15, 2009. All previous level (a)-(d) US GAAP standards issued by a standard setter are superseded. Level (a)-(d) US GAAP refers to the previous accounting hierarchy. All other accounting literature not included in the Codification will be considered non-authoritative.[4]

A direct quotation requires a citation identifying its source. It's also better to identify briefly the source of a quotation within the text itself, as the preceding examples illustrate. If a quotation comes from an individual, use his or her complete name the first time you quote from this person. You may also need to give the title or position of the person you are quoting, or otherwise explain that person's credentials. Study the following examples:

According to Richard Smith, an executive officer of the Fairways Corporation, "The industry faces an exciting challenge in meeting foreign competition."

Elaine Howard, who supervised the market research for the new product, provided this assessment of its sales potential: "Within five months from the product's introduction into the market, we expect sales to approach 500,000 units."

Notice the placement of punctuation in relation to quotation marks:

- Periods and commas should be placed inside the quotation marks:

  Allison said, "Our audit is complete."

  "Our audit is complete," Allison said.

- Semicolons should be placed outside the quotation marks:

  Allison said, "Our audit is complete"; a further examination of the files, however, revealed that additional work was necessary.

- Placement of a question mark will vary, depending on whether the question mark is part of the original quotation:

  Allison said, "How much additional work is there?"

  Did Allison say, "I'm sick and tired of this audit"?

One final remark: Some writers, especially students writing papers for academic courses, may depend too heavily on direct quotation. It's usually better to paraphrase—to express someone else's ideas in your own words—unless precise quotation would be an advantage. As a rule, no more than 10% of an academic paper should be direct quotation. To be most effective, quotations should be used sparingly, and then only for authoritative support or dramatic effect.

Chapter 8, which discusses accounting research, gives more information on the use of sources, including direct quotations and paraphrases.

SPELLING

Finished, revised writing should be entirely free of misspelled words. When you work at a word processor, use a spell-checker to catch misspelled words and typographical errors. Note that a spell-checker will not distinguish between homonyms such as *affect* and *effect* or *their* and *there*; nor will it check the spelling of most proper nouns, such as names. You may find it helpful to consult a dictionary when you aren't sure about a word's spelling.

Spelling: Always check every word!

The following short list contains words commonly misspelled or misused by accountants:

accrual, accrued

advise/advice

affect/effect

cost/costs, consist/consists, risk/risks

led, misled

occurred, occurring, occurrence

principal/principle

receivable, receive

separate, separately

The italicized words in the following sentences are often confused:

Please *advise* the customers to put the invoice number on their checks. [*Advise* is a verb.]
The *advice* we received was quite helpful. [*Advice* is a noun.]

This change in accounting policy will not *affect* the financial statements. [*Affect* is usually a verb; in the social and cognitive sciences, it can be used as a noun meaning *emotion* or *mood*.]
This change in accounting policy will have no *effect* on the financial statements. [*Effect* is usually a noun. Rarely, *effect* is a verb meaning to cause to happen.]

The replacement *cost* for the equipment is more than we had estimated. [*Cost* is singular.]
The *costs* to repair the equipment will affect the budget. [*Costs* is plural, but when you say the word aloud, you may not hear the final *s*.]

Our recommendation *consists* of three measures.
Our recommendations *consist* of three measures.

Investment is this stock carries a *risk*.
Investment in these stocks may carry several *risks*.

The ambiguous footnote may *mislead* investors. [*Mislead* is present or future tense.]
This ambiguous footnote *misled* investors. [*Misled* is past tense.]

How should we record the *principal* of this loan? [The *principal* is the face amount of the loan.]
This procedure does not follow generally accepted accounting *principles*. [*Principles* are rules.]
The *principal* reason for the investment is to generate income. [*Principal* means most important.]

HELP FROM THE COMPUTER

Some writers check their text for grammatical errors by using grammar-check software that is included in most word processing programs. These grammar-check programs can help you identify some problems with grammar, including errors with verbs, pronouns, and punctuation. These computer aids may not catch all your grammatical errors, however, and they may flag as an error a usage that is actually correct.

Using a spell-checker is another matter. As we've pointed out many times, a spell-checker is a tremendous help in correcting spelling and typographical errors.

A final word: Be sure to proofread the final hard copy of your document for errors you may have missed earlier. Computers aren't foolproof; sometimes what appears on the screen doesn't look the same on a printed page. Any errors, including those caused by the computer or printer, make work look sloppy and the writer seem careless. Effective writing should look professional: correct, neat, and polished.

In summary, Standard English—including correct grammar, punctuation, and spelling is essential for polished, professional writing. Don't just guess about the correct usage. Resolve your uncertainties with a grammar handbook, dictionary, spell-checker, or grammar checker. Remember the needs of your readers. Using Standard English is necessary for smooth, clear reading.

This chapter has provided another guideline for effective writing; we now have seventeen.

1. **Analyze the purpose of the writing, the accounting issues involved, and the needs and expectations of the readers.**
2. **Organize your ideas so that readers will find them easy to follow.**
3. **Write the draft and then revise it to make the writing polished and correct.**
4. **Make the writing unified. All sentences should relate to the main idea, either directly or indirectly. Eliminate digressions and irrelevant detail.**

5. Use summary sentences and transitions to make your writing coherent.
6. Write in short paragraphs that begin with clear topic sentences.
7. Develop paragraphs by illustration, definition, detail, and appeals to authority.
8. Be concise—make every word count.
9. Keep it simple—use simple vocabulary and short sentences.
10. Write with active verbs and descriptive nouns.
11. Use jargon only when your readers understand it. Define technical terms when necessary.
12. Be precise—avoid ambiguous and unclear writing.
13. Be concrete and specific. Use facts, details, and examples.
14. Use active voice for most sentences.
15. Vary vocabulary, sentence lengths, and sentence structures. Read the writing aloud to hear how it sounds.
16. Write from the reader's point of view. Use tone to show courtesy and respect.
17. Proofread for grammar, punctuation, spelling, and typographical errors.

TEST YOURSELF

Identify and correct the errors in the following exercises, using the guidelines discussed in this chapter. Answers are provided below.

1. Beth Cobb argued that these expenditures do not provide future benefits, thus, she expensed them.
2. Each candidate must demonstrate their mastery of communication skills.
3. One provision of the new policies are causing confusion for the auditors.
4. New SEC requirements for handling this kind of transaction forces accountants to change the way they perform some procedures.
5. We currently value our inventories according to LIFO not FIFO.
6. Many types of users rely on financial statement information, for example, investors may use the information to decide whether to purchase stock in the company.
7. If we change our marketing strategy, we would attract more customers.
8. We might suggest to the controller that he consider the FASB's Accounting Standards Codification® Topic 805 which deals with accounting standards for business combinations.
9. A statement with supplementary disclosures provide additional information to investors.

10. In spite of the uncertain outlook for the housing industry, however, we project that our sales will increase this year by at least
10%.

TEST YOURSELF: ANSWERS

(Note: Some of the errors can be corrected in more than one way. For
most sentences, this key shows only one possible correction. If you
recognize the error, you probably understand how to correct it.)

1. Comma splice. Correction:
   Beth Cobb argued that these expenditures do not provide future
   benefits; thus, she expensed them.
2. Pronoun agreement. Correction:
   Candidates must demonstrate their mastery of communication
   skills.
3. Subject-verb agreement. Correction:
   One provision of the new policies is causing confusion for the auditors. (The verb should agree with *provision*.)
4. Subject-verb agreement. Correction:
   New SEC requirements for handling this kind of transaction force
   accountants to change the way they perform some procedures.
   [The verb should agree with the subject *requirements*.]
5. Comma error. Correction:
   We currently value our inventories according to LIFO, not FIFO.
6. Comma splice. Correction:
   Many types of users rely on financial statement information. For
   example, investors may use the information to decide whether to
   purchase stock in the company.
   [Alternate: Many . . . information; for example, . . .]
7. Mood shift. Correction:
   If we changed our marketing strategy, we would attract more
   customers.
   or
   If we change our marketing strategy, we will attract more customers. [The original sentence contained a shift in mood from indicative to subjunctive. Either mood is correct here; the key is to be
   consistent.]
8. Comma error. Correction:
   We might suggest to the controller that he consider the FASB's
   Accounting Standards Codification® Topic 805, which deals with
   accounting standards for business combinations. [In this example,
   we assume we know the controller, who is a man. If we know the
   controller is a woman, the pronoun should be changed to *she*.]

9. Subject-verb agreement. Correction:
A statement with supplementary disclosures provides additional information to investors. [The verb should agree with *statement*.]
10. Correct. [*However* doesn't come between two independent clauses in this sentence.]

EXERCISES

Exercise 5–1 [General]

Join these independent clauses together in three ways.

we should file our state income taxes by April 15

for our federal taxes we can request an extension

Exercise 5–2 [General]

Identify and correct fragments, comma splices, or fused sentences. Some sentences are correct.

1. The accounting department had added several new employees, thus, we had a training session.
2. To improve our profits; therefore, we reduced expenses.
3. The proposal was unclear, so the Board requested additional information.
4. Tax season is our busiest time of the year everyone works long hours.
5. After the president announced the new policy, employees became worried.
6. Although, the new equipment has improved our rate of production.
7. The reason for our poor profit performance being that the market is saturated.
8. Accountants write many letters as part of their professional responsibilities, for example, they may write letters to the IRS.
9. Two managers postponed their vacations, and thus we were able to handle the emergency.
10. Although we increased our advertising, sales did not improve.

Exercise 5–3 [General]

Some of these sentences have verb errors, either subject-verb agreement or shifts in tense or mood. Identify these errors and correct the sentences.

1. Problems with implementing the new inventory system has frustrated everyone.

2. If we hired a consultant, we will be able to design a new system.
3. Neither the president nor the supervisors understand the new policy.
4. One problem we found in our reviews of the records were that revenues were not always recorded in the proper period.
5. A statement with supplementary disclosures provide additional information to investors.
6. The physical flow of goods generally follow the FIFO pattern.
7. Each of these statements is prepared according to GAAP.
8. We reviewed the client's system of internal control; then we will recommend ways to improve it.
9. The future benefits provided by the bond is partly due to its high interest rate.
10. Restating asset values to current costs results in realized and unrealized holding gains and losses.

Exercise 5–4 [General]

Correct any pronoun errors you find in the following sentences.

1. When an investor or creditor wishes to compare two companies, they review the companies' financial statements.
2. Hamilton Exports, Inc., increased their advertising this year.
3. The FASB deals with research and development costs in its Accounting Standards Codification® Topic 730.
4. Management is interested in improving the revenue figures for their report to the stockholders.
5. Each accountant is required to complete his report on time.
6. The Smallwood Corporation has greatly increased it's advertising expense.
7. A switch to LIFO usually results in a lower income tax liability and a lower inventory figure on the balance sheet; this would be important to our company.
8. The Board of Directors will hold its next meeting in July.
9. Every corporation coming under SEC regulations must follow certain procedures in preparing their financial statements.
10. Everyone registering for the convention will receive a package of information when they arrive.

Exercise 5–5 [General]

Revise the following sentence for parallel grammatical structure:

The hiring decision will be based on three criteria: work experience, education, and whether the applicants have good communication skills.

Exercise 5–6 [General]

a. Complete the following chart.

Singular	Singular Possessive	Plural Possessive
statement		
company		
business		
cost		
risk		
CPA		
year		
industry		

b. Use the words from the chart to fill in these sentences. The singular form of the correct word is given in the parentheses.

1. (CPA) _____ from all over the country will be at the convention.
2. (business) Investors examine a _____ statements to determine its financial condition.
3. (cost) Record all these _____ in the proper accounts.
4. (statement) Which of the _____ is in error?
5. (cost) What is the replacement _____ of this machine?
6. (risk) Investors in these bonds must accept certain _____.
7. (industry) Research and development are crucial in many _____.
8. (year) We should see a profit in two _____ time.
9. (company) The Board of Directors considered the _____ pension plan.
10. (statement) We are making changes in the two _____ totals.

Exercise 5–7 [General]

Punctuate the following sentences correctly.

1. The Board of Directors met December 12, 2014 in Charlotte North Carolina.
2. To increase the revenues from its new product the company introduced an advertising campaign in New York Chicago and Los Angeles.
3. The biggest problem in our firm however is obsolete inventories.
4. The firm hired two new auditors thus the work will be finished on time.

5. For example Elixir Products should consider the FASB's Accounting Standards Codification® Topic 840 which deals with leases.
6. The auditors revealed several problems in Thompson Company's financial records such as its depreciation policy its handling of bad debts and its inventory accounting.
7. The presidents letter contained the following warning "If our revenues don't increase soon the plant may be forced to close"
8. "We're planning a new sales strategy" the manager wrote in reply.
9. We have decided not to invest in the Allied bonds at this time instead we are considering Blackstone's common stocks.
10. Although our revenues increased during June expenses rose at an alarming rate.

Exercise 5–8 [General]

Identify and correct any misspelled words in the following list. Look up any words you are unsure of; not all of these words were included in the chapter.

1. its (the possessive pronoun)
2. recieve
3. occured
4. seperate
5. accural
6. advice (the verb)
7. existance
8. principle (the rule)
9. cost (plural)
10. mislead (past tense)
11. advise (the noun)
12. effect (the noun)
13. thier
14. intrest
15. trail balance

Exercise 5–9 [General]

Revise the following sentences, as needed, using the guidelines covered in this chapter.

1. The letter was dated May 8 2014 and mailed from Boston Massachusetts.
2. The guidelines will explain who is eligible for the benefits, costs, and how to apply.
3. We have increased our advertising thus we hope to sell more of our product.

4. The report was signed by the controller the internal auditor and the vice president.
5. Neither Susan nor Lisa are on the committee.
6. This is the employee's parking lot.
7. Either the computers or the printer are malfunctioning.
8. The benefits of this health insurance policy is obvious to employees.
9. We review the client's system of internal control. Then we will recommend ways to improve it.
10. Three new procedures were used to improve the internal control system. This was the responsibility of Hugh Tran.

Exercise 5–10 [General]

Revise the following memo, using the guidelines you've studied in this and other chapters. Your goal will be to produce a more effective memo.

FIGURE 5–1   Memo to Accompany Exercise 5–10

To:	Miss Elaine Jacobs
From:	Jonathan Brooks
Subject:	Banquet for Veteran Employees
Date:	March 12 2014

How are you doing? I am fine.

I have been asked by the Human Resources Department to organize a banquet for employees who have been with our firm ten years or more we are considering scheduling the event for May 8 which will be a convenient time for most people. Each of the honorees have already agreed that the date will work with his schedules. Being that you have experience in setting up events for our department. We hope you will take charge of the arrangement with the caterer the florist and the printer for the program. All these cost covered by the Human Resources Department.

In the past, we give special gifts to the honorees, therefore they has something tangible as a reward for their service. Please ask somebody to look into this, coordinate with Human Resources about the amount of money we can spend on each persons' gift. How many honoree's we have will effect the amount we can spend on each gift.

We want to ensure that each honoree realizes how much the firm appreciate's his service.

Please let me know if you can do this. Also can you suggest names of other people who might be willing to work on a committee for this banquet. I'm too busy with more important work to spend much time on this project.

NOTES

1. *Merriam-Webster's Collegiate Dictionary*, 11th ed. (Springfield, Mass: Merriam-Webster, Incorporated, 2004), 1216.
2. David. A. Ziebart, et al, 2nd ed., *An Introduction to Applied Professional Research for Accountants* (Upper Saddle River, NJ: Prentice Hall, 2002), 3.
3. Financial Accounting Standards Board, "Notice to Constituents about the Codification," *Accounting Standards Codification,*® v 4.1 (Stamford, Conn: FASB, April 30, 2010), 4.
4. Ibid.

CHAPTER

Format for Clarity:
Document Design

How a document looks at first glance can make a big difference in how the reader reacts to it. An attractive document generally gets a positive response, but a paper that is not pleasing to the eye may never be read. A good design does more for the readers than appeal to them visually. A well-planned format also contributes to the clarity of documents by making them easier to read. In fact, the SEC stresses the importance of document design to make financial statement disclosures useful to investors. According to an SEC commissioner, "not only is the choice of words critical, but a document's format and placement of information on the page are equally important elements of getting the message across."[1] Good design also helps a document look polished and professional after final revision, which is the seventh tip for effective writing (refer to Figure 1–2 in Chapter 1).

This chapter looks at techniques of document design that you can use to make everything you write look more appealing. These techniques can be used for any kind of document, including letters, memos, reports, and even email. We consider the choice of paper and print and the use of white space. We also show how techniques of formatting, such as headings, lists, and graphic illustrations, can make your documents clearer and more readable. Later chapters cover the conventions and formats specific to particular kinds of documents, such as the standard parts of letters, memos, and reports. Chapter 12 discusses formatting techniques for email.

GOOD DESIGN: AN ILLUSTRATION

To illustrate the difference good design can make in the readability of a document, study the example in Figures 6–1 through 6–3, which are three versions of the same memo. Figure 6–1 shows straight text, with no divisions for paragraphs, headings, or other features of good document design. Figure 6–2 divides the text into readable paragraphs with a little more white space, and Figure 6–3 uses additional white space, headings, and a set-off list. Which version of the memo do you think is most effective? Does the version in Figure 6–3 suggest formatting techniques you can use in your own writing?

FIGURE 6–1   Memo for Comparison (see Figures 6–2 and 6–3)

TO: Paul J. Streer, Partner

FROM: Billie Sanders

DATE: April 17, 2014

SUBJECT: Tax implications of Robert Burke's prospective joint
purchase of rental real estate.

Our client, Robert Burke, has expressed concern about the tax
implications of a venture he is considering, a joint purchase of real
estate with Anne Simmons. The issue that must be considered is
whether Mr. Burke will be subject to a deduction limitation because
the property will be used as a residence by Ms. Simmons. The
conclusion is that because the rental agreement is a shared equity
financing agreement, Mr. Burke will not be subject to a deduction
limitation. On January 1, 2015, Ms. Simmons and Mr. Burke plan to
purchase rental real estate, which Ms. Simmons will occupy as her
residence. They will enter into an agreement whereby Mr. Burke
will provide the down payment and one-half of the monthly mortgage payment. Ms. Simmons will pay the remaining portion of the
monthly mortgage, monthly rental payments to Mr. Burke, and the
monthly operating costs of the home. They will split the property
taxes evenly. Mr. Burke will receive one-half of the appreciation
value of the home upon its sale and has the option to demand that
his interest in the property be paid to him after five years. The issue
to be settled is whether Mr. Burke is subject to the deduction limitation in 280A(c)(5) because the rental property was used as a residence by the taxpayer. The agreement between Ms. Simmons and
Mr. Burke qualifies as a shared equity financing agreement under
280A(d)(3)(C). Because the agreement can be classified as such,
280A(c)(5) will not apply and cannot limit the deductions attributable to the rental of Mr. Burke's share of the property to the gross
income derived from the rental. This conclusion was also reached by
the IRS in Private Letter Ruling 8410038. To override the limitation
of 280A(c)(5), the shared equity financing agreement must meet certain requirements: (1) under 280A(d)(3)(D), both Ms. Simmons and
Mr. Burke must have a qualified ownership interest in the property
(an undivided interest for more than fifty years in the entire property) and (2) the rent Ms. Simmons pays to Mr. Burke must be the
fair rental at the time the agreement is entered, taking into account
Ms. Simmons' qualified interest. Because Mr. Burke will be allowed
the deductions and Ms. Simmons will not (except for expenses allowable even if the dwelling were not rented), payment of expenses
should be the responsibility of Mr. Burke. The agreement can
contain a provision that compensates Mr. Burke for this additional
encumbrance. If those expenses were paid by Ms. Simmons, the
deduction would go unused. The joint purchase Mr. Burke proposes
to enter into is sound. The agreement will not have unfavorable tax
implications for him if he is careful to follow these recommendations.

FIGURE 6–2 Memo for Comparison (see Figures 6–1 and 6–3)

TO: Paul J. Streer, Partner

FROM: Billie Sanders

DATE: April 17, 2014

SUBJECT: Tax implications of Robert Burke's prospective joint purchase of rental real estate.

Our client, Robert Burke, has expressed concern about the tax implications of a venture he is considering, a joint purchase of real estate with Anne Simmons. The issue that must be considered is whether Mr. Burke will be subject to a deduction limitation because the property will be used as a residence by Ms. Simmons. The conclusion is that because the rental agreement is a shared equity financing agreement, Mr. Burke will not be subject to a deduction limitation.

On January 1, 2015, Ms. Simmons and Mr. Burke plan to purchase rental real estate, which Ms. Simmons will occupy as her residence. They will enter into an agreement whereby Mr. Burke will provide the down payment and one-half of the monthly mortgage payment. Ms. Simmons will pay the remaining portion of the monthly mortgage, monthly rental payments to Mr. Burke, and the monthly operating costs of the home. They will split the property taxes evenly. Mr. Burke will receive one-half of the appreciation value of the home upon its sale and has the option to demand that his interest in the property be paid to him after five years.

The issue to be settled is whether Mr. Burke is subject to the deduction limitation in 280A(c)(5) because the rental property was used as a residence by the taxpayer.

The agreement between Ms. Simmons and Mr. Burke qualifies as a shared equity financing agreement under 280A(d)(3)(C). Because the agreement can be classified as such, 280A(c)(5) will not apply and cannot limit the deductions attributable to the rental of Mr. Burke's share of the property to the gross income derived from the rental. This conclusion was also reached by the IRS in Private Letter Ruling 8410038.

To override the limitation of 280A(c)(5), the shared equity financing agreement must meet certain requirements: (1) under 280A(d)(3)(D), both Ms. Simmons and Mr. Burke must have a qualified ownership interest in the property (an undivided interest for more than fifty years in the entire property) and (2) the rent Ms. Simmons pays to Mr. Burke must be the fair rental at the time the agreement is entered, taking into account Ms. Simmons' qualified interest.

Because Mr. Burke will be allowed the deductions and Ms. Simmons will not (except for expenses allowable even if the dwelling were not rented), payment of expenses should be the responsibility of Mr. Burke. The agreement can contain a provision that compensates Mr. Burke for this additional encumbrance. If those expenses were paid by Ms. Simmons, the deduction would go unused.

The joint purchase Mr. Burke proposes to enter into is sound. The agreement will not have unfavorable tax implications for him if he is careful to follow these recommendations.

FIGURE 6–3   Memo for Comparison (see Figures 6–1 and 6–2)

TO: Paul J. Streer, Partner

FROM: Billie Sanders

DATE: April 17, 2014

SUBJECT: Tax implications of Robert Burke's prospective joint purchase of rental real estate.

Our client, Robert Burke, has expressed concern about the tax implications of a venture he is considering, a joint purchase of real estate with Anne Simmons. The issue that must be considered is whether Mr. Burke will be subject to a deduction limitation because the property will be used as a residence by Ms. Simmons. The conclusion is that because the rental agreement is a shared equity financing agreement, Mr. Burke will not be subject to a deduction limitation.

Client's Situation

On January 1, 2015, Ms. Simmons and Mr. Burke plan to purchase rental real estate, which Ms. Simmons will occupy as her residence. They will enter into an agreement whereby Mr. Burke will provide the down payment and one-half of the monthly mortgage payment. Ms. Simmons will pay the remaining portion of the monthly mortgage, monthly rental payments to Mr. Burke, and the monthly operating costs of the home. They will split the property taxes evenly. Mr. Burke will receive one-half of the appreciation value of the home upon its sale and has the option to demand that his interest in the property be paid to him after five years.

Tax Issue

The issue to be settled is whether Mr. Burke is subject to the deduction limitation in 280A(c)(5) because the rental property was used as a residence by the taxpayer.

Tax Implications

The agreement between Ms. Simmons and Mr. Burke qualifies as a shared equity financing agreement under 280A(d)(3)(C). Because the agreement can be classified as such, 280A(c)(5) will not apply and cannot limit the deductions attributable to the rental of Mr. Burke's share of the property to the gross income derived from the rental. This conclusion was also reached by the IRS in Private Letter Ruling 8410038.

Recommendations

To override the limitation of 280A(c)(5), the shared equity financing agreement must meet certain requirements:

(1) Under 280A(d)(3)(D), both Ms. Simmons and Mr. Burke must have a qualified ownership interest in the property (an undivided interest for more than fifty years in the entire property).

(2) The rent Ms. Simmons pays to Mr. Burke must be the fair rental at the time the agreement is entered, taking into account Ms. Simmons' qualified interest.

Because Mr. Burke will be allowed the deductions and Ms. Simmons will not (except for expenses allowable even if the dwelling were not rented), payment of expenses should be the responsibility of Mr. Burke. The agreement can contain a provision that compensates Mr. Burke for this additional encumbrance. If those expenses were paid by Ms. Simmons, the deduction would go unused.

The joint purchase Mr. Burke proposes to enter into is sound. The agreement will not have unfavorable tax implications for him if he is careful to follow these recommendations.

A PROFESSIONAL APPEARANCE

If you already have a job, you may find models of well-designed documents written by people with whom you work. In fact, your employer may expect all documents to be written a certain way—in a standard format, for example, and on the company's letterhead and standard stock paper. You'll seem more professional if you learn your employer's expectations for document design and adhere to them.

Often, whether you're on the job or still in school, you'll have some leeway in how you design documents. The remainder of this chapter looks at techniques you can use to give your documents a professional appearance. You should choose high-quality material—the best paper and the best print. Plan your pages so that they have an attractive use of margins and white space, and be sure they are perfectly neat.

Paper and Print

If you're already employed, you might not have any choice about the paper; you'll probably use your company's letterhead stationery and standard stock for all your documents. If you are still a student, you need to select a paper that makes a good impression. For the final copy of a paper you submit for a grade, your instructor may prefer that you use 8½- × 11-inch paper of a high-quality bond, about 24-pound weight, in white or off-white.

The print of your document is another consideration. After you prepare your final manuscript, print it on a good printer that gives a professional appearance.

Whatever word processing program and printer you use, you will probably have a choice of type sizes and font styles. Choose a 12-point type size and a standard font such as Times New Roman throughout your document. Type sizes and fonts should be easy to read, and they should not draw attention to themselves, so be conservative in your choices. Never use unusual fonts for business documents.

White Space and Margins

White space is the part of a page that does not have any print. White space includes margins, the space between sections, and the space around graphic illustrations.

A document with visual appeal will have a good balance between print and white space. White space also makes a document easier to read. The space between sections, for example, helps the reader see the paper's structure.

There are no hard-and-fast rules for margin widths or the number of lines between sections. As a general guideline, plan a 1-inch margin for the sides and bottoms of your papers. The top of the first page should have a 2-inch margin; subsequent pages should have a 1-inch margin at the top.

Leave an extra line space between the sections of your document. A double-spaced page, for example, would have three lines between sections.

For any document that is single-spaced, be sure to double-space between paragraphs.

Neatness Counts!

Sloppiness in a document is unprofessional and careless. Your computer's spell-checker, will help you to find errors and make corrections with ease. (Remember, spell-checkers don't distinguish between homonyms like *bear* and *bare*. Chapter 5 discusses this problem more fully.) Always proofread the final hard copy as well, because it's possible for printing errors to appear on the printed page that don't show up on a computer screen.

FORMATTING

Some writers think of their document's format only in terms of straight text: page after page of print unbroken by headings or other divisions. If you look at almost any professional publication, including this handbook, you'll see how various formatting devices, such as headings, lists, and set-off material, make pages more attractive and easier to read.

Headings

For any document longer than about half a page, you can use headings to divide the paper into sections. Headings make a paper less intimidating to readers because the divisions break up the text into smaller chunks. Headings give readers a chance to pause and reflect on what they've read.

Headings also help readers by showing them the paper's structure and the topics it covers. In fact, many readers preview the contents of a document by skimming through to read the headings. For this reason, headings should be worded so that they indicate the contents of the section to follow. Sometimes headings suggest the main idea of the section, but they should clearly identify the topic discussed. If you look through this text, you'll see how the headings suggest the chapters' contents.

Headings can be broken down into several levels of division. Some headings indicate major sections of a paper, and others indicate minor divisions. In other words, a paper can have both headings and subheadings. In this chapter, for example, "A PROFESSIONAL APPEARANCE" indicates a major section of the chapter; "Paper and Print" marks the beginning of a subtopic, because it's just one aspect of a document's appearance. Generally, a short document needs only one heading level, but this rule can vary depending on what you are writing.

The style of the heading (how the heading is placed and printed on the page) varies with the levels of division. Some styles indicate major headings; other styles indicate subheadings. As an example, the major headings might be printed in a boldface font in all capital letters at the left margin, and subheadings might be indented, bold-faced, with only the initial letter of each main word capitalized, as follows:

FIRST LEVEL: BOLD FONT, LEFT MARGIN, ALL CAPS
   Second Level: Bold Font, Initial Letters Capitalized, Indented
   Third Level: Indented, Italicized

Here is another example of heading styles and the corresponding levels of division:

   FIRST LEVEL: CENTERED, ALL CAPS, BOLDFACED
Second Level: Left Margin, Boldfaced
   Third Level: Indented, Italicized

If you use fewer than three levels, you can follow this last system of headings, using any of the three styles, as long as they are in descending order. For example, you might use second-level headings for main topics and third-level headings for subtopics. If you are using only one level of headings, any style is acceptable.

When you write the headings for your paper, it's preferable to have all the headings of a certain level grammatically parallel: Nouns and noun phrases, such as the headings in Figure 6–3, are common for headings. Verb phrases can also be an effective choice if you're enumerating the steps in a process, or a series of actions someone will perform. For example, a memo written to summarize work done on an audit might use these verb phrases as headings for the body of the memo, which describes the steps of the inventory audit process.

> *Observing clients' inventory taking*
> *Making test counts*
> *Identifying obsolete and damaged goods*
> *Observing cutoff controls*

Chapter 5 discusses parallel grammatical structure more fully.

It's possible to overuse headings. You should not normally use a heading for every paragraph, for example.

Lists and Set-Off Material

Another formatting technique that can make a document easier to read is set-off material, especially lists. Mark each item on the list with a number, a bullet, or some other marker. Double-space before and after the list. The items can be single-spaced or double-spaced.

Here is an example using bullets:

Your firm should update its systems in these areas:

- Budgets
- Payrolls
- Fixed assets
- Accounts payable
- Accounts receivable

Set-off lists not only improve the paper's appearance by providing more white space, but they also make the paper more readable. The following example presents the same information as straight text and in a list format. Which arrangement do you prefer?

The meeting will discuss the new vacation policy. First, we'll explain who is eligible for extended vacation leave. Next we'll discuss when the policy will take effect. Finally, we'll discuss how to get vacation requests approved.

The meeting will discuss the new vacation policy:

- Eligibility for extended leave
- Effective date
- Approval process

Remember that set-off lists should be written with parallel grammatical structure (see page 93). The set-off list in the previous example uses noun phrases.

Occasionally, you'll use set-off material for other purposes besides lists. Long direct quotations are set off, and on rare occasions you might set off a sentence or two for emphasis. Chapters 2 through 6 use this technique to emphasize the guidelines for effective writing. Chapter 8 discusses the use of direct quotations.

Pagination

The next formatting technique is a simple one, but it's overlooked surprisingly often. For every document longer than one page, be sure to include page numbers. They can be placed at either the top or the bottom of the page, be centered, or be placed in the right-hand corner. Begin numbering on page 2.

GRAPHIC ILLUSTRATIONS

Graphic illustrations—such as tables, graphs, and flowcharts—can make a document more interesting and informative. They enable you to summarize a great deal of information quickly and help readers identify and remember important ideas.

TABLE 6–1 The Northeastern Beverage Company and Subsidiaries Consolidated Statements of Income

	Year ended December 31		
	2013	2012	2011
(In millions except per share data)			
NET OPERATING REVENUES	**$41,879**	$ 38,563	$ 34,121
Cost of goods sold	**12,173**	11,924	9,945
GROSS PROFIT	**29,706**	26,639	24,176
Selling, general, and administrative expenses	**15,674**	12,949	11,811
Other operating charges	**401**	357	332
OPERATING INCOME	**13,631**	13,333	12,033
Interest Income	**163**	302	283
Interest Expense	**315**	408	413
Equity income (loss)—net	**666**	15	27
Other income (loss)—net	**39**	31	(4)
INCOME BEFORE INCOME TAXES	**14,184**	13,273	11,926
Income taxes	**3,429**	2,761	2,173
CONSOLIDATED NET INCOME	**$10,755**	$10,512	$ 9,753
Less: Net income attributable to Noncontrolling interests	**98**	76	61
NET INCOME ATTRIBUTABLE TO SHAREOWNERS OF THE NORTHEASTERN BEVERAGE COMPANY	**$10,657**	$10,436	$ 9,692
BASIC INCOME PER SHARE	**$3.02**	$3.01	$ 2.87
DILUTED NET INCOME PER SHARE	**$3.00**	$2.99	$ 2.85
AVERAGE SHARES OUTSTANDING	**3,528**	3,472	3,381
Effect of dilutive securities	**26**	19	17
AVERAGE SHARES OUTSTANDING ASSUMING DILUTION	**3,554**	3,491	3,398

Refer to Notes to Consolidated Financial Statements.

Tables are an efficient way to summarize numerical data in rows and columns. When you use a table, be sure you label the rows and columns, indicate the units of measure you are reporting, and align the figures. Table 6–1, which shows the consolidated statements of income of The Northeastern Beverage Company and Subsidiaries, is an example of a table.

A pie chart shows how a whole is divided into parts, just as a pie is divided into slices. When you use a pie chart, label the wedges and show what percentages of the whole they represent. The pie chart in Figure 6–4 shows The Northeastern Beverage Company's case volume by state for 2013. The circle represents the total volume, and the slices show the percentages of that total for each state.

FIGURE 6–4   The Northeastern Beverage Company Case Volume by State

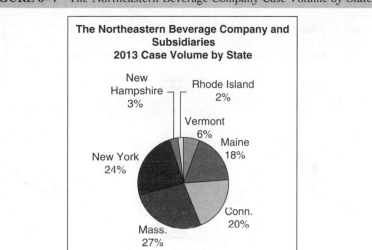

Graphs, which can take several forms, are useful for comparisons. Two of the most common types of graphs are bar graphs and line graphs. Bar graphs compare quantities or amounts. The bar graph in Figure 6–5 shows total revenue for Southeastern Sporting Goods.

A line graph, which also compares quantities, is helpful for showing trends. A line graph may have a single line or multiple lines. The line graph in Figure 6–6 compares the performance of AT&T stock to the Standard and Poor's 500 Index, a Peer Group, and the Standard and Poor's 500 Integrated Telecom Index.

FIGURE 6–5   Southeastern Sporting Goods Total Revenue

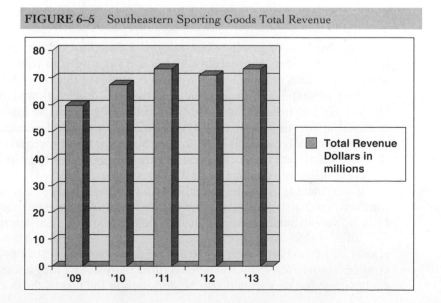

FIGURE 6–6 AT&T Stock Performance Graph

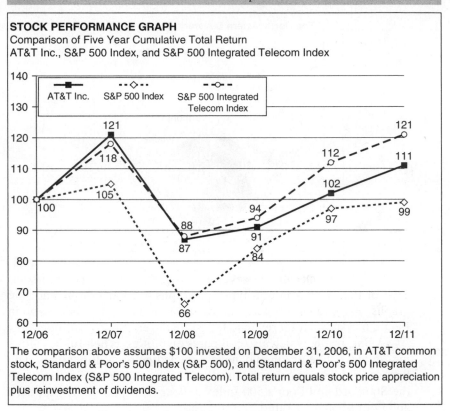

STOCK PERFORMANCE GRAPH
Comparison of Five Year Cumulative Total Return
AT&T Inc., S&P 500 Index, and S&P 500 Integrated Telecom Index

The comparison above assumes $100 invested on December 31, 2006, in AT&T common stock, Standard & Poor's 500 Index (S&P 500), and Standard & Poor's 500 Integrated Telecom Index (S&P 500 Integrated Telecom). Total return equals stock price appreciation plus reinvestment of dividends.

AT&T, "2011 AT&T Annual Report," 2012: 52. http://www.att.com/Common/about_us/files/pdf/ar2011_annual_report.pdf (15 April 2013).

Another type of graphic illustration is a flowchart, which shows the steps in a process or procedure. If you use a flowchart in your documents, use boxes or other shapes to show activities or outcomes; label each box or shape and arrange them so that the process flows from left to right and from the top to the bottom of the page. Use arrows to show the direction of the flow. Figure 6–7 shows a typical example.

Systems analyses often include very sophisticated flowcharts to show how a system works, with established symbols and formats to represent different components of the system.

If you include graphic illustrations in the documents you write, whether flowcharts, graphs, or tables, you should follow certain guidelines. Be sure to number the graphic illustrations and give them descriptive titles. Tables should be called Tables (such as Table 6–1), and graphs and flowcharts should be called Figures (such as Figure 6–7). Graphic illustrations should be labeled sufficiently so that they are self-explanatory, but they should also be discussed in the text of the docu-

FIGURE 6–7   The Cash Flow Estimation Process in Capital Budgeting

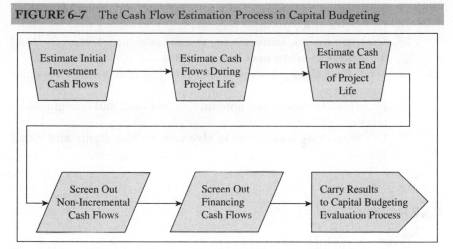

Source: Adapted with permission from Timothy J. Gallagher and Joseph D. Andrew, Jr., *Financial Management: Principles and Practice* (Upper Saddle River, NJ: Prentice-Hall, Inc. © 1996, p. 281).

ment. This discussion should refer to the illustration by description, name, and number. The discussion should precede the illustration. The illustrations can be placed either in the body of the document, close to the place in the text where they are discussed, or in an appendix.

Finally, if you use a graphic illustration from another source, identify the source fully at the bottom of the illustration.

This chapter has completed the guidelines for effective writing.

1. **Analyze the purpose of the writing, the accounting issues involved, and the needs and expectations of the readers.**
2. **Organize your ideas so that readers will find them easy to follow.**
3. **Write the draft and then revise it to make the writing polished and correct.**
4. **Make the writing unified. All sentences should relate to the main idea, either directly or indirectly. Eliminate digressions and irrelevant detail.**
5. **Use summary sentences and transitions to make your writing coherent.**
6. **Write in short paragraphs that begin with clear topic sentences.**
7. **Develop paragraphs by illustrations, definition, detail, and appeals to authority.**
8. **Be concise—make every word count.**
9. **Keep it simple—use simple vocabulary and short sentences.**
10. **Write with active verbs and descriptive nouns.**
11. **Use jargon only when your readers understand it. Define technical terms when necessary.**
12. **Be precise—avoid ambiguous and unclear writing.**

13. **Be concrete and specific. Use facts, details, and examples.**
14. **Use active voice for most sentences.**
15. **Vary vocabulary, sentence lengths, and sentence structures. Read the writing aloud to hear how it sounds.**
16. **Write from the reader's point of view. Use tone to show courtesy and respect.**
17. **Proofread for grammar, punctuation, spelling, and typographical errors.**
18. **Use formatting techniques to give your writing clarity and visual appeal.**

EXERCISES

Exercise 6–1 [Financial]

Review several annual reports issued by publicly traded corporations during the most recent year. Identify some that are examples of good document design and some that are examples of poor document design. Discuss the design strengths and weaknesses of these reports.

Exercise 6–2 [General]

Assume you are the president of your school's chapter of Beta Alpha Psi (the national accounting honorary society). You have been asked by the editor of your school's newspaper to write an article for publication discussing the attractiveness of accounting as a major and job opportunities in the accounting profession. Write the article, using techniques of document design discussed in this chapter. You may wish to refer to Chapter 15 on writing for publication.

Exercise 6–3 [General]

Assume you are the CFO of your company. Write a memo to your accounting staff discussing the importance of what the SEC has referred to as "plain English" to improve the clarity of financial statement disclosures. Use the techniques of document design discussed in this chapter. Chapter 10 discusses memo writing.

Exercise 6–4 [Tax]

A client, Carter Fowlkes, owns a second home that he has been unable to sell for quite a while. He has struck on the idea of granting the local fire department rights to use it for training, including the right to destroy it by fire or other means, if that would prove beneficial to the department. He would then like to deduct the value of the structure on his income tax return. When the fire department is finished with the structure, Mr. Fowlkes would build something else on the property. Your client has asked you to explain what effects this transaction will have on his income taxes. Write a letter to Mr. Fowlkes responding to his inquiry, using the principles of effective document design discussed in this chapter. Chapter 9 discusses letter writing.

Exercise 6–5 [Tax]

In December 2013, one of your clients, Tim Huffman, donated a valuable piece of art to a local charity to be auctioned at its annual fundraising auction. When Mr. Huffman donated the art, it was appraised for $20,000. However, at the auction held on January 20, 2014, it sold for $35,000. Mr. Huffman claims that the appraisal was obviously wrong and that the value of what he donated was obviously $35,000. Consequently, he wants to deduct $35,000 on his 2013 tax return. Write a letter to Mr. Huffman discussing the tax implications of the appraisal and subsequent sale of the art he donated. Use the principles of effective document design discussed in this chapter. Chapter 9 discusses letter writing.

Exercise 6–6 [Auditing]

Assume you are an auditing partner in a regional CPA firm. Write a memo to all audit staff members explaining how subsequent events may or may not affect a compilation and review engagement. Chapter 10 discusses memo writing. Your memo should illustrate effective document design using the techniques discussed in this chapter.

Exercise 6–7 [Auditing]

As a member of the auditing standards team of your CPA firm, you have been asked to write a memo to all audit staff discussing the distinction between technical compliance with GAAP and "fair presentation." You are expected also to include a discussion of what an auditor's obligation is when there is a conflict between these two concepts. Write the memo, paying attention to good document design. Chapter 10 discusses memo writing.

Exercise 6–8 [Auditing/Ethics]

As a member of the ethics standards team of your CPA firm, you have been asked to write a memo to all audit staff discussing the importance of ethics in auditing in general, and of compliance with Rule 501 of the AICPA's *Code of Professional Ethics* in particular. Write the memo, paying attention to good document design. Chapter 10 discusses memo writing.

Exercise 6–9 [Systems]

You are a systems consultant. One of your clients, Lynda Hill, who is comptroller of a medium-size engineering firm in town, has asked you to explain to her what cloud computing is all about and how she might use it to advantage in her accounting system. Write a letter to Ms. Hill responding to her request. Your letter should demonstrate effective document design. Chapter 9 discusses letters.

Exercise 6–10 [Systems]

You are a systems consultant. One of your clients, Ben Hill of Hill Manufacturing, is concerned about protecting his company from fraud. He has recently learned that there is fraud detection software available and has asked you whether or not he should be using such software and what it might do for his company. Write a letter to Mr. Hill responding to his request. Your letter should demonstrate effective document design. Chapter 9 discusses letters.

Exercise 6–11 [International/Managerial/Current Professional Issues]

The International Integrated Reporting Council (IIRC) (www.theiirc.org) believes the current framework of corporate reporting that emphasizes financial statements is not sufficient to answer the question of what the value of the entity is. In the IIRC's view, additional information concerning corporate strategy, governance, performance, and prospects should be reported, along with financial statements, in an "International Integrated Reporting Framework."

Write an article for your business school's newsletter defining and elaborating on this effort of the IIRC as well as evaluating its desirability. Use the techniques of document design discussed in this chapter. Chapter 15 discusses writing for publication.

NOTE

1. Cynthia A. Glassman, "Speech by SEC Commissioner: Remarks at the Plain Language Association International's Fifth International Conference," Securities and Exchange Commission, 2005. http://www.sec.gov/news/speech/spch110405cag.htm (21 January 2013).

CHAPTER

Critical Thinking

7

I n earlier chapters we've noted how important critical thinking skills are to the analysis and communication of accounting
information. We defined *critical thinking* as fair, open-minded
thinking that asks appropriate questions and considers all relevant
information before reaching a conclusion. Critical thinkers consider
problems from multiple points of view before reaching a decision, and
they are careful to avoid errors in reasoning, which are called logical
fallacies. They also use precise, clear language to construct unambiguous arguments that readers can understand and, in turn, evaluate
fairly. In other words, critical thinkers analyze issues and communicate information responsibly; critical thinking is thus a component of
ethical responsibility. And critical thinking is inseparable from effective
communication.

The AICPA recognizes the importance of critical thinking and
evaluates those skills on the CPA exam. In its "Content and Skill
Specifications for the Uniform CPA Examination," the AICPA specifies
"Complex Problem Solving and Judgment."[1] Included in this skill set
are these elements of critical thinking:

- Apply professional skepticism, which is an attitude that includes
  a questioning mind and a critical assessment of information or
  evidence obtained.
- Identify and solve unstructured problems.
- Develop reasonable hypotheses to answer a question or resolve a
  problem.
- Formulate and examine alternative solutions in terms of their
  relative strengths and weaknesses, level of risk, and appropriateness
  for a given situation.
- Develop logical conclusions through the use of inductive and
  deductive reasoning.

(For more information on writing for the CPA exam, consult Chapter 13.)

As you will see, this chapter illustrates how you can develop these
and other critical thinking skills. We will discuss the process of

constructing an argument, two approaches to logical reasoning, and some of the fallacies you should recognize and avoid. We will then show how you can use critical thinking to resolve ethical dilemmas.

MAKING AN ARGUMENT: THE PROCESS

As a practicing professional, you will sometimes be asked to recommend a course of action for your firm or for your clients. To derive a sound recommendation, you must construct an argument. This process can be divided into six steps, some of which have been introduced in earlier chapters. Here is a summary:

1. Identify the key issues.
2. Anticipate all sides to an argument.
3. Research all sides to the argument, using authoritative sources.
4. Weigh the evidence for all sides to the argument, and build support for your position.
5. Identify and respond to counterarguments.
6. Communicate your conclusions.

To illustrate the process, consider this hypothetical scenario. You are an accountant employed by a medium-size accounting firm. The firm has twenty accountants on its staff, in addition to technical and clerical support staff. The firm has had its offices in a grand old office building in the downtown heart of the city for the past sixty years. However, the owners of the building have decided to convert the building to residential condominiums, forcing your firm to relocate. You have been asked to recommend the best alternative for the new office. After researching the alternatives, you will present your recommendation in a memo to the firm's partners. How do you form and communicate your recommendation? The process listed previously will help you as you construct an argument to support your conclusions.

A word of caution is in order here: Remember that it's always important to consider the expectations of your readers and the purpose of the document you are writing. What are the expectations of the partners who asked you to investigate the relocation problem? Do they expect you to identify the one best site for the firm, or have they asked you to recommend several viable locations, giving the advantages and disadvantages of each choice? In the latter case, the partners themselves would make the final selection, based on the information you have provided. You would have narrowed the field, then, through your analysis and research. For the purposes of this hypothetical example, assume that the partners have asked you to recommend what you have identified as the best site. They will expect you to document the thoroughness with which you investigated the alternatives and the reasons for your conclusions.

1. *Identify key issues.* The first step in constructing an argument is to identify the key issues. In the situation just described, the most important issues might be, first, where in the city the new office should be located, and second, whether the firm should lease office space, purchase an office condominium, purchase its own building, or construct its own building. Each of these major issues should be further analyzed. You should consider the availability and costs of suitable space, the suitability of potential sites for the firm's business, and the accounting implications of the decision to lease, purchase, or construct.

2. *Anticipate all sides to the argument.* Before you reach your conclusions, you need to identify all the reasonable alternatives. With preliminary research, you'll gather information about the obvious choices. You also need to identify the preferences of other people involved in the decision and take account of their knowledge, experience, assumptions, and biases. It's especially important to consider the views of those who will make the final decision, in this case the firm's partners. Listen carefully to what other people say, read carefully what they have written on the issues in question, and, where appropriate, ask them to clarify their views or make preliminary suggestions for the best solution to the problem. For example, before you suggest leasing, purchasing, or constructing in this scenario, find out if the partners are willing to consider all three possibilities. You should also determine which sections of the city they believe to be viable locations for the firm. Are they determined to maintain the firm's office in the center of the city, or would they consider moving to a midtown or suburban location?

3. *Research all sides to the argument, using authoritative sources.* After you have identified the alternative solutions to your problem, you can research the possibilities, including sources for both accounting and non accounting information. Consider your firm's needs and how alternative sites would accommodate those needs. Is the location convenient to the firm's employees and clients, and is the location suitable for business? Is adequate parking and/or public transportation available for the firm's employees and clients? What other businesses are located in this area? Would proposed buildings require renovation? What are the costs, in both time and money, of these renovations, as well as other moving costs? All these decisions involve accounting considerations, which you also must research. What are the accounting and tax implications of the decision to lease, purchase, or construct? Refer to specific GAAP and tax provisions for these scenarios. (For more information on using authoritative accounting sources, see Chapter 8.)

4. *Weigh the evidence for all sides to the argument, and build support for your position.* After you've analyzed the information you find in your research, the solution may be obvious. In this example,

assume that you have identified the best site for the firm's relocation after weighing the pros and cons of all alternatives, and that you are ready to give the reasons for your conclusions. Building support for your conclusions involves organizing your ideas and materials in a logical order. This organization might take the form of an outline: the key issues, the recommendations, and the reasons to support your recommendations, from most to least important.

5. *Identify and respond to counterarguments.* In this office relocation example, some of the partners may have initial preferences for a particular location, or they may raise objections to the site you've selected. You should identify in advance the reasons why some of the partners might disagree with your conclusions. That is, you must identify the counterarguments (arguments against your recommendations). You must also decide how you will respond to these objections—whether you will agree with them (concede the counterarguments) or argue against them (refute the counterarguments).

The response to a counterargument may be a combination of concession and refutation. For instance, one of the partners in this example may object to your recommendations because the site you've chosen requires extensive, costly renovation. You might concede that those costs will be high, but also point out that over time the costs will be more than made up because the cost of the new lease (or purchase) will be considerably lower than the cost of the firm's current lease.

Sometimes people constructing an argument believe that presenting all sides of the argument will weaken their position. Just the opposite is the case, however. By presenting all sides, you'll create the impression that you are a responsible person who has carefully considered all sides of an issue before reaching a conclusion. Thus, people will find you credible and fair, and they will take your argument seriously.

To complete this step successfully, keep an open mind and imagine the situation from multiple points of view. Review the questions you asked in step 2 or ask additional questions. In our example, it might even be appropriate for you to seek preliminary feedback on your conclusions from your partners, before you present your final recommendation.

6. *Communicate your conclusions.* In this step, you present your conclusions and your reasons, along with the counterarguments to your recommendations that you have anticipated and your response to those counterarguments. You may present your conclusions orally, perhaps in a meeting, or in a written document such as a memo, letter, or report. In this example, you'll write a memo as the partners have requested. For a written document, you should apply the effective writing techniques discussed in Chapters 1–15 of this text. For an oral presentation, you should follow the guidelines given in

Chapter 16. You may, of course, be asked to present your recommendations in both oral and written formats.

Reaching Sound Conclusions:
Two Approaches to Logic

Critical thinking is the construction of an argument, often in a manner such as the process just outlined. It may also be thought of as an exercise of logic, which is defined as the practice of good reasoning. The science of logic is often divided into inductive and deductive reasoning, as discussed in Chapter 3. As we have seen, the ability to use inductive and deductive reasoning is among the skills tested on the CPA exam. In this chapter, we discuss these forms of reasoning further, as well as some of the more commonly made errors in reasoning, which are called fallacies.

Inductive Reasoning

The process used to construct an argument in the office relocation scenario discussed earlier demonstrates one form of inductive reasoning: gathering evidence, and then reaching a conclusion. More formally, inductive reasoning is defined as reaching conclusions about the entirety of something (the whole) from a study of representative examples (parts of that whole). The scientific method of research is one example of inductive reasoning: observing samples, gathering data, and drawing tentative conclusions, or hypotheses, which are then further tested for verification. Some variations of inductive reasoning include making comparisons (drawing analogies), analyzing causes, conducting surveys, referring to authoritative sources, and citing statistics. In short, inductive reasoning begins with specific facts and from these facts derives general conclusions or principles.

Deductive Reasoning

With inductive reasoning, you gather specific information and then reach a general conclusion. With deductive reasoning, you apply reasoning in the opposite direction; you begin with one or more general assumptions or premises and arrive at a specific conclusion. Consider these examples:

All accounting majors at this university must take a course in tax accounting.

Jenny is an accounting major at this university.

Therefore, Jenny must take a course in tax accounting.

Deductive reasoning is often stated in the form of a syllogism. A *syllogism* consists of a major premise, a minor premise, and a conclusion. In the preceding example, the first line is the major premise, the second line is the minor premise, and the third line is the conclusion.

Here's another example of a syllogism:

MAJOR PREMISE: Asset account balances increase with debits.
MINOR PREMISE: The asset account was debited.
CONCLUSION: The asset account balance increased.

To reach sound conclusions using deductive reasoning, you must be sure your arguments are both valid and sound. These terms—*valid* and *sound*—will become clearer with examples. First, a valid argument is one in which the conclusion has been correctly drawn from the premises. Study the following examples:

Example 1: Valid argument:

MAJOR PREMISE: All the students in this class have passed the placement test.
MINOR PREMISE: Robert is a student in this class.
CONCLUSION: Therefore, Robert has passed the placement test.

Example 2: Invalid argument:

MAJOR PREMISE: All the students in this class have passed the placement test.
MINOR PREMISE: Robert has passed the placement test.
CONCLUSION: Therefore, Robert is a student in this class.

In the valid argument in Example 1, the conclusion has been correctly drawn from the premises, unlike the invalid argument in Example 2. In Example 2, even though Robert has passed the placement test, he might not be a student in the class for any number of reasons. He might have taken the class in an earlier semester, postponed the class until a later semester, be enrolled in a different section of the class, changed his major, or transferred to another school.

Let's look at two more examples. Example 3 is a valid argument—the conclusion has been correctly drawn from the premises—but Example 4 is invalid:

Example 3: Valid argument:

MAJOR PREMISE: All publicly held companies must construct financial statements following GAAP.
MINOR PREMISE: Brite Company is a publicly held company
CONCLUSION: Therefore, Brite Company must construct its financial statements following GAAP.

Example 4: Invalid argument:

MAJOR PREMISE: All publicly held companies must construct financial statements following GAAP.
MINOR PREMISE: Brite Company constructs its financial statements following GAAP.
CONCLUSION: Brite Company is a publicly held company.

Many companies that are not publicly held also construct financial statements following GAAP. Thus, Brite Company might not be publicly held.

Deductive reasoning must be *sound*, as well as valid, for the conclusions to be true. Sound reasoning requires not only (a) that the conclusion has been correctly drawn from the premises, but also (b) that the premises are themselves true. For a sound conclusion, both the major and minor premises must be true. For instance, in the preceding Example 1, the conclusion would not be sound if either the major or minor premise is not true: (1) some students in the class have not passed the placement test, or (2) Robert is not a student in the class.

Sometimes the use of a syllogism will help you spot errors in reasoning. Consider the following example:

> The SEC has filed charges against The Gigantic National Corporation for cheating its former employees out of their pension benefits. Larry Womack, the CEO, issues this statement to the press: "The buck stops here. As CEO, I must accept responsibility for the fraud uncovered by the SEC. A few unscrupulous middle managers have violated company policy and the law by authorizing and carrying out this fraud. Those responsible will be identified, and will no longer work for this corporation. I deplore what has happened, but I will not resign."

What is wrong with the reasoning expressed in Mr. Womack's statement? We can analyze his argument in the form of a syllogism such as this one:

MAJOR PREMISE: The person(s) responsible for the fraud will no longer work for this corporation.

MINOR PREMISE: I am responsible for the fraud. (Recall the CEO's assertion: "I must accept responsibility for the fraud uncovered by the SEC.")

CONCLUSION: I will not resign.

You can see that the conclusion in this case does not follow logically from the major and minor premises. This argument is invalid. Put another way, the CEO has contradicted himself.

Fallacies: Mistakes in Reasoning

To reach sound conclusions, you must be careful to avoid mistakes in reasoning. That is, you must learn to recognize and avoid fallacies in the arguments you make or those made by others. We have already considered the requirements that a deductive argument be both valid and sound; that is, the argument must avoid the fallacies of drawing improper conclusions from the premises, or reasoning from false premises. Some other common fallacies that you should also avoid are listed here along with examples of each:

- **Fallacies involving language:** Using ambiguous word choices (vague or undefined), loaded language, labels, and slogans

  Anyone who favors the passage of this legislation is unpatriotic.

  (What does *unpatriotic* mean in this case? This word, as it is used here, is vague and loaded. That is, it may generate an emotional response unrelated to critical thinking about the legislation in question.)

- **Fallacies involving appeals to emotion:** Appealing to fear, pity, anger, or prejudice

  If we change our pension plan, widows and orphans will suffer.

  (This argument illustrates an appeal to pity. Of course, decision makers should consider the effects of the proposed change on pension recipients, but other factors should also be evaluated. It might be, for example, that the company will go bankrupt if it doesn't change its pension plan.)

- **Fallacy of appeal to tradition:** Arguing for something only because it's customary

  We shouldn't promote Joanne Risling to a partner position. Her degree is from a private university. It's tradition that our partners graduate from the state university.

- **Fallacy of false authority:** Using authorities that are unidentified, irrelevant, or lacking proper credentials

  Experts agree that all accounting firms should be involved in social media.

  (Who are these experts?)

  We should invest in this stock, because all our friends are buying it.

  (This statement illustrates a type of false authority called the bandwagon fallacy: "Get on the bandwagon and do what everybody else is doing.")

- **Ad hominem fallacy:** Attacking opponents' character, rather than their arguments

  Don't listen to what he's saying. He's an idiot.

- **Post hoc fallacy:** Assuming that because one circumstance happens before another, the first circumstance is the cause of the second

  After we hired Stan Sterling, our company's profits increased. Clearly Stan is the reason for our increased profitability.

  (Hiring Stan may indeed have affected the company's profits; however, we need more information before reaching this conclusion. What is Stan's position? What other factors, such as changes in the market, might be responsible for the growth in profits?)

- **Hasty generalization fallacy:** Using poor or inadequate sampling techniques

Professor Brown is a poor teacher. I know this because my roommate took his tax accounting course and complained about it every day.

Clearly, Jan Smith will be elected class president. I asked three of the people on my hall, and all of them plan to vote for Smith.

- *Either/or fallacy (false dilemma):* Assuming there are only two choices, when there may be several

You're either for me or against me.

(I may support you as a general rule, but disagree with you on this particular point.)

Either we adopt this measure, or we face bankruptcy.

(We might adopt a different measure and avoid bankruptcy.)

- *Slippery slope fallacy* Arguing that if one event occurs, a series of undesirable events will inevitably occur as a result

If we provide cell phones to our sales staff, the next thing you know they'll demand their own laptop computers, then company cars, and then chauffeurs to drive those cars. They'll then want unlimited expense accounts for trips to Las Vegas. The company will go bankrupt.

Earlier, we defined critical thinking as fair, open-minded thinking that asks appropriate questions and considers all relevant information before reaching a conclusion. Although there is no formula for achieving critical thinking, if you keep in mind the factors we have discussed in this chapter, your thinking will be much more responsible, enabling you to be a more effective communicator.

Critical Thinking and Ethical Dilemmas

In Chapter 1 we discussed the importance of ethics in the practice of accounting. We saw that accountants are expected to uphold a high standard of ethics in the practice of their professional responsibilities. They find guidance for making ethical decisions in legal requirements, codes of ethics (such as the AICPA's Code of Professional Ethics or the IMA's Statement of Ethical Professional Practice), and their personal ethical values. Often what constitutes ethical behavior is obvious, but sometimes accountants face complex situations for which the ethical solution is not immediately clear. Critical thinking can help resolve these ethical dilemmas.

The process for resolving ethical dilemmas resembles the steps you take to make a strong argument, as discussed earlier in this chapter. Indeed, identifying and defending a course of action as the most ethical among several alternatives is itself a kind of argument, even if one you have only with yourself. When you are faced with a situation that requires you to make an ethical decision, follow these steps:

1. Obtain all the facts relevant to the situation.
2. Identify all the ethical issues.
3. Determine who will be affected by the way these issues are resolved. Consider both individuals and groups, such as shareholders, employees, and the general public.
4. Identify alternative solutions to the issues, including arguments that might be used to support each alternative.
5. Analyze how the individuals and groups identified in step 3 would be affected by the alternative solutions.
6. Consider guidelines for ethical decisions, such as applicable legal requirements, codes of ethics, and your own ethical values. Be careful to avoid logical fallacies in your thinking.
7. Decide on the appropriate action and, when necessary, communicate your decision to the appropriate parties. If the situation is potentially contentious, be prepared to provide the reasons for your decision. When you write or speak to someone about the ethical issues, be especially tactful, courteous, and respectful to all parties concerned.

As you can see, resolving ethical dilemmas depends on critical thinking, as well as effective communication.

EXERCISES

Exercise 7–1 [General]

The following statements contain mistakes in reasoning (fallacies). Which fallacies are illustrated here? (Some statements may illustrate more than one fallacy.)

1. Ever since she changed accountants, the profits in her business have increased. Clearly the new accountant knows how to cook the books.
2. Give them an inch and they'll take a mile.
3. Either we redesign all our accounting information systems or we might as well close down the business.
4. Don't listen to him. He's just a nerdy, detail-obsessed accountant.
5. Three out of four accountants agree: *The Daily Balance Sheet* is the best source of financial news.
6. We don't need more public transportation in our city. Everyone in my office agrees they'd rather drive their own cars.
7. We've used Biddy and Bully as our firm's legal firm for four generations. Even though their work has become unsatisfactory, I wouldn't want to change firms.
8. We shouldn't hire Jim Blankenship. He's from Hick City, and everybody knows people from there are just a bunch of ignorant buffoons.

Exercise 7–2 [Ethics]

You are a partner in a medium-size CPA firm. One of your clients, Paul Garcia, who owns PG Corporation, has indicated a desire to report higher net income for his business this year because the company plans to apply for a loan at the bank. In an effort to increase reported net income, Mr. Garcia has told his accounting department to book immediately some large sales for which contracts have been signed but for which the goods will not be manufactured or shipped until after the first of the year. Write a letter to Mr. Gracia concerning your position on this issue. Chapter 9 discusses letter writing.

Exercise 7–3 [General]

Your school is considering a new attendance policy. If this policy is adopted, students will be allowed only three absences for each class during the term. After the fourth absence, the registrar's office will suspend the student. Suspended students will be allowed to appeal the suspension if they can offer documented evidence that they missed the classes for legitimate reasons, such as illness, a death in the family, or jury duty.

Do you believe the new attendance policy should be adopted? Following the guidelines for critical thinking discussed in this chapter, decide where you stand on this issue. (Remember the importance of identifying and responding to counterarguments.) After you have formed your conclusions, write your argument in the form of a letter to the Dean of Students at your school. Chapter 9 discusses letters.

Exercise 7–4 [General]

Some administrators in your school have proposed a change in grading policy for major level courses—that is, beyond the principles or introductory level. They propose that instructors be required to grade courses on a Pass/Fail basis only. What would be the advantages and disadvantages of this proposed policy? Consider both sides of this question, using critical thinking to analyze the pros and cons of the proposal. Then write a letter to the editor of your school's newspaper, or the local newspaper where your school is located, in which you summarize your findings. Chapter 9 discusses letters.

Exercise 7–5 [Financial/Ethics]

You are a staff accountant at Outrageous Corporation. The controller of the company, Howard Eino, is concerned that profits reported in the annual report will not meet those forecast at the beginning of the year. He has asked you to decrease the amount of annual depreciation charged on certain equipment by revising the estimated life. When you tell Mr. Eino that revision of useful life solely to "manage" profit is not appropriate, he responds by saying, "Oh, everybody does it." You realize that if you fail to do what your boss wants, you may receive an unfavorable annual performance evaluation. How will you resolve this dilemma?

To help yourself think through this problem, you've decided to write an outline in which you'll record the issues, relevant information, your reasoning, and the course of action you finally decide to take. You won't show the outline to anyone else, but you want it to be complete and well-organized, so that your thinking will be clear. Write the outline.

Exercise 7–6 [General]

Look for illustrations of the fallacies discussed in this chapter in print media, on radio or television, on the Internet, or in the conversations you hear. Quote or paraphrase the passage that illustrates the fallacy, giving a citation of the source. Then identify the fallacy and explain the error in reasoning the passage demonstrates. Chapter 8 discusses how to document sources.

Exercise 7–7 [Financial/Theory]

Some people would argue that historical costs should no longer be used in accounting because they are not relevant. Others argue that departing from historical cost introduces too much subjectivity into accounting. Write out a detailed outline for a presentation to your class providing a defense of both points of view and then explain why the FASB has chosen to depart from historical cost in many of its accounting standards.

To prepare for this assignment, you may wish to review Chapter 15 on Oral Presentations.

Exercise 7–8 [Auditing/Theory]

Some have suggested eliminating the provision of Rule 203 of the AICPA's professional ethics that permits non-conformance with GAAP if, in the opinion of the CPA, following GAAP would result in misleading financial statements. Thoroughly discuss the pros and cons of eliminating this provision of Rule 203 and present a convincing argument as to whether it should or should not be eliminated.

Prepare your argument in the form of a memo to the managing partner of your CPA firm, Elaine Morgan. Chapter 10 discusses memos.

Exercise 7–9 [Financial/International/Current Professional Issues]

In 2010, the International Accounting Standards Board (IASB) changed its constitution to emphasize the adoption of International Financial Reporting Standards (IFRSs), rather than simply convergence of those standards with standards issued by individual countries. Write an essay on whether the SEC should support convergence between United States GAAP and IFRSs, or whether the SEC should support adoption of IFRSs. Your essay should demonstrate your understanding of critical thinking. Assume the audience for your essay is accounting students in your class. Chapter 3 discusses essays.

Exercise 7–10 [Tax]

Write an essay that addresses the purpose, structure, and recent activities of the IRS Oversight Board. Include a discussion of its strategy to reduce the "tax gap," that is, to reduce the amount of uncollected taxes. Your essay should demonstrate your understanding of critical thinking. Assume the audience for your essay is accounting students in your class. Chapter 3 discusses essays.

Exercise 7–11 [Systems]

Write a brief article for your accounting honorary society's Web page about the kinds of issues that must be considered when designing an accounting information system. Your purpose is to generate interest among the students in taking an accounting information systems course. Chapter 15, which discusses writing for publication, will help you prepare your article.

Exercise 7–12 [Managerial]

Your accounting honorary society's Web page is running a series of articles about various careers in accounting that accounting students might choose. You have been asked to write an article about the advantages of a career in management accounting. Write the article with the purpose of persuading students to seek a career in management accounting without discouraging them from considering other career choices. Chapter 15 discusses writing for publication.

NOTE

1. American Institute of Certified Public Accountants (AICPA), *Content and Skill Specifications for the Uniform CPA Examination,* Update Approved October 1, 2011, Effective Date January 1, 2013. (New York: AICPA), 37–38.

CHAPTER

Accounting Research

8

Accountants and business services professionals often do research to solve technical accounting or tax problems or to gather information on some general topic of interest, such as the feasibility of offering a new service to their clients. This chapter discusses how to conduct research and write a research paper, report, or technical memorandum. If you have written documented papers or reports before, much of this material will be review. However, the suggestions should be helpful to anyone who must conduct research and write a summary of the results.

The first part of the chapter discusses basic guidelines for all research, including using electronic and printed sources of information, taking and using notes, using direct quotations and paraphrases, and documenting your sources. The remainder of the chapter focuses on specific steps in the technical accounting research process, including determining relevant facts, identifying key issues, researching the literature, considering alternative solutions, and communicating results. These steps in the research process are similar to the guidelines given in Chapter 7 for critical thinking and resolving ethical dilemmas. Accountants need all these skills to solve problems encountered in practice.

RESEARCH: BASIC GUIDELINES

If your project requires research, chances are you already know something about the topic you will research. If you don't, you may need to do some initial reading so that you have a basic familiarity with your subject. After you have a general idea of what your topic involves, you're ready to begin your research in more depth.

One author said this about research:

Research . . . is the process of obtaining information systematically. That process is deliberate and is conducted carefully and with diligence. Usually, research implies an exhaustive search for and collection of information to resolve a problem and includes the collection of that pertinent information.[1]

The key here is that good research requires deliberation, care, and diligence. You should look at all possible sources of information so that you don't overlook something important.

Often it's a good idea to write out a research plan before you begin your research. In your research plan, you can list sources of information with which you're already familiar, as well as references you can consult that will guide you to additional resources. For example, let's assume your research topic is "forensic services" and that you are aware that the AICPA has published a report on this topic. You also realize that professional journals have published articles on forensic services. Initially, your research plan might list the following:

- Check the AICPA Web site to see if the report on forensic services is posted. You can also check the Web site for other information on forensic services or links to such information.
- Check the *Journal of Accountancy* and other professional journals for past articles. These articles may be available online, or you may have to locate printed copies of the journals.
- Do a keyword search of any electronic literature indexes available at the library or online for articles or reports from the past two years.
- Do a topical and keyword search of the Web.

As you begin to follow your research plan, you should modify it to include references to other resources you find. Thus, you may add references to specific articles, reports, Web sites, indexes, or searchable databases. As you come across specific sources, such as published articles and reports, look at the bibliographical, footnote, or endnote references they contain. These will often lead you to useful material you may not otherwise find.

As you conduct your research, you should keep track of what you have done by checking off the steps listed in your plan. If your research includes a keyword search of an electronic index or database, be sure to keep a log of the keywords and keyword combinations you have used in your search and the results they have obtained. Keeping good records will increase the efficiency of your research because you can avoid duplicating searches; at the same time, you can critique the search process you have followed to determine what you may have missed or how to refine the process. Keeping records of your sources will also help you write the citations for your final document.

FASB Accounting Standards Codification®

In 2009, the Financial Accounting Standards Board (FASB) released a new codification system for Generally Accepted Accounting Principles

(GAAP) called the *FASB Accounting Standards Codification®* ("ASC" or "Codification" for short). The FASB now refers to the Codification as "the single source of authoritative nongovernmental U.S. Generally Accepted Accounting Principles (US GAAP)." The Codification supersedes all existing non-Securities and Exchange Commission (non-SEC) standards. The FASB now issues all authoritative US GAAP in the form of "Accounting Standards Updates" (ASUs), rather than FASB Statements, FASB Interpretations, Emerging Issues Task Force (EITF) Abstracts, and such. ASUs are used to revise the Codification and are not by themselves considered to be authoritative.[2]

The FASB's Codification affects the way you cite accounting standards for papers you prepare for your accounting courses or for any other accounting writing you may complete. The Codification uses a system of Topic numbers, Subtopic numbers, Section numbers, and Paragraph numbers. So, for example, the definition of goodwill may be found in Topic 310 ("Intangibles—Goodwill and Other"), Subtopic 10 ("Overall"), Section 05 ("Overview and Background"), Paragraph 01, and would be cited as "FASB ASC par. 310-10-05-01."

The Codification is available in both printed and electronic form. (See "Online Database Services," Appendix 8–B, for more information on this source.)

Electronic Sources of Information

Electronic sources of information include the Internet and online databases (including the electronic version of the *FASB Accounting Standards Codification®*). The quantity and availability of these electronic sources, along with how quickly and easily they can be searched, should place them high on your list of resources for most research.

The Internet

One step in your research plan should be to search the Internet for material related to your topic. Search engines such as Google enable you to locate documents on the Web. Tailor the search to your needs by using keywords or phrases associated with your research topic.

The Internet may lead you to publications available at your library or to documents that you can download. Read the material you find on the Internet carefully and take accurate notes of your findings, including references to the sources you are using. A later section of this chapter discusses note taking and how to properly indicate references in more detail. Print out useful material you find unless the length of a particular source makes this impractical, in which case you should save it on your computer or an external drive. When you save this material, be sure to record the Web address (URL).

Appendix 8–A at the end of this chapter shows some of the better Web sites available on the Internet that offer information related to accounting and finance as well as links to other useful sites.

Online Databases

Many information databases are available online. The FASB Accounting Standards and AICPA Professional Standards are available in this manner.

The *FASB Accounting Standards Codification® Research System* covers accounting literature issued by several standard setters. FASB publications included are Statements, Interpretations, Technical Bulletins, Staff Positions, Staff Implementation Guides, and Statement 138 Examples. Abstracts and Topic D of the Emerging Issues Task Force are included, as are Derivatives Implementation Group Issues, Accounting Principles Board Opinions, Accounting Research Bulletins, and Accounting Interpretations. AICPA Statements of Position, Audit and Accounting Guides, Practice Bulletins, and Technical Inquiry Service issuances are also available here, along with "relevant portions of authoritative content issued by the SEC and selected SEC staff interpretations and administrative guidance."[3]

CCH's Accounting Research Manager® contains "analytical accounting, auditing, governmental, internal controls, and SEC information as well as primary source data."[4] The *CCH® Tax Research NetWork*™ or CCH's *Standard Federal Tax Reporter*, which is available in print or accessible electronically through CCH's *IntelliConnect®*, can be indispensable for tax research. Thomson Reuters' *Checkpoint* is another good online data-base for tax research.[5]

Many other databases are available. Appendix 8–B lists many of the most useful online references and databases available for accounting and finance research.

Printed Sources of Information

Although electronic media can provide excellent sources for your research, don't limit your research to electronic sources, because some important information may not be available in electronic form. You'll have to use printed resources, which will require conventional library research.

Even if your library doesn't have specialized electronic databases, it most likely has a general database, which lists articles published in most periodicals, including accounting periodicals. You'll access this database by a keyword search, so be imaginative in looking for articles on your topic; consider the different headings under which articles might be listed.

One print source of information about technical accounting topics is official accounting standards. The *FASB Accounting Standards Codification®* is available in both printed and electronic form. You can also study printed versions of government regulations or laws to find out how to handle a client's technical problem. In either case, read the material carefully and take accurate notes of your findings, including references to the sources you use.

Appendix 8–C lists some of the popular printed sources of accounting information. The library probably has other references that you may find helpful as well. For example, some newspapers publish an index. Many of these indexes are available both as reference books and as electronic reference services.

A librarian can help you find references that will help you to prepare your paper.

Note Taking

After you have located a useful source, take notes on what you read. You may decide to take notes on a laptop that you can take to the library or keep next to the computer terminal at which you are conducting an electronic search. Using a computer can help you write your notes and organize them at the same time, which will save you time later. Any good word processing or database program can be used to take notes.

Some people prefer to take notes by hand instead of using a computer. Most of the techniques discussed here apply in either case.

If you take notes on a computer, you'll need two computer files—one for the bibliography (the list of sources you used) and another for your notes. (If you take notes by hand, you can use two sets of cards—4- × 6-inch cards for your notes and 3- × 5-inch cards for your bibliography.)

Be sure to include in the *bibliography file* all the information you will need for the bibliography (see the section on documentation later in this chapter). The following are examples of entries you might make in your bibliography file:

1. Financial Accounting Standards Board (FASB). *Accounting Standards Codification®*, Topic 350, "Intangibles—Goodwill and Other." Stamford, Conn.: FASB 2013.

2. Financial Accounting Standards Board (FASB). *Objectives of Financial Reporting by Business Enterprises, Statement of Financial Accounting Concepts No. 1.* Stamford, Conn.: FASB 1978.

Give each of your sources a number. The number will save time when you take notes from that source and later when you draft your paper. The sources just illustrated are numbered *1* and *2*.

The *note file* contains the information you will actually use in your paper. Notice the parts of this note file entry:

II. A. 1.—Goodwill definition
[1] Subtopic 10, Sect. 05, Par. 01

"An asset representing the future economic benefits arising from other assets acquired in a business combination or an acquisition by a not-for-profit entity that are not individually identified and separately recognized."

The first line of the note file entry gives an outline code (II. A. 1.) that corresponds with the section in your outline where the note fits, and a short description of what the note is about. The second line gives the number of the source for this note as contained in your bibliography file and the page or paragraph numbers where this information was found ([1] Subtopic 10, Sect. 05, Par. 01). The note itself is taken from the source and is the material you will use in your paper.

Direct Quotation and Paraphrase

You can take notes in two ways: as a direct quotation (the exact words from the source) or as a paraphrase (your own words and sentence structures). If you take notes as direct quotations, you can decide later whether to use a direct quotation or paraphrase in your paper. However, if you're sure you won't need a direct quotation in your paper and you take the time to paraphrase as you research, you'll save time when writing the draft. Remember, too, that no more than about 10 percent of most papers should be direct quotation.

Here's a good way to paraphrase. Read a section from your source (or quotation copied earlier into your notes)—perhaps several short paragraphs. Then look away and try to remember the important ideas. Write them down. Then look back to check your notes for accuracy.

If you take notes as quotations, use quotation marks so you'll know later that these are someone else's words. Copy the quotation exactly, including capitalization and punctuation. It's important that direct quotations be accurate in every way and that paraphrases be your own words and sentence structures, not just a slight variation of your source.

Plagiarism

It's important to give credit for material you borrow from someone else, whether you paraphrase or quote directly, and whether you've used electronic or printed sources. You must also give credit for visual materials, as well as language and ideas. If you don't give credit, you'll be guilty of plagiarism. *The Prentice Hall Guide for College Writers* contains the following discussion of plagiarism:

> Plagiarism occurs when you use the language, ideas, or visual materials from another person or text without acknowledging the source—even if you do this unintentionally. . . . Do not use language, ideas, or graphics from any essay, text, or visual image that you find online, in the library, or from commercial sources without acknowledging the source.[6]

Plagiarism can thus involve the unacknowledged (undocumented) use of someone else's ideas, opinions, research, or graphics—not just the use of someone's exact words.

The key to avoiding plagiarism is to document your sources adequately with either internal documentation or notes (see the section on documentation). In actual practice, however, sometimes you might not know whether you should identify the source of information you want to use in your paper. The difficulty arises because information that is considered common knowledge in a given field need not be documented.

Obviously the problem is to decide what is common knowledge. One guideline says that if you can find the same information in three different sources, that information is considered common knowledge and therefore needs no documentation.

There are many gray areas when it comes to issues of plagiarism. Perhaps the safest rule is to document your sources whenever there is any question of possible plagiarism.

Remember: plagiarism is theft of another person's words or ideas. In some situations, it's punishable by law. If you plagiarize at school, the repercussions are very serious: You may fail the assignment, fail the course, or be expelled, depending on your school's policies. Plagiarism on the job may lead to termination.

Organizing Your Notes and Ideas

As you are taking notes, you will probably form some idea of the major divisions of the paper. That is, you should be getting a rough idea of its outline.

Go ahead and write down your ideas for an outline. The more reading you do, the more complete the outline will become. Stop and evaluate the outline from time to time. Are you covering all the important areas of your topic? Is the outline getting too long? Should you narrow the topic? Are some sections of the outline irrelevant to the topic? Answering these questions will guide you as you continue your research.

Writing Your Research Report or Memo

When your research is complete, you are ready to begin writing your report or memo. Your first step should be to refine your outline. Be sure that your topic is completely covered and that the ideas are arranged in the most effective order. Think about the introduction and conclusion to your paper, as well as any other relevant parts. Do you want to include charts, tables, or graphs?

Next, arrange your notes in the order of the outline and write the appropriate outline code beside each note.

With a completed outline and an orderly arrangement of your notes, you're ready to write the draft of your report or memorandum.

Integrating Notes into Your Writing

The draft of a research paper is written just like that of any other kind of writing, except that you are incorporating notes taken from your sources into your own ideas. If you have already paraphrased the notes, your task is much easier.

Include in your draft an indication of where your notes came from. In other words, you must give credit for words or ideas that are not your own. In the final version of your paper, these references will be footnotes, endnotes, or parenthetical citations. In the draft, you can indicate your sources with a parenthetical notation like this: *([1] p. 403)*. The numbers come from your notes and refer to the source and page or paragraph number of each note.

Revising

After you have completed the draft, you'll need to revise it to perfect the organization, development, style, grammar, and spelling. You might also ask a colleague to review your paper and suggest ways it can be improved.

Documentation

As noted earlier, any information you get from a source other than your own knowledge must be documented; that is, you must say where you got the information. Styles for documentation vary, but we'll look at two of the most common: internal documentation and notes.[7] The format we illustrate for both styles is consistent with *The Chicago Manual of Style*[8] and Kate L. Turabian's *A Manual for Writers of Term Papers, Theses, and Dissertations*[9] or, in the case of electronic citations, Walker and Taylor's *The Columbia Guide to Online Style.*[10] You may want to consult one of these works as you write your paper.

Internal Documentation

Many writers prefer to use internal documentation, which places abbreviated information about sources within the text, using parentheses ( ) or brackets [ ], followed by a list of references at the end of the paper. What goes within the parentheses or brackets depends on the kind of source you are using. Appendix 8–D at the end of this chapter gives sample citations and reference list entries for sources typically used by accounting professionals.

It's a good idea to introduce quotations or paraphrases within the text itself, such as in this example:

> According to the *FASB Accounting Standards Codification®*, current assets are "cash and other assets or resources commonly identified as those that are reasonably expected to be realized in cash or sold or consumed during the normal operating cycle of the business" (FASB ASC, par. 210-10-45-01).

Note that the end punctuation for the quotation, in this case the period, comes after the parentheses. The numbers shown in this citation refer to Codification Topic (210), Subtopic (10), Section

(45), and Paragraph (01). This is the standard way of citing the Codification. If readers check the reference list at the end of the paper, they will find:

> Financial Accounting Standards Board (FASB), 2010. *Accounting Standards Codification*®. Stamford, Conn.: FASB.

Here's one reminder about the use of technical sources. Consider whether the readers of your paper will be familiar with the literature cited. If they won't be, you should identify the source more fully and briefly explain its significance.

Endnotes or Footnotes

The other style of documentation in wide use is endnotes or footnotes. The difference between these two note forms is that footnotes come at the bottom of the page where the references occur, whereas endnotes come at the end of the paper. Most authorities consider endnotes acceptable. If you prefer footnotes, your word processor should be able to place footnotes on the right pages, in the acceptable format. With either endnotes or footnotes, you have the option of adding a bibliography at the end of your paper, listing your sources in alphabetical order.

Appendix 8–E at the end of this chapter gives examples of notes and bibliographical entries for typical accounting sources.

As with internal documentation, you should introduce your paraphrased or quoted material:

> According to an article in *The Wall Street Journal*, many accounting firms find the poor writing skills of their new employees to be a serious problem.[11]

The introduction to this paraphrase tells generally where the information came from; the note and bibliographical entry give complete information about the source.

Citing Online Sources

Online sources have become so important to the research process that you'll probably need to cite material that you have found online.

An acceptable form of citation for documents available from online sources usually resembles the pattern of citations for hard-copy sources, but you need to provide additional information so that your readers can find the file or document online.

It's important to provide the date you accessed the document, because the document may be modified or even removed from online availability after you have accessed it. For the same reason, it's also a good idea to save a copy of the document you are citing.

Examples of citations for online sources are illustrated in Appendices 8–C and 8–D at the end of this chapter.

CRITICAL THINKING AND TECHNICAL ACCOUNTING RESEARCH

In Chapter 7, we discussed critical thinking in general. In this section, we examine its importance and application to accounting research.

In *An Introduction to Applied Professional Research for Accountants,* Professor David A. Ziebart has this to say about technical accounting research:

> [Technical accounting] research . . . is a *process*, and its result is a defensible solution to the problem or issue at hand. By process we mean a systematic routine of identifying the problem or issue, specifying alternative plausible solutions, conducting an inquiry into the propriety of the alternatives, evaluating the authoritative literature found, making a choice among the alternatives, and communicating the results. Since the solution must be defensible, the accounting professional must be certain that the search of the professional literature is exhaustive and the reasoning employed in determining the solution is sound.[12]

Notice the importance of critical thinking skills to the process of accounting research. Professor Ziebart specifies these steps of the research process that involve critical thinking: identifying the issues or problems; identifying alternative solutions; evaluating the best solution; and communicating the recommended solution, giving reasons for its preference.

Technical accounting research is most often done in either financial or tax accounting. The following discussion, which focuses on financial accounting, will give you an idea of the complexity of this kind of research, as well as a strategy you can use when faced with a difficult accounting problem.

Financial Accounting Research

Research in financial accounting is often necessary (particularly in larger accounting firms and industry) because financial transactions may not always be directly covered by generally accepted accounting principles (GAAP). In other words, you may not always find guidance in published accounting standards that fits a particular transaction or that fairly represents the conditions under which the transaction occurred. When this situation occurs, you must devise an accounting solution that can be defended based on accounting theory and logic found elsewhere in GAAP. The following section suggests a procedure you can use for this research.

Steps in the Financial Accounting Research Process

Financial accounting research involves the following steps:

1. Determine all the relevant facts.

2. Identify all the issues involved.
3. Research the issues in the accounting literature.
4. Identify alternative solutions and arguments for and against each.
5. Evaluate alternative solutions and choose the one that can be best defended.
6. Communicate the results of your research to interested parties.

Note that these steps are similar to those presented in Chapter 7, but applied more directly to financial accounting research. Let's discuss these steps one at a time.

Determine All the Relevant Facts

Determining the relevant facts is often fairly straightforward. If you realize that research is necessary, you're probably already aware of most facts of the transaction. Be sure you have *all* the facts before you begin your research. Do you fully understand the transaction and the conditions under which it was made? If the transaction is supported by a contract or other documents, be sure you have examined them thoroughly. Are there any hidden contingencies, liabilities, or unperformed duties on the part of any participants? What motivated the parties to make the transaction?

Identify All the Issues Involved

It often comes as a surprise to many people that identifying the issues can be one of the more difficult steps in the accounting research process. It's not uncommon for facts (or a lack of facts), terminology, and researcher bias to obscure some issues rather than clarify them. Ethical issues may also become apparent as you gather additional information and consider alternative solutions. Attention to critical thinking will help you ensure that all the issues are identified.

Consider the case of a custom machine parts manufacturer that routinely manufactures more parts than its customers order, expenses the cost of these extra parts as part of cost of goods sold, and physically holds the parts in inventory at a carrying value of zero. If a customer later has an emergency need for another part or two, the parts can be delivered immediately; however, this almost never happens, and the additional revenue from the sale of these extra parts is of no consequence. The question is whether the manufacturer's method of accounting for this situation is appropriate. What are the issues?

A quick reading of the facts presented may suggest that the issue is whether the cost of manufacturing the extra parts is properly accounted for by expensing it as part of cost of goods sold and carrying the inventory at zero, or whether the cost of the extra parts should be attributed to the inventory. Certainly the questions of inventory valuation and accounting for cost of goods sold will be answered by our research and the conclusions we draw from it. However, the central issue is best stated quite differently.

The basic issue in this case is the nature of the expenditure involved in producing the extra parts. That is, which one of the elements discussed in *Statement of Financial Accounting Concepts No. 6* best describes the expenditure? Does the expenditure result in an asset (not necessarily the physical parts)? This is the question to start with because definitions of the other elements depend on the definition of an asset. If an asset has resulted from the expenditure, the type of asset is still in question: Is it inventory, goodwill, or some other intangible asset? If an asset has not been the result, has an expense been incurred? If so, is it appropriate to include it as part of cost of goods sold, or is it some other type of expense? If an expense has not been incurred, the expenditure must be accounted for as a loss.

Research the Issues in the Accounting Literature

After you have identified the issues, the next step is to research the accounting literature to gather all relevant material. If the issues involve theoretical questions, as most probably will, you should consult relevant parts of the *Statements of Financial Accounting Concepts*. Certainly you should review the *FASB Accounting Standards Codification®* to identify GAAP bearing directly or indirectly on the issues.

Sometimes you may find useful information in GAAP covering an unrelated area. For example, if an issue involves revenue recognition of an entity in the software industry, GAAP covering the music industry or some industry even further removed from the software industry may contain logic or guidance that could serve as a basis for a solution.

It's possible that your research may take you beyond the materials just discussed. SEC regulations, regulations of other federal agencies, accounting books, and articles in accounting journals all may prove useful. SEC regulations may be controlling if the entity involved falls under SEC jurisdiction. Online databases such as those listed in Appendix 8–B are good sources for much of this material.

Identify Alternative Solutions and Arguments For and Against Each

It's important to realize that if you're engaged in technical accounting research, you're probably dealing with issues for which there are no established solutions. You must identify all alternative solutions, determine the best solution, and defend that solution against all others.

Evaluate Alternative Solutions and Choose the
One That Can Be Best Defended

In the end, you must be able to present a well-reasoned defense of your accounting method. Although accounting is not law (except as governed by the SEC), just as a lawyer may prepare a well-reasoned defense of an issue using legal precedent and logic, an accountant doing technical accounting research must use many of the same skills in preparing a defense of a proposed solution to an accounting issue.

Indeed, it's possible that the solution you choose may have to be defended in a court during some legal proceeding.

If you expect that your readers will oppose your recommended treatment or will prefer an alternative, your written document should anticipate and answer such objections. You should explain the reasons that support your recommendation, as well as why alternatives are not acceptable.

Communicate the Results of Your Research to the Interested Parties
You will usually communicate the results of your research in a report, letter, or memo, and occasionally you may report orally as well. However you report your research, incorporate all the elements of effective communication discussed in this text. Audience analysis, precision, clarity, and logical development are particularly important.

EXERCISES

Exercise 8–1 [Managerial/Systems]

In May 2013, the Committee of Sponsoring Organizations (COSO) of the Treadway Commission issued an update to its Internal Control—Integrated Framework. The controller of your company, Mr. Dennis Patterson, has asked you to write a report discussing this document and explaining how it might be used by the Board of Directors and higher level management to better design the company's system of internal control. Write the report, inventing any facts that may be necessary.

Exercise 8–2 [Financial/Theory]

Harmon Industries manufactures and sells industrial machinery around the world. The company is heavily dependent on contracts with transatlantic and transpacific shipping companies to deliver its products. Because fuel prices are unpredictable, several of the shipping companies Harmon uses have included a clause in their contracts allowing them to impose a fuel supplement if the price of West Texas Intermediate fuel exceeds a stipulated price per barrel. Although the supplement has never been imposed, the price of fuel has been increasing fast, and Harmon's controller, Trent Johnson, is concerned about how he will account for the supplement if it is imposed. Typically, contracts state that the supplement may be imposed on June 30 each year to cover the shipping company's fuel purchases during the preceding 12 months. The amount of the surcharge levied on any one shipper, such as Harmon, would be based on a formula that takes into account the number of shipments and tonnage shipped by that shipper during the period. Based on Harmon's projections, such a levy, if ever made, could result in several million dollars of additional expense.

Harmon has a fiscal year end of December 31. Mr. Johnson has asked you, a member of his accounting staff, to research the problem of accounting for any fuel supplement that might be imposed. He has asked you to look into these questions:

- Should the supplement be treated as an expense of the period in which it is imposed, or should it be apportioned between the current and preceding periods in some manner?
- How should the supplement be reported (classified) in the financial statements?
- What type of risk disclosure (if any) should be included in the financial statements?

Mr. Johnson has indicated that you should look into all accounting and reporting aspects of the situation and not just his list of questions. If he has left anything significant out of his list, you should cover that as well.

Write a report to Mr. Johnson responding to his concerns.

Exercise 8–3 [General]

Choose one of the following topics and narrow it if necessary. Write a documented research paper on your topic, using the steps discussed in this chapter.

- Congressional attempts to affect the accounting standard setting process
- The future of eXtensible Business Reporting Language (XBRL) and how it might be used to support the development of other comprehensive bases of accounting (OCBOA) outside of GAAP
- The Public Company Accounting Oversight Board (PCAOB)
- The International Auditing and Assurance Standards Board (IAASB) and its role in establishing International Standards on Auditing (ISAs)
- The use of fair value measurements in Generally Accepted Accounting Principles
- The future of "integrated reporting" and the possible expansion of the attest function
- The role of judgment in the application of accounting standards and whether that role should be reduced or expanded
- The impact of the Committee of Sponsoring Organizations' (COSO) Internal Control—Integrated Framework

Exercise 8–4 [Financial/Theory]

American Petroleum Company (AP Oil) owns and operates deep-water drilling rigs in international waters off the coast of Euromania, a Western European country. Several months ago, it experienced a disastrous explosion and fire at one of its rigs that resulted in a monumental oil spill, which has yet to be contained. The spill is expected to have dire effects on hundreds of miles of the Euromanian coastline, putting untold thousands of people in fishing, tourist, and supporting industries out of work. Because the disaster occurred in international waters, the ability of the Euromanian courts to impose liability judgments against AP is probably limited to its ability to seize whatever AP assets are located within its jurisdiction. These assets are carried on AP's books at $20 billion. In addition, Euromanian law limits liability in such cases to a maximum of €96 million ($115 million). However, out of a feeling of ethical obligation and in an effort to salvage the good name of the company, AP's Board of Directors has agreed to honor all damage claims in an unlimited fashion. It is estimated that the value of such claims could reach €83 billion ($100 billion).

Your firm has served as the auditors for AP for several years. AP's Board of Directors has requested that your firm prepare a report for the Board discussing how its decision should be reflected in AP's financial statements under U.S. GAAP. Your supervisor, Charles Brogan, has asked you to research the technical issues involved and prepare a memo for him recommending how the issues should be handled; he will subsequently prepare the report for AP. He has told you not to be concerned with the issue of foreign currency translation, as that is well understood by AP. Prepare the memo for Mr. Brogan. Chapter 10 discusses memos.

Exercise 8–5 [Financial/Theory]

Your client, Smooth Brew Company, has just purchased a brewery known for the unique taste of its beer. This taste is primarily the result of using sparkling spring water that flows from a particular stream made famous in the brewery's advertisements. The brewery is located on 20 acres at the foot of a large mountain. The famous stream flows down the mountain out of North Carolina and through the brewery's property in Georgia.

Your client paid a high price for these brewing operations—$1 million above the fair market value of the tangible assets acquired. The president of Smooth Brew has made it clear that the main reason he agreed to pay the price is to get access to the special water. Accordingly, he has requested that an account entitled "Water" be set up in the balance sheet and valued at $1 million.

As Smooth Brew's CPA, you know your firm will have to take a position on this issue. Should your firm allow the client to account for the $1 million the way he suggests? If not, what will be the position of your firm on how the transaction should be accounted for?

Write a memo to your boss, Claire Sanders, recommending what position your firm should take with this client and why. Chapter 10 discusses memos.

Exercise 8–6 [Auditing]

Prepare a research report on the subject of independence in auditing. Cover the necessity for independence in general, what professional standards say about independence, what the SEC's role has been to foster independence, and anything else you may find appropriate. Assume your report will be distributed to entry-level accountants recently hired by your firm, as part of their in-house training materials. Chapter 11 discusses reports.

Exercise 8–7 [Managerial]

Prepare a research report on the use of GPK (Grenzplankostenrech-nung) and ABC (Activity Based Costing) cost systems. Discuss some actual experiences of companies as well as some advantages and disadvantages of using each system. Assume your report will be made available to your manufacturing clients. Chapter 11 discusses reports.

Exercise 8–8 [Tax]

Marquette Corporation, a tax client since its creation three years ago, has requested that you prepare a memorandum explaining its estimated tax requirements for the current year. The corporation is in the fabricated steel business. Its earnings have been growing each year. Marquette's taxable income for the last three tax years has been $500,000, $1.5 million, and $2.5 million, respectively. The Chief Financial Officer, Greg Patterson, expects its taxable income in the current year to be approximately $3 million.

Write a memo to Mr. Patterson explaining Marquette's estimated tax requirements for the current year, providing the necessary supporting authorities for your findings.[13] Chapter 10 discusses letters.

NOTES

1. David. A. Ziebart, et al, 2nd ed., *An Introduction to Applied Professional Research for Accountants* (Upper Saddle River, NJ: Prentice Hall, 2002), 2.
2. This information is taken from the "FASB Accounting Standards Codification®, Notice to Constituents (v 4.1), About the Codification."
3. Ibid.
4. CCH, "timely complete inter-pretive," CCH, http://www. accountingresearchmanager. com/ARMMenu.nsf/vwHTML/ ARMSplash?OpenDocument (23 January 2013).
5. See http://ria.thomsonreuters.com/ IntegratedSolutions (23 January 2013).
6. Stephen Reid, *The Prentice Hall Guide for College Writers,* Brief Tenth Edition (Upper Saddle River, NJ: Pearson Education, Inc., 2014), 492.
7. There are many documentation styles in current use. The sample entries in this chapter illustrate

acceptable usage, but you may use another acceptable style as long as you're consistent within each paper.

8. *The Chicago Manual of Style*, 16th ed. Chicago: The University of Chicago Press, 2010.

9. Kate L. Turabian, *A Manual for Writers of Term Papers, Theses, and Dissertations*, 7th ed. Chicago: The University of Chicago Press, 2007.

10. Janice R. Walker and Todd Taylor, *The Columbia Guide to Online Style*, 2nd ed. New York: Columbia University Press, 2006.

11. Lee Burton, "Take Heart, CPAs: Finally a Story That Doesn't Attack You as Boring," *The Wall Street Journal* (13 May 1987), 33.

12. David. A. Ziebart, et al, 2nd ed., *An Introduction to Applied Professional Research for Accountants* (Upper Saddle River, NJ: Prentice Hall, 2002), 3.

13. Adapted and modified with permission from Thomas R. Pope, Kenneth E. Anderson, and John L. Kramer, *Federal Taxation 2013* (Upper Saddle River, NJ: Pearson Education, Inc., 2013), 3-70.

Appendix 8 – A

Sources of Accounting and Financial Information on the Internet[*]

Accounting and auditing organizations
Academy of Accounting Historians   http://www.aahhq.org
Advancing Government Accountability   http://www.agacgfm.org/
    (Formerly: Association of Government   homepage.aspx
    Accountants)
American Accounting Association   http://aaahq.org/index.cfm
American Institute of CPAs   http://www.aicpa.org
Center for Audit Quality, The   http://www.thecaq.org
Committee of Sponsoring Organizations   http://www.coso.org
    (COSO)
Financial Accounting Standards Board   http://www.fasb.org
Government Accounting Standards Board   http://www.gasb.org
International Forum of Independent   https://www.ifiar.org/Home.aspx
    Audit Regulators (IFIAR)
Institute of Internal Auditors, The   http://www.theiia.org
IMA (Formerly: Institute of   http://www.imanet.org
    Management Accountants)
National Association of State Boards   http://www.nasba.org
    of Accountancy (NASBA)
Public Company Accounting   http://pcaobus.org/Pages/default.
    Oversight Board   aspx

Business and accounting news network services
Accounting Today for the WebCPA   http://www.accountingtoday.com
AccountingWEB   http://www.accountingweb.com/
CNNMoney.com   http://money.cnn.com
MSN Money   http://money.msn.com

Business newspapers
Barrons Online   http://online.barrons.com/
       home-page

Financial Times of London   http://www.ft.com/home/us
Investors.com (Investors Business Daily)   http://www.investors.com/
       default.htm?formad=1
The Wall Street Journal   http://online.wsj.com/home-page

Business magazines
Business 2.0   http://money.cnn.com/magazines/
       business2
Business Week   http://www.businessweek.com

---

[*]These Web addresses were accurate when this book went to press. However, Web addresses change frequently.

Fortune Magazine	http://money.cnn.com/magazines/fortune
Money Magazine (CNNmoney)	http://money.cnn.com/magazines/moneymag
Worth	http://www.worth.com

Data on the economy, industries, market indexes, and financial statistics—domestic and foreign

Bloomberg.com	http://www.bloomberg.com
Briefing.com	http://www.briefing.com
Dow Jones	http://www.dowjones.com
International Monetary Fund (IMF)	http://www.imf.org
New York Federal Reserve Bank	http://www.newyorkfed.org/index.html
The World Bank	http://www.worldbank.org

Information about stocks—company performance, corporate financial data, charts, company home pages, etc.

Hoover's Inc.	http://www.hoovers.com
Internetnews.com	http://www.Internetnews.com/bus-news/
INVESTools	http://www.investools.com
Morningstar.com	http://www.morningstar.com
NASDAQ	http://www.nasdaq.com
NYSE	https://nyse.nyx.com/
OTC Bulletin Board	http://www.otcbb.com/
StockMaster	http://www.stockmaster.com
Zacks Investment Research	http://www.zacks.com

Information about bonds

Bonds Online	http://www.bonds-online.com

Information about mutual funds

Morningstar.com	http://www.morningstar.com
Standard and Poor's Rating Service	http://www.standardandpoors.com/home/en/us
StockMaster	http://www.stockmaster.com

Securities exchanges

NASDAQ	http://www.nasdaq.com
New York Stock Exchange (NYSE)	https://nyse.nyx.com/

Government sites

Federal Accounting Standards Advisory Board	http://fasab.gov
Fed World (National Technical Information Service)	http://www.fedworld.gov
General Accounting Office (GAO)	http://www.gao.gov
Internal Revenue Service (IRS)	http://www.irs.ustreas.gov/
Securities and Exchange Commission (SEC)	http://www.sec.gov
Thomas (Legislature)	http://thomas.loc.gov/home/thomas.php

USA.gov (Index of Government Departments & Agencies)	http://www.usa.gov/directory/federal/index.shtml
U.S. House of Representatives	http://www.house.gov
U.S. Senate	http://www.senate.gov

International accounting and finance organizations and sites

European Financial Reporting Advisory Group	http://www.efrag.org/Front/Home.aspx
IFRS (International Financial Reporting Standards) Foundation/International Accounting Standards Board (IASB)	http://www.ifrs.org/Pages/default.aspx
International Association of Financial Executive Institutes	http://www.iafei.org
International Auditing and Assurance Standards Board (IAASB)	https://www.ifac.org/auditing-assurance/about-iaasb
International Ethics Standards Board for Accountants (IESBA)	http://www.ifac.org/Ethics/
International Federation of Accountants (IFAC)	http://www.ifac.org
International Integrated Reporting Council	http://www.theiirc.org/
International Monetary Fund (IMF)	http://www.imf.org/external/index.htm
International Public Sector Accounting Standards Board (IPSASB)	http://www.ifac.org/public-sector
World Bank	http://www.worldbank.org

Links to other organizations, firms, journals, newspapers, etc.

accountancylive [UK]	http://www.accountancylive.com/
AccountantsWorld	http://www.accountantsworld.com/power/Practice/User/Default.aspx
Accounting Historians Journal	http://www.olemiss.edu/depts/general_library/dac/files/ahj.html
Accounting Review	http://aaajournals.org/loi/accr
Accounting Today	http://www.accountingtoday.com/
AccountingWEB	http://www.accountingweb.com/
AICPA (accounting publications)	http://www.cpa2biz.com/index.jsp
Big 4	http://www.big4.com/blog
CA Magazine [CANADA]	http://www.camagazine.com/index.aspx
CPA Journal, The	http://www.cpajournal.com/
CPA Trendlines	http://cpatrendlines.com/
International Integrated Reporting Council (IIRC)	http://www.theiirc.org/
International Journal of Accounting	http://www.sciencedirect.com/science/
The Journal of Accountancy	http://www.journalofaccountancy.com/

Journal of Accounting Research	http://onlinelibrary.wiley.com/ journal/10.1111/(ISSN) 1475-679X
Management Accounting Quarterly	http://www.imanet.org/resources_ and_publications/management _accounting_quarterly.aspx
New York Times, The (Accounting)	http://topics.nytimes.com/topics/ reference/timestopics/ subjects/a/accounting_and_ accountants/index.html
Rutgers Accounting Web	http://accounting.rutgers.edu/
Social Science Research Network	http://www.SSRN.com
Smart Brief	http://www.smartbrief.com/news/ accounting
SmartPros Accounting	http://www.accountingnet.com
Sustainability Accounting Standards Board	http://www.sasb.org/
Thomson Reuters	http://ppc.thomson.com/ sitecomposer2/
Wall Street Journal, The (Accounting)	http://online.wsj.com/public/page/ news-accounting-industry.html

Online Database Services[*]

- *ABI/INFORM*® provides online indexing to business-related material occurring in thousands of publications from 1923 to the present. For additional information go to http://www.proquest.com/en-US/catalogs/databases/detail/abi_inform.shtml.
- *Accounting Research Manager*®, by Commerce Clearing House (CCH), contains "analytical accounting, auditing, governmental, internal controls and SEC information as well as primary source data." For additional information go to http://www.accountingresearchmanager.com/ARMMenu.nsf/vwHTML/ARMSplash?OpenDocument.
- *Accounting Standards Codification*® *Research System*, by the FASB, covers accounting literature issued by several standard setters. FASB publications included are Statements, Interpretations, Technical Bulletins, Staff Positions, Staff Implementation Guides, and Statement 138 Examples. Abstracts and Topic D of the Emerging Issues Task Force are included as are Derivatives Implementation Group Issues, Accounting Principles Board Opinions, Accounting Research Bulletins, and Accounting Interpretations. AICPA Statements of Position, Audit and Accounting Guides, Practice Bulletins, and Technical Inquiry Service issuances are also available here, along with "relevant portions of authoritative content issued by the SEC and selected SEC staff interpretations and administrative guidance."[†] For additional information go to https://asc.fasb.org.
- *Business Source*, by EBSCO Information Services, provides citations and abstracts to articles in about 600 business periodicals and newspapers. Full text is provided from selected periodicals, covering accounting, communications, economics, finance, management, marketing, and other business subjects. For additional information go to http://www2.ebsco.com.
- *Capital IQ Compustat*, by Standard and Poor's. Financial data on publicly held U.S. and some foreign corporations. For additional information go to http://www.compustat.com/?gclid=COL10NyyvaACFUFM5QodxDySUQ.
- *Checkpoint*, by Thomson Reuters, is a good online research database for tax research. For additional information go to http://ria.thomsonreuters.com/IntegratedSolutions/.
- *EconLit*, by the American Economic Association, covers the worldwide literature of economics. Subjects include microeconomics, macroeconomics, economic history, inflation, money, credit, finance, accounting theory, trade, natural resource economics, and regional economics. For additional information go to http://www.aeaweb.org/econlit/index.php.
- *FRED*® *Economic Data (Federal Reserve Economic Data)*, by the St. Louis Federal Reserve, contains 61,000 U.S. and international economic time series. For additional information go to http://research.stlouisfed.org/fred2.

---

[*]These Web addresses were accurate when this book went to press. However, Web addresses change frequently.

[†]Financial Accounting Foundation, "Notice to Constituents (v 4.1)—About the Codification." 2010. (Stamford, Conn.: Financial Accounting Foundation, 2010), 8.

- *Governmental Accounting Research System*™ (GARS), by the Governmental Accounting Standards Board (GASB), provides online access to accounting standards and related literature for state and local governments including GASB Codification, Original Pronouncements, and Implementation Guides. For additional information go to http://gars.gasb.org.
- *International Financial Statistics,* by the International Monetary Fund (IMF), provides statistical data on "all aspects of international and domestic finance." For additional information go to http://www.imf.org/external/pubs/cat/longres.cfm?sk=397.0.
- *IntelliConnect*®, by Commerce Clearing House (CCH), can be indispensable for tax and accounting research. For more information go to http://tax.cchgroup.com/IntelliConnect-Tax-Research/default.
- *Investext*® *Archive,* by Dialog, LLC contains full text of investment research reports from hundreds of sources, including leading brokers and investment bankers. Reports are available on approximately 60,000 publicly traded companies. Separate industry reports are available. For additional information go to http://library.dialog.com/bluesheets/html/bl0545.html.
- *NAARS Annual Reports (AICPA Annual Reports)*, contains "portions of annual reports to shareholders and information extracted from SEC filings, including financial statements, footnotes, auditor's opinions, material incorporated by reference and management responsibility letters." For additional information go to http://libguides.mit.edu/content.php?pid=63012&sid=466611.
- *ProQuest Banking Information Source*™ provides indexing, abstracting, full text, and images of more than 690 publications from 1971 to present, with weekly updates. Covers the financial services industry, including banks, savings institutions, investment houses, credit unions, insurance companies, and real estate organizations. Emphasis is on marketing and management. For additional information go to http://www.proquest.com/en-US/catalogs/databases/detail/pq_banking_info.shtml.
- *U.S. Basic Economics Database* presents more than 6,000 statistical series relating to business, industry, finance, and economics. Time period is 1947 to present, with daily updates. For additional information go to http://www.bsu.edu/mcobwin/econ/database/dri/index.html.
- *CCH*® *Tax Research NetWork*™, hosted by The University of Texas, is a powerful research tool for tax research. For additional information go to http://www.lib.utexas.edu/indexes/titles.php?id=74.
- *World Economic Outlook Database,* by the International Monetary Fund (IMF) contains "data series on national accounts, inflation, unemployment rates, balance of payments, fiscal indicators, … for countries and country groups … whose data are reported by the IMF." For additional information go to http://www.imf.org/external/pubs/ft/weo/2009/01/weodata/index.aspx.

Other Printed Sources of Accounting and Financial Information

Business news, articles, market data;
stock, bond, and mutual fund price quotes

Barron's

USA Today

Investor's Business Daily

The Wall Street Journal

Business news, articles

Business Week

Forbes Magazine

Fortune Magazine

Money Magazine

Data on the economy and industries;
financial and economic statistics

Business Conditions Digest

Economic Report of the President

Federal Reserve Bulletin

Standard & Poor's Industry
  Surveys

Standard & Poor's Statistical Surveys

Statistical Abstract of the
  United States

US Industrial Outlook

World Almanac

Summary data about industries, companies;
advice on industries, stocks; analyses and forecasts

Standard & Poor's Outlook

Value-Line Investment Survey

Stock information, company performance;
corporate financial data

Annual reports of companies

Moody's Bank & Finance Manual

Moody's Bond Record

Moody's Bond Survey

Moody's Handbook of Common Stocks

Moody's Industrial Manual

Moody's International Manual

Moody's OTC Manual

Moody's Public Utility Manual

Moody's Transportation Manual

Standard & Poor's Corporation
  Records

Standard & Poor's Stock Reports

Bond information

Moody's Bond Record

Moody's Bond Survey

Mutual fund information

Morningstar Mutual Funds

Internal Documentation Style

C = Citation within the text
R = Entry in reference list

Book—Single Author
C   (Pacter 1994, 12)
R   Pacter, P. 1994. *Reporting financial information by segment.* London, UK: International Accounting Standards Committee.

Book—Single Editor
C   (Frankel 1994, 64)
R   Frankel, J. A., ed. 1994. *The internationalization of equity markets.* Chicago: University of Chicago Press.

Book—Two Authors
C   (Romney and Steinbart 2003, 621)
R   Romney, Marshall B., and Paul John Steinbart. 2003. *Accounting Information Systems,* 9th ed. Upper Saddle River, N.J.: Prentice Hall.

Book—More Than Two Authors
C   (Ahrens, Elder, and Beasley 2014, 84)
R   Ahrens, Alvin A., Randal J. Elder, and Mark S. Beasley. 2014. *Auditing and Assurance Services,* 15th ed. Upper Saddle River, N.J.: Pearson Education, Inc.

Book—Author Is an Association, Institution, or Organization
C   (AICPA 1993, 2)
R   American Institute of Certified Public Accountants (AICPA). 1993. *The information needs of investors and creditors: A report on the AICPA special committee's study of the information needs of today's users of financial reporting, November, 1993.* New York: AICPA.

Article in a Journal—Single Author
C   (Schwartz 1996, 20)
R   Schwartz, Donald. 1996. The future of financial accounting: Universal standards. *Journal of Accountancy* 181, no. 5 (May): 20–21.

Article in a Journal—Two Authors
C   (May and Schneider, 1988, 70)
R   May, G. S., and D. K. Schneider. 1988. Reporting accounting changes: Are stricter guidelines needed? *Accounting Horizons* 2, no. 3 (September): 68–74.

Article in a Journal—More Than Two Authors
C   (Barth, Landsman, and Rendleman, 1998, 75)
R   Barth, Mary E., Wayne R. Landsman, and Richard J. Rendleman, Jr. 1998. Option pricing-based bond value estimates and a fundamental components approach to account for corporate debt. *The Accounting Review* 73, no. 1 (January): 73–102.

Article in a Magazine
C   (Blinder 1988, 25)
R   Blinder, Alan S. 1988. Dithering on Hill is crippling a key agency. *Business Week,* 26 September, 25.

Article in a Newspaper—Author Not Identified
C   (*The Wall Street Journal,* 16 July 1986)
R   *The Wall Street Journal,* 16 July 1986, Words count.

Article in a Newspaper—Author Identified
C   (May 1987)
R   May, Gordon S. 1987. No accounting for poor writers. *The Wall Street Journal,* 29 May.

Primary Source Reprinted in a Secondary Source
C   (FASB, *SFAC 1,* par. 3)
R   Financial Accounting Standards Board (FASB). 1978. *Objectives of financial reporting by business enterprises, statement of financial accounting concepts no. 1.* Stamford, Conn.: FASB. Reprinted in *Original Pronouncements, as Amended, 2005/2006 Edition: Accounting Standards as of June 1, 2006,* Vol. II. New York: John Wiley & Sons, 2006.

FASB Accounting Standards Codification®‡
C   (FASB ASC par. 350-10-05-01)
R   Financial Accounting Standards Board (FASB), 2014. *Accounting Standards Codification®.* Stamford, Conn.: FASB.

Legal Citation
C   (*Aaron v. SEC,* 446 U.S. 680, 1980)
R   Aaron v. SEC, 446 U.S. 680 (1980).

Internal Revenue Code Section
C   (*Internal Revenue Code* Sec. 6111(a))
R   *Internal Revenue Code.* Sec. 6111(a).

Government Document
C   (SEC 1995, 3)
R   United States Securities and Exchange Commission (SEC). 1995. *Self-regulatory organizations; notice* of filing and order granting accelerated approval of proposed rule change by the National Association of Securities Dealers, Inc., relating to an interim extension of the OTC Bulletin Board (R) service through September 28, 1995. Securities Exchange Act Release No. 35918, 60 FR 35443. Washington, D.C. (July 7).

Federal Register
C   (61 Fed. Reg. 1996, 208:55264)
R   "Revision to NASA FAR supplement coverage on contractor financial management reporting." *Federal Register* 61, no. 208 (25 Oct. 1996): 55264.

---

‡The numbers shown in the in-text citation refer to the Codification Topic (350), Subtopic (10), Section (05), and Paragraph (01). The date in the accompanying reference list entry is the date of the edition of the ASC. Because the ASC is continuously updated, this will usually be the date you consulted it.

World Wide Web
C   (Cohn, 2013)
R   Cohn, Michael. "Council Proposes Accounting Standards Modifications for
      Private Companies," Accounts Media Group. 2013. http://www.
      accountingtoday.com/news/Council-Proposes-Accounting-Standards-
      Modifications-Private-Companies-66631-1.html (30 May 2013).

E-mail
C   May, Gordon S. "The PCAOB." Personal email (3 Aug. 2004).
R   Personal email messages are usually not included in reference lists.

More Than One Work in Reference List by Same Author or Authors—Different
Years
C   (Lang and Lundholm, 1993)
R   Lang, M., and R. Lundholm. 1993. Cross-sectional determinants of analyst
      ratings of corporate disclosures. *Journal of Accounting Research* 31, no. 2
      (Autumn): 246–271.
      _____. 1996. Corporate disclosure policy and analyst behavior.
      Accounting Review 71, no. 4 (October): 467–492.

More Than One Work in Reference List by Same Author or Authors—Same Year
C   (Frost and Pownall, 1994b, 61)
R   Frost, C. A., and G. Pownall. 1994a. Accounting disclosure practices in the
      United States and United Kingdom. *Journal of Accounting Research* 32,
      no. 1 (Spring): 75–102.
      _____. 1994b. A comparison of the stock price response to earnings
      measures in the United States and the United Kingdom.
      Contemporary Accounting Research 11, no. 1 (Summer):
      59–83.

Appendix 8 – E

Endnotes or Footnotes and Bibliography Style

N – Endnote or footnote (Endnotes are numbered with full-sized or superscript Arabic numerals in a Notes section at the end of each chapter or at the end of the paper.)

B = Bibliographical entry

Book—Single Author

N   [1]P. Pacter, *Reporting Financial Information by Segment* (London, UK: International Accounting Standards Committee, 1994), 12.

B   Pacter, P. *Reporting Financial Information by Segment.* London, UK: International Accounting Standards Committee, 1994.

Book—Single Editor

N   [1]J. A. Frankel, ed., *The Internationalization of Equity Markets* (Chicago: University of Chicago Press, 1994), 64.

B   Frankel, J.A., ed. *The Internationalization of Equity Markets.* Chicago: University of Chicago Press, 1994.

Book—Two Authors

N   [1]Marshall B. Romney and Paul John Steinbart, *Accounting Information Systems*, 11th ed. (Upper Saddle River, NJ: Pearson Prentice Hall, 2009), 622.

B   Romney, Marshall B., and Paul John Steinbart. *Accounting Information Systems*, 11th ed. Upper Saddle River, NJ: Pearson Prentice Hall, 2009.

Book—More Than Two Authors

N   [1]Alvin A. Ahrens, Randal J. Elder, and Mark S. Beasley, *Auditing and Assurance Services,* 15th ed. Upper Saddle River, NJ: Pearson Education, Inc., 2014.

B   Ahrens, Alvin A., Randal J. Elder, and Mark S. Beasley. *Auditing and Assurance Services,* 15th ed. Upper Saddle River, NJ: Pearson Education, Inc., 2014.

Book—Author Is an Association, Institution, or Organization

N   [1]American Institute of Certified Public Accountants (AICPA), *The Information Needs of Investors and Creditors: A Report on the AICPA Special Committee's Study of the Information Needs of Today's Users of Financial Reporting, November, 1993.* (New York: AICPA, 1993), 2.

B   American Institute of Certified Public Accountants (AICPA). *The Information Needs of Investors and Creditors: A Report on the AICPA Special Committee's Study of the Information Needs of Today's Users of Financial Reporting, November, 1993.* New York: AICPA, 1993.

Article in a Journal—Single Author

N   [1]Donald Schwartz, "The Future of Financial Accounting: Universal Standards," *Journal of Accountancy* 181, no. 5 (May 1996): 20.

B   Schwartz, Donald, "The Future of Accounting: Universal Standards." *Journal of Accountancy* 181, no. 5 (May 1996): 20–21.

Article in a Journal—Two Authors
N   [1]G. S. May and D. K. Schneider, "Reporting Accounting Changes:
     Are Stricter Guidelines Needed?" *Accounting Horizons* 2, no. 3 (Sept.
     1988): 70.
B   May, G. S., and D. K. Schneider. "Reporting Accounting Changes:
     Are Stricter Guidelines Needed?" *Accounting Horizons* 2, no. 3 (Sept.
     1988): 68–74.

Article in a Journal—More than Two Authors
N   [1]Mary E. Barth, Wayne R. Landsman, and Richard J. Rendleman,
     Jr., "Option Pricing-Based Bond Value Estimates and a Fundamental
     Components Approach to Account for Corporate Debt," *Accounting
     Review* 73, no. 1 (January 1998): 75.
B   Barth, Mary E., Wayne R. Landsman and Richard J. Rendleman, Jr.
     "Option Pricing-Based Bond Value Estimates and a Fundamental
     Components Approach to Account for Corporate Debt." *Accounting
     Review* 73, no. 1 (January 1998): 73–102.

Article in a Magazine
N   [1]Alan S. Blinder, "Dithering on Hill is Crippling a Key Agency," *Business
     Week*, 26 September 1988, 25.
B   Blinder, Alan S. "Dithering on Hill is Crippling a Key Agency." *Business
     Week,* 26 September 1988, 25.

Article in a Newspaper—Author Not Identified
N   [1]*The Wall Street Journal,* 16 July 1986, "Words Count."
B   *The Wall Street Journal,* 16 July 1986, "Words Count."

Article in a Newspaper—Author Identified
N   [1]Gordon S. May, "No Accounting for Poor Writers," *Wall Street Journal,*
     29 May 1986.
B   May, Gordon S. "No Accounting for Poor Writers," *Wall Street Journal* 29,
     May 1986.

Primary Source Reprinted in a Secondary Source
N   [1]Financial Accounting Standards Board (FASB). *Objectives of Financial
     Reporting by Business Enterprises, Statement of Financial Accounting
     Concepts No. 1.* (Stamford, Conn.: FASB, 1978), par. 3; reprinted in
     *Original Pronouncements, As Amended, 2005/2006 Edition: Accounting
     Standards as of June 1, 2005,* Vol. II. (New York: John Wiley & Sons,
     2005), 1005-1020.
B   Financial Accounting Standards Board (FASB). *Objectives of Financial
     Reporting by Business Enterprises, Statement of Financial Accounting
     Concepts No. 1.* Stamford, Conn.: FASB. Reprinted in *Original
     Pronouncements, As Amended, 2005/2006 Edition: Accounting Standards
     as of June 1, 2005,* Vol. II, 1005-1020. New York: John Wiley & Sons, 2005.
N   [1]Financial Accounting Standards Board (FASB). *Accounting for Income
     Taxes, Statement of Financial Accounting Standards No. 109.* (Stamford,
     Conn.: FASB, 1992), par. 17; available in *Financial Accounting Research
     System (FARS).* Stamford: Financial Accounting Standards Board, 2010.
B   Financial Accounting Standards Board (FASB). *Accounting for Income
     Taxes, Statement of Financial Accounting Standards No. 109.* Stamford,
     Conn.: FASB. Available in *Financial Accounting Research System
     (FARS).* Stamford: Financial Accounting Standards Board, 2010.

Legal Citation
N   [1]*Aaron v. SEC.* 446 U.S. 680 (1980).
B   *Aaron v. SEC.* 446 U.S. 680 (1980).

Internal Revenue Code Section
N   [1]*Internal Revenue Code* Sec. 6111(a).
B   *Internal Revenue Code.* Sec. 6111(a).

Government Document
N   [1]United States Securities and Exchange Commission (SEC), *Self-Regulatory Organizations; Notice of Filing and Order Granting Accelerated Approval of Proposed Rule Change by the National Association of Securities Dealers, Inc., Relating to an Interim Extension of the OTC Bulletin Board (R) Service Through September 28, 1995.* Securities Exchange Act Release No. 35918, 60 FR 35443 (7 July 1995): 3.
B   United States Securities and Exchange Commission (SEC). *Self-Regulatory Organizations; Notice of Filing and Order Granting Accelerated Approval of Proposed Rule Change by the National Association of Securities Dealers, Inc., Relating to an Interim Extension of the OTC Bulletin Board (R) Service Through September 28, 1995.* Securities Exchange Act Release No. 35918, 60 FR 35443 (7 July 1995).

Federal Register
N   [1]"Revision to NASA FAR Supplement Coverage on Contractor Financial Management Reporting." *Federal Register* 61, no. 208 (25 Oct. 1996): 55264.
B   "Revision to NASA FAR Supplement Coverage on Contractor Financial Management Reporting." *Federal Register* 61, no. 208 (25 Oct. 1996): 55264.

World Wide Web
N   [1]Michael Cohen, "Council Proposes Accounting Standards Modifications for Private Companies," Accountants Media Group. 2013. http://www.accountingtoday.com/news/Council-Proposes-Accounting-Standards-Modifications-Private-Companies-66631-1.html (30 May 2013).
B   Cohen, Michael. "Council Proposes Accounting Standards Modifications for Private Companies," Accountants Media Group. 2013. http://www.accountingtoday.com/news/Council-Proposes-Accounting-Standards-Modifications-Private-Companies-66631-1.html (30 May 2013).

E-mail
N   [1]Gordon S. May, "The PCAOB." Personal email (3 Aug. 2009).
B   May, Gordon S., "The PCAOB." Personal email (3 Aug. 2009).

More Than One Work in Bibliography by Same Author or Authors
N   [1]M. Lang and R. Lundholm, "Cross-Sectional Determinants of Analyst Ratings of Corporate Disclosures," *Journal of Accounting Research* 31, no. 2 (Autumn 1993): 246–271.
B   Lang, M., and R. Lundholm, "Cross-Sectional Determinants of Analyst Ratings of Corporate Disclosures," *Journal of Accounting Research* 31, no. 2 (Autumn 1993): 246–271.
        _____. "Corporate Disclosure Policy and Analyst Behavior," *The Accounting Review* 71, no. 4 (October 1996): 467–492.

CHAPTER

Letters

All accountants, no matter what their specialty, write letters to a variety of people, including clients, government agencies, and fellow professionals. Auditors write engagement letters, letters regarding deficiencies in internal control, management letters, and other letters to clients. Tax accountants may write letters seeking data about a client's tax situation, or to clarify issues for a client. Accountants may also write letters to communicate the results of research into a technical accounting problem or for a wide variety of other reasons.

For any letter to get the best results, of course, it must be well written. This chapter begins with principles of good letter writing: organization, style, tone, and format. We then look at some typical letters that accountants write.

PRINCIPLES OF LETTER WRITING

Effective letters have the characteristics of any good writing: They contain correct, complete information, and they are usually written with specific readers in mind. They are also written in an active, direct style. In other words, they are coherent, clear, and concise. The letters are also neat and attractive, with a professional appearance.

Planning a Letter

A letter can vary in length from one paragraph to several pages, although many business letters are no longer than a page. Whatever the length, think carefully about what the letter should cover before you begin so that you won't forget something important.

As in other writing tasks, analyze the purpose of the letter before you write it. If you are answering another person's letter, keep that letter on hand and note any comments for which a reply is needed. Finally, jot down a brief outline to organize the material logically.

It's also important to think about the reader of your letter, especially when writing about a technical topic. The reader's knowledge and experience should determine how much detail you use when explaining the technical material in the letter.

Sometimes you must explain complex accounting procedures in words that a non-accountant can understand. *Tax Research Techniques*, a study published by the AICPA, discusses user needs in writing letters to clients about tax problems:

> Like a good speaker, a good writer must know the audience before beginning. Because tax clients and their staff vary greatly in their tax expertise, it is important to consider their technical sophistication when composing a tax opinion letter. The style of a letter may range from a highly sophisticated format, with numerous technical explanations and citations, to a simple composition that uses only layperson's terms. In many situations, of course, the best solution lies somewhere between the two extremes.[1]

Organization

Like other kinds of writing, a letter is organized into an introduction, a body, and a conclusion. Each section uses summary sentences to emphasize main ideas and help the reader follow the train of thought.

The *introduction* of a letter establishes rapport with the reader and identifies the subject of the letter or the reason it was written. You can mention previous communication on the subject, such as an earlier letter or phone call, or remind the reader of a recent meeting or shared interest. The introduction should also briefly summarize the main ideas or recommendations discussed in the letter. If the letter is longer than a page, it's also a good idea to identify in the introduction the main issues or topics the letter will cover.

The *body* of the letter is divided logically into discussions of each topic. Arrange the topics in descending order of importance *from the reader's point of view*. Start with the most important issue and work your way down to the least important. Begin the discussion of each issue with a summary sentence stating the main idea or recommendation.

Paragraphs should be short, usually a maximum of four or five sentences, and each should begin with a topic sentence that summarizes the paragraph's main idea.

The letter's *conclusion* may be a conventional courteous closing:

> Thank you very much for your help.

The conclusion is also a good place to tell your correspondent exactly what you want him or her to do, or what you will do to follow up on the subjects discussed in the letter:

> May I have an appointment to discuss this matter with you? I'll be in Chicago next week, October 7–11. I'll call your administrative assistant to see whether we can set up a time that is convenient for you.

If your letter is very long, the conclusion may also summarize your main ideas and recommendations.

Conciseness and Clarity

Conciseness and clarity, two qualities of all good writing, are particularly important in letters. You don't want to waste your readers' time, nor do you want them to miss important ideas. Come to the point quickly and say it in a way they will understand.

Many techniques already presented in this handbook are useful for writing short, clear letters. Your writing should be unified: paragraphs with a central idea that is easy to spot. The letter should also be as brief and simple as possible, while still conveying an unambiguous, precise meaning.

Tone

One of the most important characteristics of a well-written business letter is its tone, or the way it makes the reader feel. Chapter 4 discussed writing from your reader's point of view, emphasizing the reader's interests and needs. Courtesy and respect are important qualities of business letters, as they are in all forms of communication.

In general, effective letters reflect a personal, conversational tone. However, the best tone to use for a given letter depends to some extent on the purpose and reader of that letter. Review the discussion of tone in Chapter 4 to see how the content of the letter and your relationship with the reader can affect the tone you choose for your correspondence.

Form and Appearance

One of the primary characteristics of an effective letter is a neat appearance. Good stationery is important: 8½- × 11-inch, unlined paper of a high-quality bond, about 24-pound weight. Envelopes, 4 × 10 inches, should match the stationery. White or cream is usually the best color choice. Software programs now make it possible to design and print your own letterhead stationery. If you design your own letterhead, be conservative when you select font styles and sizes.

Business letters should be printed on a good-quality printer. Envelopes should also be printed. Both the letter and the envelope should be free of errors. Neatness is essential!

A letter is usually single-spaced, with double-spacing between paragraphs, although letters can be double-spaced throughout (see the sample formats in Figures 9–1 and 9–2). Margins should be at least 1 inch on all sides and as even as possible without justifying the right margin, although a shorter letter may allow you to set wider margins.

One-page letters should be placed so that the body of the letter, excluding the heading, is centered on the page or slightly above center. A computer makes it easy to experiment with margins and spacing until you get the best arrangement.

FIGURE 9–1   Diagram of a Letter Format — Block Style

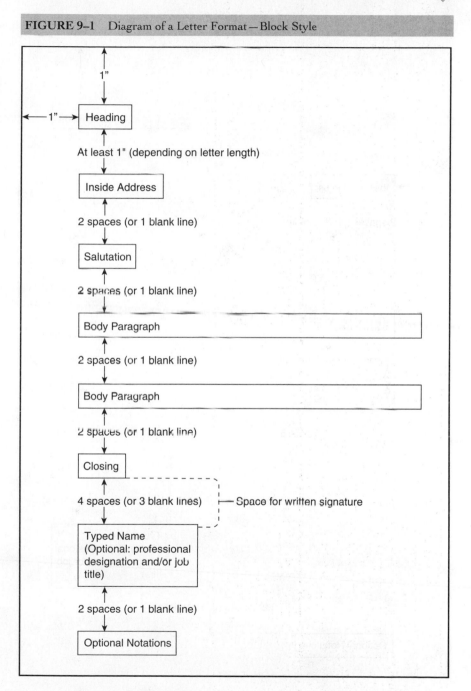

FIGURE 9–2   Diagram of a Letter Format — Modified Block Style

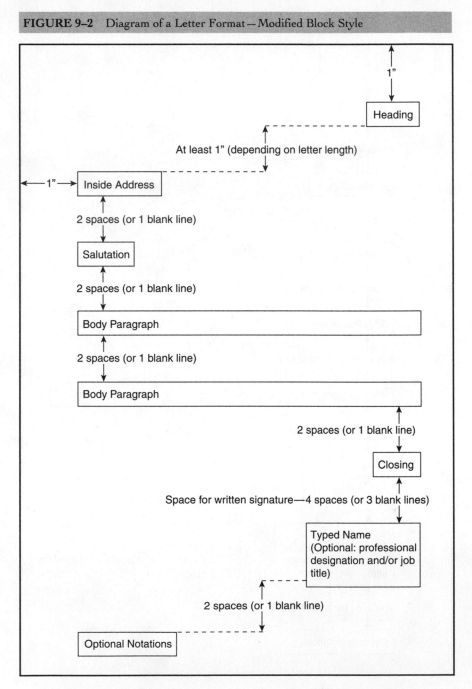

Parts of the Letter

Study the diagrams in Figures 9–1 and 9–2, which illustrate the parts of a letter and their proper placement for two formats, the block and the modified block styles. The following sections describe each part of the letter in more detail. Remember also that formatting techniques, such as headings and set-off lists, can make your letters attractive and easy to read.

Heading

The heading contains your address (not your name) and the date of the letter. If you use stationery without a letterhead, place the heading on the left margin (for block style) or next to the right margin (for modified block style). If you use letterhead stationery, omit the heading except for the date. Center the date below the letterhead or place it next to the left margin for block style.

Inside Address

The inside address is a reproduction of the address on the envelope. Place the title of the person to whom you are writing either on the same line as his or her name, or on the following line:

Anna O'Rourke, President
Excellent Consulting Services
2110 Winners Circle
Atlanta, GA 30378

-or-

Anna O'Rourke
President
Excellent Consulting Services
2110 Winners Circle
Atlanta, GA 30378

It's better to address a letter to a specific person rather than to an office or title. You can usually find the name of the person to whom you are writing by phoning the company or organization, or by consulting its Web page. You should also verify the spelling of the name and the gender of the person, if gender isn't obvious from the name.

Salutation

If possible, address your correspondent by name:

Dear Ms. O'Rourke:

or

Dear Mr. Smith:

For a female correspondent, use Ms. unless she prefers another title. If you know your correspondent well, you may use his or her first name in the salutation:

Dear Anna:

Be careful with the use of first names, however, especially when writing to someone you haven't met in person. A title and last name may be especially appropriate for an older person or one in a position of greater authority than yours. In many situations, a respectful, courteous tone requires using a title and last name.

If you don't know the name of the correspondent, use a salutation such as the following:

Dear Human Resource Division:
Dear Registrar:

Note that a colon (:) always follows the salutation in a business letter.

Closing

The letter's formal closing is placed at the left margin for a block-style letter and next to the right margin for the modified block style. Capitalize the first word of the closing and put a comma at the end. Either of the following closings is correct:

Sincerely yours,
Sincerely,

Signature

Your name should be printed four lines below the closing; your position or professional designation (or both) can be added in one of the ways shown below:

Sincerely,

Anna O'Rourke
Anna O'Rourke
President

or

Sincerely yours,

Anna O'Rourke
Anna O'Rourke, CPA
Managing Partner

The space between the closing and printed name is for your hand-written signature.

Optional Parts of a Letter

Sometimes you'll need additional notations, which are placed below the signature at the left margin. First, if someone else types your letter, a notation is made of your initials (all capital letters) and the typist's (all lowercase):

AO'R:lc

or

AO'R/lc

Second, if the letter includes an enclosure, make a notation:

Enclosure(s)

Finally, if you will distribute copies of the letter to other people, note the people who will receive a copy:

cc: John Jones

Second Page

Many business letters are only one page long. If you need to write additional pages, each should have a heading identifying the addressee, the date, and the page number. This information is printed at the left margin:

Mr. Richard Smith
November 18, 2014
Page 3

A second page (and any subsequent pages) should have at least three lines of text, in addition to the heading and closing.

RESPONDING TO CORRESPONDENCE

When you reply to a letter written by someone else, it's important to respond in a way that will build a good working relationship between you and the correspondent. Many of the techniques for effective letters already discussed apply to responses. Here is a summary of those techniques, as well as a few pointers that particularly apply when you are answering someone else's letter:

1. Respond promptly, by return mail if possible.
2. Reread carefully the letter you received, noting questions that need answers or ideas that need your comment.
3. For the opening paragraph:
   • Refer to the earlier correspondence, such as the date of the letter you received.
   • If your letter is good news, or at least neutral, state clearly and positively the letter's main idea.

- If your letter contains bad news, such as the denial of a request, identify the subject of the letter in the opening paragraph. State the explicit refusal later in the body of the letter.
4. Answer all your correspondent's questions fully and cover all relevant topics in sufficient detail. However, the letter should be as concise as possible.
5. End with a courteous closing.

TYPICAL ACCOUNTING LETTERS

Before we begin this section, we should note that many accounting firms have standardized letters for some situations. The management of a firm may have decided on the organization and even the specific wording that it requires its staff to use for engagement letters, management advisory letters, and the like. If your firm uses standardized letters, simply adapt the basic letter to the specific case you are concerned with, adding dates, names, figures, and other relevant facts.

Sample letters for various situations are presented in the following pages, along with general comments on the content and organization of these letters.

Engagement Letters

Engagement letters put into writing the arrangements made between an accounting firm and a client. Engagement letters can confirm the arrangements for a variety of services: audit, review, compilation, management advisory services, or tax. The main advantage of an engagement letter is that it clarifies the mutual responsibilities of the accountant and client and thus prevents possible misunderstandings.

Engagement letters can vary a great deal in content, depending on the firm writing the letter, the type of services to be provided, and the facts of the case. However, most engagement letters will include the following:

- A description of the objectives and nature of the service the accountants will provide, including any non-audit services such as the preparation of tax returns or management consulting
- A description of the responsibilities of both the client and the auditor
- A description of any limitations, restrictions, or deadlines imposed on the work to be done
- A description of any assistance to be provided by the client
- A statement that an audit will possibly not uncover all acts of fraud

In addition to these elements, an engagement letter may also include other information, such as information about the fee and a space for the client to indicate acceptance of the arrangements outlined in the engagement letter.

Figure 9–3 shows a sample engagement letter for an audit.

FIGURE 9–3   Engagement Letter for an Audit[2]

Collins & Yancey
Certified Public Accountants
356 Woodale Avenue
Austin, Texas 78712

July 15, 2014

Robert Samson, President
Samson Manufacturing Company
167 Abbey Road
Austin, Texas 78712

Dear Mr. Samson:

You have requested that we audit the financial statements of Samson Manufacturing Company, which comprise the balance sheet as of December 31, 2014, and the related statements of income; changes in stockholders' equity and cash flows for the year then ended; and the related notes to the financial statements. We are pleased to confirm our acceptance and our understanding of this audit engagement by means of this letter. Our audit will be conducted with the objective of our expressing an opinion on the financial statements.

Our Responsibilities

We will conduct our audit in accordance with auditing standards generally accepted in the United States of America (GAAS). Those standards require that we plan and perform the audit to obtain reasonable assurance about whether the financial statements are free from material misstatement. An audit involves performing procedures to obtain audit evidence about the amounts and disclosures in the financial statements. The procedures selected depend on the auditor's judgment, including the assessment of the risks of material misstatement of the financial statements, whether due to fraud or error. An audit also includes evaluating the appropriateness of accounting policies used and the reasonableness of significant accounting estimates made by management, as well as evaluating the overall presentation of the financial statements.

Because of the inherent limitations of an audit, together with the inherent limitations of internal control, an unavoidable risk that some material misstatements may not be detected exists, even though the audit is properly planned and performed in accordance with GAAS.

In making our risk assessments, we consider internal control relevant to the entity's preparation and fair presentation of the financial statements in order to design audit procedures that are appropriate in the circumstances, but not for the purpose of expressing an opinion on the effectiveness of the entity's internal control. However, we will communicate to you in writing concerning any significant deficiencies or material weaknesses in internal control relevant to the audit of the financial statements that we have identified during the audit.

FIGURE 9–3 *(Contd.)*

Robert Samson, President
July 15, 2014
Page 2

Management Responsibilities

Our audit will be conducted on the basis that management acknowledges and understands that they have responsibility

  a. for the preparation and fair presentation of the financial statements in accordance with accounting principles generally accepted in the United States of America;

  b. for the design, implementation, and maintenance of internal control relevant to the preparation and fair presentation of financial statements that are free of material misstatement, whether due to fraud or error; and

  c. to provide us with

   i. access to all information of which management is aware that is relevant to the preparation and fair presentation of the financial statements such as records, documentation, and other matters;

   ii. additional information that we may request from management for the purpose of the audit; and

   iii. unrestricted access to persons within the entity from whom we determine it necessary to obtain audit evidence.

As part of our audit process, we will request from management written confirmation concerning representations made to us in connection with the audit.

Other Services

As part of our engagement for the year ending December 31, 2014, we will also prepare the federal and state income tax returns for Samson Manufacturing Company.

Our fees will be billed as work progresses and are based on the amount of time required at various levels of responsibility, plus actual out-of-pocket expenses. Invoices are payable upon presentation. We will notify you immediately of any circumstances we encounter that could significantly affect our initial estimate of total fees of $150,000.

We will issue a written report upon completion of our audit of Samson Manufacturing Company's financial statements. Our report will be addressed to management and the board of directors of Samson Manufacturing. We cannot provide assurance that an unmodified opinion will be expressed. Circumstances may arise in which it is necessary for us to modify our opinion, add an emphasis-of-matter or other-matter paragraph(s), or withdraw from the engagement.

Please sign and return the attached copy of this letter to indicate your acknowledgement of, and agreement with, the arrangements for our audit of the financial statements including our respective responsibilities.

Accepted:	Yours very truly:
Robert Samson	*Mary Collins*
By: Robert Martinez	Mary Collins
Date: July 27, 2014	Partner

Management Advisory Letters

At the conclusion of an audit, an accountant often writes a letter to the client suggesting ways the client can improve the business. This type of letter may contain suggestions on a variety of topics:

- Internal control
- The accounting and information system
- Inventory control
- Credit policies
- Budgeting
- Tax matters
- Resource management
- Operating procedures

Sometimes, if the auditor includes many recommendations in the management letter, the letter may be quite long. If you write a management letter that is more than three pages long, consider organizing it into a report with a transmittal letter. Address the transmittal letter to the president or board of directors of the client company and summarize in the letter the major recommendations made in the report. Chapter 11 provides information on report writing.

In any case, whether the management letter is a single document or a report with a transmittal letter, remember that long letters are more attractive and easier to read if they contain headings. These headings divide the letter into logical sections.

Whatever the format of the management letter, write it in a way that is helpful to the client and builds a good professional relationship between the client and your firm. The techniques for effective writing discussed so far in this text certainly apply to management letters: clear and logical organization, readable style, and specific and concrete explanation.

An article in the *Journal of Accountancy* has noted that management letters may anger clients if they don't give enough specific information to support the accountants' suggestions.[3] The authors stress the importance of answering three questions about each recommendation:

- Why is the change needed?
- How can it be accomplished?
- What benefits will the client receive?

An example of a short, but effective, management advisory letter appears in Figure 9–4.

Tax Research Letters

Accountants who provide tax services often write letters to their clients communicating the results of the research into some tax question. These letters can be for either tax planning or after-the-fact tax situations.

FIGURE 9–4 Management Advisory Letter[1]

JADAU AND HERNANDEZ
Certified Public Accountants
1553 W. Ellis Street
Atlanta, Georgia 30316

March 15, 2014

Arthur Sanders, President
Art Products, Inc.
24 N. Broad Street
Atlanta, Georgia 30327

Dear Mr. Sanders:

Our examination of Art Products' financial statements for the year
ended December 31, 2013, revealed two areas where we believe
you could improve your business:

- Stronger budgeting system
- Review of credit policies

The following paragraphs explain these recommendations in
greater detail.

Budgets

Operating, selling, and general administrative expenses for 2013
as compared with 2012 increased from $1 million to $1,050,000, a
change of 5 percent. Although management has been able to control
expenditures, we believe efforts in this area would be assisted by
implementation of a strong system of budgeting.

Under such a system, responsibility for actual performance is
assigned to the employees most directly responsible for the expenditures involved. (It is best that such employees have a role in establishing the budgets.) Periodic reports reflecting actual and budgeted
amounts, together with explanations of significant variances, should
be provided to the management personnel responsible for approving
the budgets initially. We cannot overemphasize the value of sound
budgeting and planning in all areas of the company's activities.

Credit Policies

The history of write-offs of bad accounts over the past few years
indicates that the write-off percentage has declined. Considering
the low net earnings margin under which the company operates
(slightly less than 0.6 percent of net sales), it is most important that
this favorable record continue because a significant increase in bad
debts could have a substantial negative impact on net earnings.

FIGURE 9–4   *(Contd.)*

Arthur Sanders
March 15, 2014
Page 2

In view of the high cost of money for business in general, management should consider reviewing its credit policies to reasonably ensure that the risk inherent in continued sales to customers of questionable credit standing is justified. This is a delicate area of policy; it is not desirable to so restrict sales representatives that profitable sales are lost because of overly stringent credit policies. However, the credit and collection department should exercise a reasonable amount of control to ensure a minimum of bad accounts. For example, a limit could be set on the amount sales representatives could extend to customers whose accounts have reached a certain balance.

We will be glad to discuss these suggestions with you and help you implement them.

Sincerely,

Juan Hernandez

Juan Hernandez
Jadau and Hernandez
Certified Public Accountants

The content and organization of these letters can vary, but the following basic outline is a good one:

- The facts on which the research was based.
- Caution that the advice is valid only for the facts previously outlined.
- The tax questions implicit in these facts.
- The conclusions, with the authoritative support for the conclusions.
- Areas of controversy that the IRS might dispute. (Tax accountants do not all agree that the letter should identify the vulnerable areas in the client's situation. *Tax Research Techniques* suggests that if the letter does identify these weaknesses, the accountant should caution the client to control access to the letter.)[5]

In addition to a logical organization, such as the one outlined here, tax research letters should be understandable to the client. Tax questions are often highly technical, and you may need to explain the conclusions in terms a businessperson will understand.

Figure 9–5 illustrates a letter written to a client to report the results of tax research. The letter, which is written to the chief administrator of a large hospital, deals with a technical tax question, but is clearly written with a friendly, courteous tone.

FIGURE 9–5 A Letter Reporting the Results of Tax Research[6]

Professional Accounting Associates
2701 First City Plaza
Suite 905
Dallas, Texas 75019

December 12, 2014

Elizabeth Fegali, Chief Administrator
Mercy Hospital
22650 West Haven Drive
Arlington, Texas 75527

Dear Ms. Fegali:

It was great to see you at last Thursday's football game. If not for that last minute fumble, the Longhorns might have taken the conference championship!

In our meeting of December 6, you asked us to research whether the value of the meal vouchers that Mercy provides to its medical employees is taxable to the employees. I regret to inform you that if the vouchers are redeemed at MacDougal's, their value is likely to be taxable to the employees. On the other hand, if the vouchers are redeemed in the hospital cafeteria, their value is likely to be excludible from the employee's income.

In reaching this conclusion, we consulted relevant provisions of the Internal Revenue Code (IRC), applicable Treasury Regulations under the IRC, and a pertinent Supreme Court case. In addition, we reviewed the documents on employee benefits that you submitted to us at our earlier meeting.

Facts

The facts as we understand them are as follows: Mercy provides meal vouchers to its medical employees to enable them to eat while on emergency call. The vouchers are redeemable either in the hospital cafeteria or at MacDougal's. MacDougal's is a privately owned institution that rents business space from the hospital. Although Mercy's employees are not required to remain on or near the premises during their meal hours, they generally do.

Applicable Laws

Under the IRC, the value of meals is excludible from an employee's income if two conditions are met: first, the meals are furnished "for the convenience of the employer," and second, they are provided "on the business premises of the employer." Although the IRC does not explain what is meant by "for the convenience of the employer," "business premises of the employer," and "meals," other authorities do. Specifically, the Treasury Regulations define "business premises of the employer" to be the place of employment of the employees.

FIGURE 9–5   *(Contd.)*

Elizabeth Fegali
December 12, 2014
Page 2

The regulations state that providing meals during work hours to have
an employee available for emergency calls is "for the convenience of
the employer."

Moreover, under the IRC, if more than half the employees satisfy
the "for the convenience of the employer" test, all the employees
will be regarded as satisfying the test. The Supreme Court has
interpreted "meals" to mean food-in-kind. The Court has held that
cash allowances do not qualify as "meals."

<u>Analysis</u>

Clearly, the meals furnished by Mercy are "for the convenience
of the employer." They are furnished during the employees' work
hours to have the employees available for emergency calls. Although
the meals provided in the hospital cafeteria appear to be furnished
"on the business premises of the employer," the meals provided
at MacDougal's do not appear to be. The hospital is the place of
employment of the medical employees. MacDougal's is not. What is
unclear is whether the meal vouchers are equivalent to food-in-kind.
On the one hand, they are redeemable at more than one institution
and thus resemble cash allowances. On the other hand, they are
redeemable only in meals and thus resemble food-in-kind.

<u>Recommendation</u>

Because of this lack of clarity, we suggest that you modify your
employee benefits plan to allow for the provision of meals-in-kind
exclusively in the hospital cafeteria. In this way, you will dispel any
doubt that Mercy is furnishing "meals," "for the convenience of the
employer," "on the premises of the employer."

Please call me at (817) 475-2020 if you have any questions concerning this conclusion. I also suggest that we meet next week to discuss
the possibility of revising your employee benefits plan.

U.S. Treasury Regulations require us to advise you that, unless otherwise specifically noted, any federal tax advice in this communication
(including any attachments, enclosures, or other accompanying materials) was not intended or written to be used, and it cannot be used, by
any taxpayer for the purpose of avoiding penalties; furthermore, this
communication was not intended or written to support the promotion
or marketing of any of the transactions or matters it addresses.

Very truly yours,

Rosina Havacek

Rosina Havacek, Junior Associate
Professional Accounting Associates

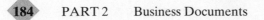

STANDARDIZED LETTERS: A CAUTION

As already mentioned, many organizations have standardized letters that they use for situations that occur often, such as engagement letters. These form letters save time, and they also convey the message precisely and reliably. If your employer expects you to use these standardized letters, then, of course, you should do so.

One word of caution: Remember that in many situations personalized letters are more appropriate than standardized letters. If you use standardized letters, be sure they are responsive to the reader's needs and concerns.

If you know your correspondent personally, a friendly reference to a topic of mutual interest can add warmth to your letter. The opening paragraph of the letter in Figure 9–5 provides a friendly, personalized opening to a client letter:

> It was great to see you at last Thursday's football game. If not for that last minute fumble, the Longhorns might have taken the conference championship!

LETTERS SENT BY EMAIL

Until a decade or two ago, business letters were always printed on paper and sent via the postal service. Today, much business correspondence is sent electronically, either as the body of an email or as an email attachment, as might be the case for a formal letter. The use of email correspondence is often convenient, but it must be done carefully, with attention to possible breaches of security. Chapter 12 provides detailed information on the use of email communication.

EXERCISES

Exercise 9–1 [General]

Suppose you received the letter shown in Figure 9–6. How would you react? What, specifically, is wrong with this letter? What about it is effective?

After you have analyzed the strengths and weaknesses of the letter as it is shown in Figure 9–6, revise it so that it would make a better impression on a reader.

Exercise 9–2 [General]

A friend of yours, Greg Burleson, has a daughter, Elaine, who wants to major in accounting. She believes that the only skills she needs for success as an accountant are technical skills: knowledge of accounting principles, the ability to research accounting issues, and computer expertise. Your friend Greg suspects that success in accounting requires a wider range of skills than Elaine realizes. However, Elaine isn't receptive to suggestions from her father.

FIGURE 9–6   Letter for Exercise 9–1

Smith, Barnum, and Bailey
Certified Public Accountants
301 MacDonald Place
Atlanta, Georgia 36095

Members
American Institute of   Telephone: (306) 782-5107
Certified Public Accountants

May 21, 2014

Mr. John W. Simmons
234 Myers Hall, UGA
Athens, Georgia 30609

Dear John:

   After considerable debate about our needs, we have decided to offer the internship to someone else. Our offer was excepted, so the position is now filled. I enjoyed talking with you and felt you would of been a positive impact to our firm and would work well with our present staff. Upon graduation we would be most interested in talking with you regarding full-time employment. If I can be of assistance in the near future, please feel free to call.

Sincerely,

Jason A. Smith

Jason A. Smith
JASjr/mlk
Enclosures

   You are a successful CPA who has been in practice for over twenty years, and your family has been friends with the Burleson family for a long time. Greg asks you to write a letter to Elaine about the skills necessary to become a successful accountant. He is sure Elaine will take your advice seriously.

   Write a letter to Elaine, a freshman at State University.

Exercise 9–3 [General]

Assume you are an undergraduate accounting major in a state university. The Future Leaders Group, an educational support organization, is offering a scholarship for which you may qualify, and the additional funds the scholarship would provide would be of significant help in financing your education. The application materials for the scholarship require that you write a letter to the chair of the scholarship awards committee, Allison Yang. Your letter will explain your choice of careers. You are also asked to describe possible career specialties in your chosen major, as well as projections for future employment opportunities.

Write the letter as requested, after you research the topics you will discuss.

Exercise 9–4 [Managerial]

Your client, Janice Rush, is the owner/manager of a store that sells jewelry, fine china, sterling silver flatware, and other gifts. The store has ten employees, mostly sales personnel who advise customers and handle the sales transactions. Ms. Rush is an astute business person, but she has little training in business. She has asked for your help because she has begun to notice discrepancies between the amount of sales she believes have occurred and the amount of money deposited in the bank. After talking with Ms. Rush, you realize that she needs a better system of internal control over cash.

Write a letter to Ms. Rush in which you explain the concept of internal control and outline a system that she can put in place.

Exercise 9–5 [Financial]

Lori Tripp wants to invest in an annuity for her grandchild Charles, who is ten years old. She wants the annuity to pay exactly $10,000 a year for five years, beginning on Charles's 21st birthday (September 15, 2024). She wants to know how much money she will have to invest on March 15, 2014, when she expects to receive an inheritance check, in order to provide such an annuity. You have already determined that the annuity will earn three percent interest, compounded annually.

Write a letter to Ms. Tripp explaining annuities and the amount she would need to invest on March 15, 2014, to set up the plan she has in mind. Invent any facts you may need to complete the letter.

Exercise 9–6 [Auditing]

Assume that you are a partner of Black and White, CPAs. During the last year, you were part of the team that audited Parker and Smith, Inc., a small publicly held company. The audit went quite well, and the client had high praise for the work done by you and the other members of the audit team. One day six months after the completion of the audit, you receive this email from Jerome Parker, president of Parker and Smith:

Hi [your name],

   We are still talking around here about the good job you and the other members of the audit team did on our audit. You all seemed to have a thorough understanding of our business, and we found working with you a pleasure. Based on the good experience we had with the audit, we would like to engage your firm to do additional work for us. Specifically, we'd like your help in designing a new financial information system for our company. We're also considering investing in stock being offered by one of our suppliers, and we'd like your input into that decision.

   Hope you can help us here! Looking forward to hearing from you.

   Regards,
   Jerome

   Write a letter to Mr. Parker in response to his email. Remember that you want to maintain a good working relationship with Parker and Smith. You also want to maintain proper professional and ethical standards.

Exercise 9–7 [Tax]

Assume you are a CPA specializing in tax accounting for individuals in your community. One of your clients, Alicia Evans, has sent you the following email.

As you know, I have recently returned to work full time and need to hire someone to help me with house cleaning. I need to know what, if any, obligations I will have for withholding social security. Will I have any other tax or reporting obligations? I am considering the following possibilities:

1. Hiring an individual who has a business license and is self-employed as a contractor. This person would clean my house weekly. In return, I would pay this person $100 a week for 50 weeks of the year.
2. Using a cleaning service, who would send one of its employees to my home. I would use this service biweekly at $125 per visit, for a total of 26 visits per year.
3. Hiring my neighbor, who does not have a business license. She would clean my house biweekly, and I would pay her $75 each visit, for a total of 26 visits each year.

(contd.)

I have one more question. Can I deduct any of the above expenses for house cleaning from my own income tax? After all, if I were not working I would not need to hire someone else to clean my house. It seems to me the house cleaning should be a legitimate business expense.

Please send the answer to the above questions to my home by registered mail. You have my address on file.

Write a letter to Ms. Evans in which you answer her questions.

Exercise 9–8 [Auditing/Ethics]

In the process of completing a tax return, your client, Sam Rhodes, refused to provide evidence to support some rather large deductions for business travel, saying, "Oh, I don't know about receipts. Just put it down and if and when the IRS questions me, I'll worry about receipts then."

Write a letter to Mr. Rhodes explaining why you cannot prepare a tax return showing these deductions unless he can provide the receipts. Remember the importance of tact and diplomacy in an awkward situation such as this. Use the proper format, effective organization, and appropriate style. Invent any information you feel is necessary to make your letter complete.

Exercise 9–9 [Auditing]

You are a partner in the firm of Shipley, Pyburn & Bynum, a local CPA firm. Your firm has received a letter from George Rayburn of Rayburn Industries, a potential audit client, that asks the following questions:

- What are the objectives of auditing your firm follows?
- How much responsibility does your firm take for the financial statements you produce as a result of an audit? Will your firm guarantee the accuracy of financial statements following your audit?
- What sort of guarantee does your firm provide that it will find any and all errors and fraud during the completion of an audit?

It is evident that Mr. Rayburn has sent a similar letter with the same questions to several CPA firms and plans to select a firm based on the answers he receives.

Write a letter to Mr. Rayburn responding to his questions. Invent any information you feel is necessary to make your letter complete.

Exercise 9–10 [Auditing]

During your first audit of a new client, Capital Food Supplies, a small restaurant food supply company, you become aware of a major weakness in internal control: One employee keeps the accounts receivable and payable records, pays bills, and does the bank reconciliation each month.

When you casually mention the problem to Scott Devin, the owner and general manager, he dismisses the issue. He says he trusts all his employees, has never had any problems, and can't afford to hire another employee just to deal with such a small internal control technicality.

Write a letter to your client tactfully explaining why you do not consider the problem to be "a small technicality." Explain the possible ramifications of not dealing with the issue, both in terms of the audit and in terms of asset protection. Use the proper format, effective organization, and appropriate style. Invent any information you feel is necessary to make your letter complete.

Exercise 9–11 [Financial/Theory]

Your boss, John Creedy, is a partner in the small local CPA firm for which you work. One morning a client, Jeff Altman, the owner of Altman Manufacturing, storms into Mr. Creedy's office and delivers a complaint. An edited version follows:

> This morning at my breakfast club I spoke with my competitor, Tony Dodd. He uses the LIFO inventory method just as I do. He boasted that his accountant had told him that by speeding up his purchases of raw materials at year-end he could significantly increase reported profits. If he can do that, why can't I? And why haven't you discussed this gimmick with me? I don't expect to rely on Dodd for financial advice; I pay you for that.

After Altman's departure, Mr. Creedy calls you, the accountant-in-charge of the Altman account, into his office to discuss Mr. Altman's complaint. You explain to your boss that your concern is your client's very large raw material inventory and slow turnover rate caused by years of over-buying. Mr. Creedy advises you that Mr. Altman needs new capital in his business and is trying to interest another local businessperson in becoming a limited partner. An increase in reported profits could be advantageous to Mr. Altman's plans. Therefore, left to his own devices, Mr. Altman would likely follow Mr. Dodd's accountant's advice.

Mr. Creedy asks you to draft a letter to Mr. Altman. The letter should provide a discussion of the problems of maintaining an overly large inventory as well as the disadvantage of a low turnover rate. Although you are not familiar with Mr. Dodd's company, you are reasonably certain his accountant would not have made the comment he did if Mr. Dodd's company had the same existing inventory problems as Altman Manufacturing. Use the proper format, effective organization, and appropriate style for your letter. Invent any information you feel is necessary to make your letter complete.

Exercise 9–12 [Financial]

Your audit client, Steven Dabbs, has written a letter to you. He is concerned because he has just received an offer to purchase his business for $1,000,000 more than the net carrying value of the assets as reported in the most recent financial statements that you had audited. He is not interested in selling the business, but he is now convinced that you have certified financial statements that do not properly reflect the value of his company.

Write a letter to your client explaining why the figures in the balance sheet should not be changed. You may assume your client is an astute businessman with no background in accounting. Use good format, effective organization, and appropriate style. Invent any information you feel is necessary to make your letter complete.

Exercise 9–13 [Tax]

Jennifer Davies, one of your tax clients, is contemplating making the following gifts: $25,000 to her church, $30,000 to each of her two grandchildren, $10,000 to her sister, and $15,000 to the local symphony orchestra. Ms. Davies has asked your firm what the tax consequences of these gifts will be to her and her husband. Among the issues you will want to discuss is the possibility of splitting some or all of the gifts with her husband. Ms. Davies is already aware of the term "gift splitting" because one of her friends has mentioned it to her. However, she does not understand how it works or whether it may be advantageous to her. She has also asked why she can't simply treat the gifts as "charitable contributions."

Write a letter to Ms. Davies replying to her inquiry. Invent any information you feel is necessary to make your letter complete.

Exercise 9–14 [Systems]

James Gipper, one of your consulting clients, is the CEO of Glassplex, a rapidly growing glass manufacturing company. Because his company is quickly developing its Internet presence, he is becoming increasingly concerned about Internet security. At his request, you are to write a letter to him outlining the basics of Internet security. Write the letter using good format, effective organization, and appropriate style. Invent any information you feel is necessary to make the letter complete.

Exercise 9–15 [Cost/Managerial]

One of your clients is Corporate Sentry, Inc., which manufactures alarms and other security devices. Because of competitive pressures, it plans to reduce costs so that it can more competitively price its products. In preparation for its internal deliberations, the CFO of the company, Charles Sargent, has asked your consulting firm to write a letter to him explaining the difference between engineered costs and discretionary costs and how such a distinction may be relevant to their downsizing plans. Write the letter using proper format, effective organization, and appropriate style. Invent any information you feel is necessary to make your letter complete.

Exercise 9–16 [Systems]

One of your clients, Jim Vaught, owns a very successful regional medical supply business. He has recently become interested in implementing an image processing system to improve cash collections. Mr. Vaught has asked you to write a letter to him describing the basics of a good image processing system. Write the letter using proper format, effective organization, and appropriate style. Invent any information you feel is necessary to make your letter complete.

Exercise 9–17 [Managerial/International/Current Professional Issues]

You are a successful management accountant employed by a large international corporation. The son of a good friend of yours is considering majoring in accounting in college. He is interested in accounting and international business and has recently learned that the AICPA and the Chartered Institute of Management Accountants jointly offer a Chartered Global Management Accountant (CGMA) designation, but knows nothing more about it. Your friend has asked you to write his son, Mitch Wilson, a letter explaining what a CGMA designation is, how to obtain it, and what benefit this credential might be to him if he is eventually employed in an international business environment. Write the letter using proper format, effective organization, and appropriate style. Invent any information you feel is necessary to make your letter complete.

NOTES

1. Robert L. Gardner, Dave N. Stewart, and Ronald G. Worsham, Jr., *Tax Research Techniques,* 8th ed. (New York: American Institute of Certified Public Accountants, 2008), 185–186. This source provides additional information on other letters that tax accountants may write, such as tax protest letters and requests for rulings.

2. Alvin A. Arens, Randal J. Elder, and Mark S. Beasley, *Auditing and Assurance Services*, 15th Ed., © 2014, pp. 168, 212. Reprinted and Electronically reproduced by permission of Pearson Education, Inc., Upper Saddle River, New Jersey.

3. Robert T. Lanz and S. Thomas Moser, "Improving Management Letters," *Journal of Accountancy* 149 no 3 (March 1980): 39–42.

4. The recommendations included in this letter are taken from Lanz and Moser, pp. 41-42.

5. These points are discussed in Gardner, Robert L., Dave N. Stewart, and Ronald G. Worsham, Jr., *Tax Research Techniques*, 8th ed. (New York: American Institute of Certified Public Accountants, 2008), 186–187.

6. Thomas R. Pope and Kenneth E. Anderson, *Prentice Hall's Federal Taxation 2013 Comprehensive*, 26th Ed., © 2013. Reprinted and Electronically reproduced by permission of Pearson Education, Inc., Upper Saddle River, New Jersey. A-7

CHAPTER

Memos

Memos, also called memoranda or memorandums, are often used for communication within an organization—between departments, for example, or between a supervisor and other members of the staff. Memos may be of any length, from one sentence to several pages. They may be printed and distributed as hard copy, or they may be circulated via email. (Chapter 12 covers special considerations for email and other forms of electronic communication.) Memos may be less formal than letters written to people outside the organization, but well-written memos have the same qualities as good letters: clarity, conciseness, coherence, and courtesy.

In this chapter, we first discuss some basic principles of effective memos. Then we look at a special kind of memo that accountants often write: a memo to a client's file.

MEMOS: SOME BASIC PRINCIPLES

Often memos are quite short—from one sentence, perhaps, to several paragraphs. Figure 10–1 is an example of a short memo. Notice the heading of the memo: the person or persons addressed, the writer, the subject, and the date. The writer's initials may replace a formal signature.

Sometimes memos are much longer than the one in Figure 10–1; in fact, they can be used for short reports. For longer memos, organization and structure are more complicated, so you need to think of writing the memo in terms of the writing process discussed in Chapter 2. Take the time to plan your memo: Analyze its purpose, considering the needs and interests of your readers; complete any needed research; and, finally, organize the material into a good outline. After you have planned the memo, you can then draft and revise it using the techniques covered in Chapters 2 through 7.

The Parts of a Memo: Organizing for Coherence

Like most kinds of writing, a memo is organized into an introduction, a body, and a conclusion. Summary sentences are used throughout the memo to make it more coherent. Even very short memos have

FIGURE 10–1   Sample Short Memo

> To: Fourth-floor employees
>
> From: Skip Waller *SW*
>
> Subject: Scheduled painting
>
> Date: September 12, 2014
>
> Our painting contractors are scheduled to repaint the offices and public areas on our floor next week, September 22-26. The contractors understand that we will continue to work in the offices during this time and will try to disturb us as little as possible. But the work is bound to be disruptive, so let's all stay flexible and keep a sense of humor during this time that is bound to be somewhat inconvenient.
>
> Thanks for your cooperation as we complete this much-needed maintenance.

this structure. The memo shown in Figure 10–1, which contains only two paragraphs, begins by summarizing the main idea of the memo. The remainder of the first paragraph provides additional information, and the final paragraph, which is only one sentence, concludes by thanking the readers for their cooperation.

The *introduction* of a memo may vary from one sentence to one or more paragraphs. The introduction should identify what the memo is about and why it was written. If the memo will discuss more than one topic or be divided into several subtopics, the introduction should identify all important issues to be covered. The introduction might contain a sentence such as the following to indicate the memo's contents:

> This memo explains how to account for patents, copyrights, and trademarks.

An introduction should also identify the main ideas or recommendations of your memo. Sometimes the main idea can be summarized in one or two sentences, but in some situations, you might need an entire paragraph. If the summary of your main ideas is longer than a paragraph, it's better to put it in a separate section immediately following the introduction. This section would have a heading such as "Summary" or "Recommendations."

The *body* of the memo can be divided into sections, each with a heading that describes the contents of that section. Remember to begin by summarizing the main idea of the section.

A section can have one or many paragraphs. Paragraphs should usually be no more than four or five sentences long, and each should begin with a topic sentence.

Memos often end with a *conclusion*, which can be very brief. Consider this example:

Let me know if you have any further questions about these procedures.

A conclusion such as this one brings the memo to a close and ends in a courteous, helpful tone. A word of caution, however, about conclusions like the one just given: Be careful not to end all your memos with the same sentence (or some slightly altered variation). The conclusion should be a meaningful addition to the memo, not just an empty string of words added out of habit. Also, be sure your conclusion (like the rest of the memo) is appropriate to your reader. Consider why the conclusion in Figure 10–1 might be unsuitable for a memo you're sending to your boss. The sample memos in this chapter show several different conclusions; all are appropriate to the content of the memo and the reader.

One misconception some people have about conclusions is that they should always repeat the memo's main ideas. For short memos, this repetition is usually not necessary, although for longer memos, such an ending summary can be helpful.

Whatever the length of the memo, the conclusion is a good place to tell your readers what you want them to do, or what you will do, to follow up on the ideas discussed in the memo. The memo shown earlier in Figure 10–1 has such a conclusion. It implies tactfully that readers should cooperate with the painting project, without complaining.

Concise, Clear, Readable Memos: Style and Tone

Memos should be as concise as possible: no unnecessary repetitions, digressions, or wordiness. They should be written in a clear, direct style, so that readers find them interesting and informative. Finally, memos should have flawless grammar and mechanics.

Memos can vary considerably in tone, depending on what they are about and how they will be circulated. Some memos, such as the one shown previously in Figure 10–1, are informal. For these memos, a conversational, personal tone is appropriate.

Other memos are more formal and might serve as short reports. Some memos, such as the one shown in Figure 10–3, may report the results of research or work performed, and may thus become part of the permanent records in a client's file. These memos are usually written with a more impersonal, formal tone. Whether formal or informal, however, all memos should be clear and concise.

Formats

Memos can be written in a variety of formats, as the examples in this chapter show. The memo in Figure 10–2[1] is typical of the format used in many organizations. Notice especially how the headings and set-off list make this memo attractive and easy to read.

FIGURE 10-2   A Memo

MEMORANDUM   August 16, 2014

TO: FLOYD JONES
FROM: DENNIS SMITH *DS*
SUBJECT: PURCHASING SHERATON MANUFACTURING

This memo is in response to your questions concerning the purchase
of Sheraton Manufacturing. The memo will first explain goodwill
and then discuss how to determine its value. After you determine
the value of Sheraton's goodwill, you will be better able to decide
how much you want to offer for the company as a whole.

<u>What Is Goodwill?</u>

Goodwill is an intangible asset made up of items that may contribute to
the value and earning power of a company, but that are not otherwise
listed on the company's balance sheet. Here are some possible items
that may contribute to goodwill for Sheraton Manufacturing:

1. Highly capable engineering staff
2. Strong reputation for quality work
3. Good management
4   A large number of loyal customers

These items are not separately identified on Sheraton's balance
sheet. However, they obviously have value and therefore should be
included in the purchase price of the business.

<u>Determining the Value of Goodwill</u>

The value of goodwill is established by comparing the present
value of future cash earnings (the purchase price of Sheraton
Manufacturing) with the total value assigned to the separately
identified assets acquired, less liabilities. The difference between
the two is the value of goodwill.

   The key to determining the value of goodwill is, of course, the
determination of the purchase price for Sheraton (estimating the
present value of future cash earnings). We can do this by completing a cash-flow analysis similar to the ones we perform in our capital budgeting process.

   Let me know if you have any further questions about goodwill or
the Sheraton Manufacturing acquisition.

FIGURE 10–3   A Memo to a Client's File[2]

Memorandum to the File

Date: December 9, 2014

From: Rosina Havacek *RH*

Re: The taxability of meal vouchers furnished by Mercy
         Hospital to its medical staff.

Facts

Our client, Mercy Hospital ("Mercy"), provides meal vouchers to
its medical employees to enable them to remain on emergency call.
The vouchers are redeemable at Mercy's onsite cafeteria and at
MacDougal's, a privately owned sandwich shop. MacDougal's rents
business space from the hospital. Although Mercy does not require
its employees to remain on or near its premises during their meal
hours, the employees generally do. Elizabeth Fegali, Mercy's Chief
Administrator, has asked us to research whether the value of the
meal vouchers is taxable to the employees.

Issues

The taxability of the meal vouchers depends on three issues:

• Whether the meals are furnished "for the convenience of the
  employer."
• Whether they are furnished "on the business premises of the
  employer."
• Whether the vouchers are equivalent to cash.

Applicable Law

Section 119 provides that the value of meals is excludible from an
employee's income if the meals are furnished for the convenience
of, and on the business premises of, the employer. Under Reg. Sec.
1.119-1, a meal is furnished "for the convenience of the employer" if it
is furnished for a "substantial noncompensatory business reason." A
"substantial noncompensatory reason" includes the need to have the
employee available for emergency calls during his or her meal period.
Under Sec. 119(b)(4), if more than half the employees satisfy the "for
the convenience of the employee" test, all employees will be regarded
as satisfying the test. Regulation Sec. 1.119-1 defines "business premises
of the employer" as the place of employment of the employee.

A Supreme Court case, *Kowalski v. CIR*, 434 U.S. 77, 77-2 USTC
9748, discusses what constitutes "meals" for purposes of Sec. 119.
In *Kowalski*, the State of New Jersey furnished cash meal allowances to its state troopers to enable them to eat while on duty. It
did not require the troopers to use the allowances exclusively for
meals. Nor did it require them to consume their meals on its

FIGURE 10–3   *(Contd.)*

business premises. One trooper, R.J. Kowalski, excluded the value of his allowances from his income. The IRS disputed this treatment, and Kowalski took the IRS to court. In court, Kowalski argued that the allowances were excludible because they were furnished "for the convenience of the employer." The IRS contended that the allowances were taxable because they amounted to compensation. The U.S. Supreme Court took up the case and decided for the IRS. The Court held that the Sec. 119 income exclusion does not apply to payments in cash.

Analysis

Issue 1: The meals provided by Mercy seem to be furnished "for the convenience of the employer." They are furnished to have employees available for emergency calls during their meal breaks. This is a "substantial noncompensatory reason" within the meaning of Reg. Sec. 1.119-1.

Issue 2: Although the hospital cafeteria appears to be the "business premises of the employer," MacDougal's does not appear to be. The hospital is the place of employment of the medical employees. MacDougal's is not.

Issue 3: Based on the foregoing authorities, it is unclear whether the vouchers are equivalent to cash. On the one hand, they are redeemable only in meals. Thus, they resemble meals-in-kind. On the other hand, they are redeemable at more than one institution. Thus, they resemble cash. Nor is it clear whether a court deciding this case would reach the same conclusion as the Supreme Court did in *Kowalski*. In the latter case, the State of New Jersey provided its meal allowances in the form of cash. It did not require its employees to use the allowances exclusively for meals. Nor did it require them to consume their meals on its business premises. In our case, Mercy provides its meal allowances in the form of vouchers. Thus, it indirectly requires its employees to use the allowances exclusively for meals. On the other hand, it does not require them to consume their meals on its business premises.

Conclusion

Although it appears that the meals acquired by voucher in the hospital cafeteria are furnished "for the convenience of the employer" and "on the business premises of the employer," it is unclear whether the vouchers are equivalent to cash. If they are equivalent to cash, or if they are redeemed at MacDougal's, their value is likely to be taxable to the employees. On the other hand, if they are not equivalent to cash, and they are redeemed only in the hospital cafeteria, their value is likely to be excludible.

Some organizations may prefer another format that has become customary within the organization. You should prepare your memos according to your employer's expectations. The examples in Figures 10–2 and 10–3 illustrate formats some CPA firms prefer when the memos are part of a client's file. Note that in Figure 10–3 the section labeled "Conclusion" appears before the section labeled "Discussion."

If you are free to design the format of your memos, be conservative; avoid oversized fonts and a great deal of inked space.

SAMPLE MEMOS

The memo shown in Figure 10–2 was written in response to the hypothetical situation described here:

Situation:

Floyd Jones is the proprietor of the firm for which you work. Mr. Jones wants to acquire a manufacturing business. The business he wants to acquire, Sheraton Manufacturing, is insisting that Floyd pay not only for the identifiable net assets of the business, but also for "goodwill." Floyd asks you: "What is goodwill? Should I pay for it? If I should pay for it, how much should I pay?"

Study the memo shown in Figure 10–2 to see how it illustrates the principles of memo writing already discussed. Do you think Mr. Jones will be pleased with the memo?

Memos to Clients' Files

Accountants often record information about a client's situation in a memo that is placed in the client's file for later reference. Other members of the staff may refer to the information recorded in these memos months or even years later, so the information must be recorded clearly, accurately, and correctly.

For example, a client might write or call an accounting firm about a tax question. The person receiving the letter or handling the call might then write a memo to record the pertinent facts of the client's situation. Later, another member of the staff can research the question. The researcher needs adequate information to identify the issues and solve the client's problem.

A sample memo written for a client's file appears in Figure 10–3. This memo summarizes research into an accountant's tax question.

MEMOS SENT BY EMAIL

Memos circulated in today's firms and offices are often sent electronically, as the body of an email or as an email attachment. Memos may occasionally be sent as email to persons outside the organization as well. Chapter 12 discusses email and other forms of electronic communication.

EXERCISES

Exercise 10–1 [General]

Two years ago, you were hired as an accountant in the tax department of a small regional accounting firm. This year you have been asked to help mentor an intern from the local university. This intern, Jeff Golightly, has been following your progress as you've researched a client's tax problem. Your conclusions, which are complex and technical, have been approved by your supervisors.

Jeff sent you an email to suggest that you and he meet with the client over lunch and present the results of your research orally. That way, he argues, you can avoid the work and aggravation of putting your findings into a written client letter.

Write a memo to Jeff in which you explain why his idea is not a good one.

Exercise 10–2 [General]

You are a manager in a local CPA firm, Barry, Peters, & Travis. While attending the symphony in your city, you noticed in the program that a couple of other CPA firms in the area were listed among the donors; one had given $100,000 and another had given $40,000. As a fan of the symphony, you would like to see your firm also make a donation. However, beyond wanting to support the symphony, you want to encourage such a donation because you think it would enhance the image of your firm and be a good marketing move. You note that several of your firm's clients have also made donations.

Write a memo to the partner-in-charge of your firm, John Hoffman, persuading him to support such a donation.

Exercise 10–3 [General]

You have just graduated from college and been hired as an entry-level accountant in a local CPA firm, Olde, Aged, and Outofit, CPAs. When you arrived on the job, you were shocked to learn that the firm's partners, Elmer Olde, Thaddeus Aged, and Ethel Outofit, know almost nothing about social media, especially as it is now being used in business. They boast that they do business "the old-fashioned way" and regard social media as the trendy hobby of inexperienced young people.

At a recent meeting with one of the firm's main clients, however, Mr. Olde heard some disturbing news. This client, Rodney Current, believes that all businesses, if they are to remain competitive and effective, must understand and in some cases incorporate social media into their business practices. Mr. Olde was horrified to hear Mr. Current's views, but he and his partners have begun to suspect that their own views might be just a little behind the times.

Mr. Olde called you into the office because he knows you are fully up-to-date on the use of electronic communication and social media. He has asked you to research the use of social media in business, especially in professional accounting practices. He has not asked you to recommend whether the firm should embrace these media; after all, what could a young whippersnapper like you possibly know? However, he does want to be fully informed about the topic, so that he and the other partners can evaluate whether their firm will need to update their attitudes, and possibly their practices.

Research the topic and write a memo to Mr. Olde, as he has requested.

Exercise 10–4 [Managerial]

You are a staff accountant for Mitchell Manufacturing, Inc., a large electronics manufacturing company. Mitchell has four sales divisions, three manufacturing plants, and a home office in Dearborn, Michigan, which houses all the administrative offices. Management is considering employing responsibility accounting methods for the first time. Jeff Smart, Chief Operating Officer of Mitchell, has asked you to answer the following questions in a memo:

- What is responsibility accounting?
- How might Mitchell Manufacturing employ responsibility accounting for control and management evaluation purposes?
- Assuming responsibility accounting techniques are used, are there any precautions that should be taken to ensure that the techniques are used properly? If so, what are they?

Write a memo to Mr. Smart containing the answers to these questions.

Exercise 10–5 [Financial]

You are newly hired as an accountant for the Hill Business Technologies, Inc., a small service business that has no formal capital budgeting system. The president of your company, Janice Hill, has requested that you write a memo to her explaining what the net present value method of investment evaluation is, how it differs from the payback period method, and why Hill Business Technologies should use the net present value method for capital budgeting purposes instead of the payback method. Write the memo.

Exercise 10–6 [Managerial]

You are the controller of Beemer's Car Dealerships. Recently, you have become aware that your company needs to evaluate and perhaps redesign its internal control system. To familiarize the dealership's managers with the need for a good internal control system, you have decided to write a memo explaining what internal control is and why it's important to a business like Beemer's. Write the memo. You can make up hypothetical examples to illustrate your memo.

Exercise 10–7 [Managerial]

You are a managerial accountant at Gourmet Restaurant Supplies, which supplies fresh produce, meat, seafood, and food staples to the area's finest restaurants. You have been asked by the controller to write a memo to the company's regional managers that will explain cost-volume-profit (CVP) analysis. In particular, the controller hopes that managers will understand how CVP analysis can help them perform their responsibilities.

Write the memo to Gourmet's three regional managers: Lupe Garcia, Sybil Alexander, and Paul Chan. You can make up hypothetical examples if needed to illustrate your memo.

Exercise 10–8 [Tax]

The CPA firm you work for, Sutton, Alexander, and Jones, has been in practice for five years. The majority of the tax work done for its clients, who are mostly small businesses, is the preparation of state and federal income tax returns. One of the firm's tax partners, Hugh Sutton, mentioned to you the possibility that the firm might expand its services to offer tax planning for the owners of small businesses. Write a memo to Mr. Sutton in which you discuss the advantages and disadvantages of offering tax planning as an additional service.

Exercise 10–9 [Financial]

Daniel Gordon, the president of the Skinner Company, is considering a bond issue to raise $1,000,000 for the company. Mr. Gordon notes that long-term Treasury bonds yield 3%, which he thinks is a good loan rate. Before proceeding with the bond issue, however, Mr. Gordon wants to know more about it. Specifically, he wonders what the annual interest payments would be on the bonds.

You are a financial analyst at Skinner Company. Write a memo to Mr. Gordon explaining what the interest payments on a $1,000,000, 20-year bond issue would be if the bonds were issued at a 3% yield. Also, explain in your memo why the Skinner Company would probably not be able to issue the bonds at 3%.

Exercise 10–10 [Systems]

You are a new employee at Southwest Parts Distributors, Inc. As a specialist in accounting information systems, one of your responsibilities is to recommend adequate controls to ensure the safety of Southwest's data, including the data it keeps on suppliers and customers. You recently recommended that the company adopt a new set of control procedures. However, Southwest's regional manager, Bill Tomlinson, has expressed impatience with your recommendations. He views the new procedures as "unnecessary red tape."

Write a memo to Mr. Tomlinson that explains the advantages of strong controls to protect the company's data.

Exercise 10–11 [Systems]

You are employed by a regional systems consulting firm. Charles Drummond, the president of Drummond Industries, a successful local manufacturing company, has asked for your help. The company is experiencing systems problems, and he wants you to prepare a memo that he can use in a meeting with other top management that will address those problems.

Over the years Drummond has developed an accounting information system (AIS) that records the journal entries for sales along with the dates of the transactions. Other information about the sale is collected and processed by three other different AISs. This has led to a problem of redundancy and data discrepancies among systems.

Write a memo to Charles Drummond that recommends the development and implementation of an enterprise resource planning (ERP) system and explains how an ERP system can overcome the problems the company is experiencing. Invent any facts necessary to complete the memo.

Exercise 10–12 [Auditing]

Assume you are a staff accountant working for Kim & Kirkpatrick, Inc. (K&K), a small publicly traded company that will soon have its financial statements audited by a local CPA firm, Young, Mitchell, and Gregory. Eleanor Lee, a rising manager at K&K, expects to work closely with the auditors. Ms. Lee has a general business background and several years experience working for K&K, but her knowledge of auditing is limited. She sees you in the hall one day, and during the conversation, she tells you she is confused about a term she's heard of that will somehow affect the upcoming audit. The term she refers to is *materiality*. You talk with her briefly about materiality, but as she walks away she still seems to be a little confused. Later she asks you to write her a memo explaining the concept of materiality and possible ways it might affect the audit of K&K.

Write the memo, inventing any details you need to make your discussion clear and readable.

Exercise 10–13 [Auditing/Current Professional Issues]

You are an audit partner in a medium-size CPA firm, Kilmer, Kissenger, and Kennedy. Several of your larger audit clients have read in the news about the possibility that audit firm rotation might at some time be required and have asked whether they should be prepared to comply with such a requirement in the near future. You have been asked by your partners to prepare a memo for distribution to your firm's clients that discusses the pros and cons of such a requirement and your evaluation of the likelihood of its occurrence in the near future.

Write the memo, inventing any details you need to make your discussion clear and readable.

NOTES

1. Adapted from Pete Wardlaw, "Purchasing DCL Broadcasting" (unpublished student paper, University of Georgia, 1987).
2. Thomas R. Pope and Kenneth E. Anderson, *Prentice Hall's Federal* *Taxation Comprehensive*, 26th Ed., © 2013. Reprinted and Electronically reproduced by permission of Pearson Education, Inc., Upper Saddle River, New Jersey, A-6.

CHAPTER

11

Reports

Sometimes accountants prepare formal reports, such as a report for a client that a CPA in public practice might prepare. Managerial accountants might prepare reports for other departments in their firm or perhaps for a group of managers with a particular need. Auditors prepare various reports to summarize their findings for auditing engagements. Figure 11–1 shows an example of an auditor's report—in this case, a standard unqualified report on comparative financial statements.

An auditor's report, such as the one illustrated in Figure 11–1, is a special type of report that uses standard wording required by AICPA auditing standards.

Other reports you may write may involve analyzing an accounting problem and applying accounting principles, or applying provisions of the tax code to a particular situation. A report may also require researching professional literature or other material, so the research techniques discussed in Chapter 8 are often part of report preparation as well.

Reports may vary in length, but all reports should meet certain basic criteria. The technical content should be accurate and complete, the organization should be coherent, the report should be presented attractively, and the writing style should be clear and concise. Like all forms of writing, a report should be designed and written with the readers' needs and expectations in mind.

PLANNING A REPORT

If you are preparing a report on the job, your company may have an established format for you to follow for all reports. Find out your organization's expectations and policies before you begin work on your report. Even if the organization doesn't require employees to follow a certain report format, you may find your job easier if you use several well-written reports as models.

If you are free to design your own report format, or if you are preparing the report for a class assignment, the format presented in

FIGURE 11–1   A Standard Auditor's Unqualified Report on Comparative
Financial Statements

Coffey & Nelson, P.C.
Certified Public Accounts
2300 Peachtree St., Suite 100
Atlanta, GA 30000

Independent Auditor's Report

To the Stockholders
DVD Enterprises, Inc.

We have audited the accompanying balance sheets of DVD
Enterprises, Inc., as of December 31, 2013 and 2012, and the related
statements of income, changes in stockholders' equity, and cash flows
for the years then ended and the related notes to the financial statements.

Management's Responsibility for the Financial Statements
Management is responsible for the preparation and fair presentation of the financial statements in accordance with the accounting
principles generally accepted in the United States of America; this
includes the design, implementation, and maintenance of internal
control relevant to the preparation and fair presentation of financial statements that are free from material misstatement, whether
due to fraud or error.

Auditor's Responsibility
Our responsibility is to express an opinion on these financial statements based on our audits. We conducted our audits in accordance
with auditing standards generally accepted in the United States of
America. Those standards require that we plan and perform the
audit to obtain reasonable assurance about whether the financial
statements are free of material misstatement.

An audit involves performing procedures to obtain audit evidence
about the amounts and disclosures in the financial statements. The
procedures selected depend on the auditor's judgment, including
the assessment of the risks of material misstatement of the financial
statements, whether due to fraud or error. In making those risk
assessments, the auditor considers internal control relevant to the
entity's preparation and fair presentation of the financial statements in order to design audit procedures that are appropriate in
the circumstances, but not for the purpose of expressing an opinion
on the effectiveness of the entity's internal control. Accordingly,
we express no such opinion. An audit also includes evaluating the
appropriateness of accounting policies used and the reasonableness
of significant accounting estimates made by management, as well as
evaluating the overall presentation of the financial statements.

FIGURE 11–1   *(Contd.)*

We believe that the audit evidence we have obtained is sufficient and appropriate to provide a basis for our audit opinion.

Opinion
In our opinion, the financial statements referred to above present fairly, in all material respects, the financial position of DVD Enterprises, Inc., as of December 31, 2013 and 2012, and the results of their operations and cash flows for the years then ended in accordance with accounting principles generally accepted in the United States of America.

COFFEY & NELSON, P.C., CPAs
Atlanta, Georgia

February 23, 2014

---

this chapter can serve as a generic model that is typical of those used in business and industry.

When planning the report, you must also consider the purpose of the report and who its readers will be. Analyzing the purpose and audience for a report may be more difficult than it is for letters and memos because a report can have many groups of readers, and each group will have different interests and needs.

For example, a report recommending that a firm invest in a new information system might be circulated to the management information systems (MIS) department, the accounting department, the departments that would actually use the system, and senior management. The accounting department would be interested in the accounting information aspects of the acquisition as well as how the system could be used for various accounting tasks. The MIS department would be interested in the technical features of the system and how it would affect MIS personnel. Other departments would want to know how the system would make their work easier or more difficult, whether it would affect their budgets, and what additional training, if any, their personnel would need to use the system. Senior management would be interested in the bigger picture, such as how the system would affect the firm's efficiency, competitiveness, and cash flow.

To write this report, you would need to identify clearly who the readers are and what information they want the report to include. You would obviously be writing to readers with different degrees of knowledge about the technical features of the new system and with different interests and concerns as well. The way to handle this complicated situation is to write different parts of the report for different groups of readers.

Fortunately, many reports are not as difficult to plan and write as this one, but this example shows how important it is to analyze carefully the needs and expectations of different groups of readers.

Most reports require a great deal of research. They may report the results of empirical studies or pilot projects, or report research involving generally accepted accounting principles or other technical literature. Organizing this research into a coherent outline is essential. Review the organization principles discussed in Chapter 3, and then apply the following questions to your report as you plan the outline and structure your draft.

1. Is the subject covered adequately?
   - Background information when necessary
   - Adequate explanations, supporting data, and examples
   - Citations from GAAP and other authoritative sources, as needed
   - Application to the specific needs and interests of the readers
2. Is the report too long?
   - Digressions—off the subject
   - Too much explanation or detail
   - Repetitions or wordiness
3. Is the report logically organized?
   - In order from most to least important—from the readers' point of view
   - Summary sentences where helpful
   - Transitions to link ideas
   - Short, well-organized paragraphs with topic sentences

The format of a report—how its various parts are put together—also determines how coherent the report is.

THE PARTS OF A REPORT

Reports can be presented in a variety of formats that are all designed to make the report easy to read. The format presented in this handbook is typical of how reports are structured.

A report may include these sections:

Transmittal document

Title page

Table of contents

List of illustrations

Summary section

Introduction

Body of the report
Conclusion
Appendices
Notes
Bibliography
Graphic illustrations

Transmittal Document

The transmittal document can be either a cover letter or memo, depending on whether you are sending your report to someone within or outside your organization. It presents the report to the people for whom it was written and adds any other information that will be helpful.

The transmittal document will not be long, but it should include essential information, such as the report's title, topic, and purpose; you might also identify who requested or authorized the report. You should usually summarize the report's main idea or recommendation if you can do so in a few sentences. You may want to add other comments about the report that will be helpful to the readers, but always end with a courteous closing.

Whereas the style of the actual report is usually formal and impersonal, the transmittal document can usually be more conversational, including the use of personal pronouns.

Title Page

In a professional report, the title page might look something like this:

Title of Report
Prepared for...
Prepared by...
Date

For a student's report, the instructor might prefer information such as this:

Title of Report
Student's Name
Course and Period
Instructor
Date

Table of Contents

The table of contents appears on a separate page with a heading. The contents listed are the major parts of the report, excluding the transmittal document, with the appropriate page numbers.

List of Illustrations

The list of illustrations, if applicable, includes titles and page numbers of graphs, charts, and other illustrations.

Summary Section

All formal reports have a section near the beginning of the report that summarizes the main ideas and recommendations. This section can vary in length from one paragraph to several pages and can come either immediately before or immediately after the introduction. The summary section may be called an executive summary, abstract, synopsis, summary, or some other term.

An executive summary is especially helpful for long reports. This section gives the readers an overview of the report's contents without the technical detail. Busy managers may read the executive summary to decide whether they should read the entire report.

The executive summary identifies the purpose and scope of the report and possibly the methods used for research. It includes the major findings of the research, the conclusions of the researcher, and the recommendations, if any.

The length of an executive summary varies with the length of the report, but it's generally about one to three pages. The summary begins on a separate page following the table of contents or list of illustrations and is entitled *Executive Summary*. The sample report at the end of this chapter uses this kind of summary.

For shorter reports, a section right after the introduction can provide a summary of the report's main ideas and recommendations. This section is labeled *Summary*; it's usually one or two paragraphs long.

Introduction

The introduction of a formal report is longer than that of a letter or memo—usually at least two or three short paragraphs, and for long reports, even longer than a page. The introduction identifies the subject of the report and states why it was written—who requested or authorized it, or for whom it was prepared. The introduction states the purpose of the report in specific terms:

The purpose of this report is to discuss the feasibility of offering a stock bonus plan to employees of Gulf Coast Industries.

Not:

The purpose of this report is to discuss stock bonus plans.

Sometimes an introduction includes additional information to help the reader, perhaps a brief background of the report's topic.

However, if it's necessary to include a great deal of background information, this material should be presented in a separate section in the body of the report.

Finally, the introduction of a report should end with a plan of development that gives the reader an overview or forecast of the topics the report covers and the order in which they are presented. A simple plan of development can be in sentence form:

This report describes the proposed pension plan and then discusses its costs and benefits.

Sometimes a set-off list makes the plan of development easier to read:

This report discusses the following topics related to the proposed pension plan:

- Major provisions
- Benefits to employees
- Benefits to the corporation
- Cost
- Accounting for the plan

Body of the Report

The body of the report should be divided into sections, and possibly subsections, each with an appropriate heading. Remember to begin each section with a statement that summarizes the main idea to be covered in that section.

The body of the report can also contain graphic illustrations, as discussed later.

Conclusion

In addition to the summary section at the beginning, a report should have a conclusion to remind the reader of the report's main ideas and recommendations. This section may be from one paragraph to several pages long.

Appendices (Optional)

Depending on the report's audience and purpose, you may want to place technical information and statistics in appendices at the end of the report. If you use an appendix, give it a title and refer to it in the body of the report.

Notes and Bibliography

What to put at the end of the report depends in part on the style of documentation you use. If you use endnotes, they should usually begin on a separate page and be labeled *Notes*.

Almost all reports have some sort of bibliography or reference list. This list identifies the sources you cited in your paper, and it may also include additional references the reader might want to consult. This section should begin on a separate page following the notes (if any) and should have a title such as *Bibliography* or *References*.

Appendix 8–E in Chapter 8 demonstrates the proper form for endnotes or footnotes and bibliographical entries.

Graphic Illustrations

Sometimes graphic illustrations, such as graphs or tables, make a report easier to read and more interesting, especially if you are presenting statistical or numerical data or if the subject of the report concerns a process. You can place graphic illustrations either in an appendix or in the body of your report, just after the place in the text where they are discussed.

Graphic illustrations are discussed more fully in Chapter 6.

APPEARANCE

Presenting your report as attractively as possible is important. Use good-quality paper and a high-quality printer.

Reports can be single-spaced or double-spaced, depending on the situation. Students' reports are usually double-spaced to provide space for annotations when they are graded. In all reports, the transmittal document and any set-off material are single-spaced. Pages should be numbered, using lowercase Roman numerals for front matter (table of contents, list of illustrations, executive summary) and Arabic numerals for the remainder of the report, from the introduction through the end matter.

STYLE AND TONE

The tone of a formal report is usually just what its name implies: formal, and therefore impersonal. You probably won't use personal pronouns or contractions in a formal report, for example. However, a formal style should still be readable and interesting, so you should use the effective style techniques discussed in Chapter 4. Even a formal document can be written simply, clearly, and concretely.

Unlike the actual report, the transmittal document may be written in a personal, more informal style.

The report in Figure 11–2 illustrates many effective report writing techniques.

FIGURE 11–2 A Report

B&H Financial Consultants
125 Easy Street
Athens, Georgia 30601
August 8, 2014

Mr. Sam Hamilton
Hamilton Manufacturing
1890 Meerly Avenue
Atlanta, Georgia 30306

Dear Mr. Hamilton:

Enclosed is the report about convertible bonds that you requested
in your letter of July 21. The report, titled *Convertible Bonds:
Financial and Accounting Considerations*, examines the nature
of convertible debt, the pros and cons of such an issue, and the
accounting treatment of the securities.

The report shows that convertible bonds may represent a relatively
less expensive method of raising capital than nonconvertible bonds.
Another advantage is that should the convertible bonds be converted, the existing shares of common stock will not be diluted as
severely as they would if common stock had been issued. However,
as the report makes clear, these effects are by no means certain.

I believe the report will provide you with the information you need.
If you have any further questions, however, don't hesitate to give
me a call.

Sincerely yours,

Joyce Samuels

Joyce Samuels
jhw

FIGURE 11–2   *(Contd.)*

CONVERTIBLE BONDS:
FINANCIAL AND ACCOUNTING CONSIDERATIONS

Prepared for Hamilton Manufacturing

by

JOYCE SAMUELS

AUGUST 8, 2014

FIGURE 11–2 *(Contd.)*

CONTENTS

EXECUTIVE SUMMARY ii

INTRODUCTION 1

NATURE OF CONVERTIBLE BONDS 1

FINANCIAL ADVANTAGES AND DISADVANTAGES 2

    Advantages 2

    Disadvantages 2

ACCOUNTING TREATMENT 2

CONCLUSION 3

WORKS CITED 4

FIGURE 11–2   *(Contd.)*

EXECUTIVE SUMMARY

This report provides information about convertible bonds for the managers of Hamilton Manufacturing. Included is information about the nature of convertible bonds, financial advantages and disadvantages of issuing such bonds, and their accounting treatment.

A convertible bond is a debt security that carries the option of exchange for an equity security, usually common stock. The bond indenture specifies when the bonds may be converted and a conversion ratio.

Convertible bonds would offer Hamilton several advantages:

- The company could issue the bonds at a premium or at a low stated interest rate, which investors would accept because of the conversion privilege.
- The company could avoid another stock issue now, when the price of Hamilton's stock is low.
- The company may avoid a decrease in share price caused by issuing a large number of new shares on the market at one time.
- Total stock issuance costs may be less.
- Management would avoid possible conflict with its major stockholders.

There are also potential disadvantages management should consider before issuing the convertible bonds:

- Before conversion, the uncertain conditions of the economy make a future increase in the market price of the company's stock uncertain. If conversion does not occur, Hamilton may have difficulty meeting the debt requirements.
- Bond conversion will reduce basic earnings per share. Conversion will also increase Hamilton's income tax liability because of the loss of interest expense.
- The required accounting treatment of convertible bonds may have an unfavorable effect on the company's financial statements: a high level of debt may be presented alongside a lowered diluted earnings per share (DEPS).

ii

FIGURE 11–2 (*Contd.*)

CONVERTIBLE BONDS:
FINANCIAL AND ACCOUNTING CONSIDERATIONS

Introduction

The purpose of this report is to provide information for the management of Hamilton Manufacturing about convertible debt as a means of financing. Convertible debt is an issue of debt securities (bonds) with the option to exchange those debt securities for equity securities (usually common stock).

This report covers three major topics:

- The nature of convertible bonds.
- Financial advantages and disadvantages Hamilton can expect if it issues the bonds.
- Accounting treatment for the bonds.

Nature of Convertible Bonds

When convertible bonds are issued, the bond indenture defines a time period after issuance during which the bonds may be converted. The indenture also gives a conversion ratio, which is the number of shares of stock for which each bond may be exchanged. The effective price of stock to the bondholder is determined by dividing the par value of the bond by the number of shares exchangeable for one bond.

The indenture usually includes a call provision so that the issuing entity can force bondholders to convert (usually at a premium over par). Thus, entities that issue convertible debt often do so as a means of raising equity capital. The following sections discuss why Hamilton might choose to issue convertible debt.

1

FIGURE 11–2   (*Contd.*)

Financial Advantages and Disadvantages

Advantages

Use of convertible debt would offer Hamilton advantages over straight debt or stock issues.

Investors in bonds that are convertible into stock are usually willing to accept a lower stated interest rate on such bonds, to pay a premium and accept a lower yield, or to accept less restrictive covenants. Thus, by issuing convertible debt, Hamilton will probably be able to obtain funds at a lower cost than if it issued debt that is not convertible.

Depending upon economic conditions, there may also be a timing advantage to issuing convertible debt. If current conditions make it unfavorable to sell stock because of depressed value, issuing convertible debt will allow Hamilton to raise capital debt now that may later be converted into stock when the stock price has recovered.

In addition, by issuing convertible debt, Hamilton may avoid a decrease in stock price caused by a large new issue of stock being made available on the market all at once.

Another advantage to Hamilton of issuing convertible bonds is that the company might avoid creating a conflict with major stockholders, who want to maintain their percentage interests. The stockholders might vote against a large issue of stock. However, the bond issue could be convertible into a number of shares small enough not to significantly injure the stockholders' interests.

Disadvantages

Most disadvantages of issuing convertible bonds are related to the uncertainty of conversion. If Hamilton's stock price does not rise, conversion may not occur without call, the company may not obtain the equity financing it desires, and Hamilton might then be saddled with long-term debt obligations.

Another disadvantage is the impact on either diluted earnings per share (DEPS) before conversion, or basic earnings per share (BEPS) after conversion. In either case the earnings per share figure will be reduced. After conversion, income tax expense will increase because of the reduction in interest expense.

2

FIGURE 11–2 *(Contd.)*

Accounting Treatment

According to Generally Accepted Accounting Principles (GAAP), if convertible bonds are "sold at a price or have a value at issuance not significantly in excess of the face amount…[n]o portion of the proceeds from the issuance…shall be accounted for as attributable to the conversion feature" (ASC pars. 470-20-25-10b and 470-20-25-12). In other words, the expectation that some or all of the bonds will be converted into stock is not recognized in the accounts.

Because convertible bonds are normally sold at a premium, the amount of the cash proceeds from the issue is usually greater than the face value of the bonds. The premium is amortized over the life of the bonds. The effect of the amortization is that the interest expense recorded by Hamilton each period would not equal the amount of the interest *payment*, but would reflect the effective yield to the bondholders.

When the bonds are converted, Hamilton will remove from the accounts the balance associated with those bonds. The value assigned to the stock equals the book value of the bonds, and no gain or loss is recognized or recorded (Kieso, Weygandt, and Warfield 2012, 907).

If Hamilton decides to retire its convertible bonds for cash before their maturity date, the transaction will be recorded in the same way as the early bonds, and the cash paid to retire them will be a gain or a loss on the income statement.

Although convertibles are accounted for solely as debt, Hamilton must also consider the equity characteristics of such issues in computing diluted earnings per share (DEPS). GAAP require that corporations having issued securities that are potentially dilutive of EPS, such as convertible bonds, must present both basic earnings per share (BEPS) and diluted earnings per share (DEPS) for income from continuing operations and for net income in the income statement "with equal prominence" (ASC par. 260-10-45-2).

The DEPS figure represents EPS *as if* the bonds had been converted into stock. If they had been converted, the removal of the bonds would have caused a reduction of interest expense, which would have increased earnings. However, the positive effect of the earnings adjustment may not offset the negative effect of the shares adjustment. Thus, convertibles reduce reported DEPS.

3

FIGURE 11–2   *(Contd.)*

Conclusion

In deciding whether to finance with convertible debt, Hamilton must consider whether it would benefit from using convertibles rather than straight debt or stock issues and whether it can meet the debt requirements, should conversion not occur as expected. In addition, management should analyze carefully the effect of the issue on readers of the financial statements, because until the bonds are converted, a possibly high level of debt will exist alongside a lowered presentation of DEPS.

WORKS CITED

Financial Accounting Standards Board (FASB), 2013. *Accounting Standards Codification®*. Stamford, Conn.: FASB.

Kieso, Donald E., Jerry J. Weygandt, and Terry D. Warfield. *Intermediate Accounting*, 14th ed. Hoboken, NJ: John Wiley & Sons, Inc., 2012.

4

EXERCISES

Exercise 11–1 [Financial]

Assume you are a recently hired accountant working for Growing Bigger, Inc., a national business consulting firm with ambitions to expand into an international market. The president of Growing, Elizabeth Golightly, calls you into her office with a request. She has been asked to participate in a seminar on international accounting standards and wants to update her knowledge of the topic. She asks you to research the topic, with particular emphasis on the position taken recently by U.S. agencies and other authorities. She would like to know what the arguments are in favor of international accounting standards, as well as the disadvantages, especially to businesses based in the United States. She is not asking you to take a position on whether the United States should endorse international accounting standards, but she does want a balanced report on the topic.

Ms. Golightly has asked you to research the topic and prepare a report for her, which she will use to help her prepare for her seminar participation. Respond to her request.

Exercise 11–2 [Financial]

A client, Manuel Rodriguez, has just inherited some money and has decided to invest it in stock. He is not interested in mutual funds because he prefers to have personal control over his stock investments. He currently has a diversified portfolio of stock to which this new investment will be added. Your client wants to invest about $50,000, but in keeping with his conservative investing strategy, he wishes to keep his risk as low as possible.

Mr. Rodriguez has asked you to evaluate the most recent annual reports of several corporations as possible investment options. Choose three corporations whose stock is listed on the NYSE or the NASDAQ and whose annual reports you can study. Compare the information found in these reports and then write a report for Mr. Rodriguez that explains which of the companies is likely to be his best investment. Explain your conclusions thoroughly, quoting from the annual reports as necessary.

Exercise 11–3 [Financial]

You have received an inquiry from a prospective client, Lazy Sofa, Inc., concerning the accounting for investments. Betty Jason, owner of Lazy Sofa, is considering investing some of her company's idle cash in either equity or debt securities. Write a report for Ms. Jason, explaining briefly how the types of investments and her purpose for investing might affect the accounting methods used. Remember that your client knows very little about accounting.

Exercise 11–4 [Auditing][1]

Saylor & Company is a brokerage firm registered under the Securities Exchange Act of 1934, which requires Saylor to file audited financial statements with the SEC annually. Your firm, O'Brien and Sherrill, Saylor's CPAs, performed the annual audit for the year ended December 31, 2013, and rendered an unqualified opinion, which was filed with the SEC along with Saylor's financial statements. During 2013, a Saylor employee engaged in a massive embezzlement scheme that eventually bankrupted the company and resulted in substantial losses suffered by its customers and shareholders, including some shareholders who had purchased shares of Saylor & Company after reviewing the company's 2013 audit report. O'Brien and Sherrill's audit was deficient; if it had fully complied with auditing standards, the embezzlement would have been discovered. However, the CPA firm had no knowledge of the embezzlement, and their conduct cannot be characterized as reckless.

Hugh O'Brien, partner-in-charge of O'Brien and Sherrill, has asked you to write a report discussing the different theories of liability available to the customers and stockholders of Saylor & Company under common law and what liability your firm may have under the Securities Exchange Act of 1934.

Write the report requested by Mr. O'Brien.

Exercise 11–5 [Financial]

Write a report analyzing the most recent financial aspects of a publicly traded company of your choice. Include an analysis of (1) liquidity, (2) profitability, (3) productivity, and (4) debt management. If your analysis uncovers any problems, include recommendations on how they may be overcome.

Assume you are preparing the report for Cindy Baer, the president of the company you are analyzing. Ms. Baer is knowledgeable about business and her company's industry, but does not have a strong background in accounting.

Exercise 11–6 [Systems]

Your employer, Nalley, Nellie & Nicholson, CPAs, is considering the use of cloud-based systems to grow its business and better serve its clients. As one with some knowledge of information technology, you have been asked to prepare a report for the managing partners of your firm evaluating the pros and cons of cloud-based systems. Your managing partners have asked that you give specific attention to the ability of cloud-based solutions to cut costs, build client and employee relationships, improve the exchange of information with clients, and build sales capabilities and sales management. You have also been

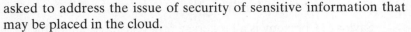

asked to address the issue of security of sensitive information that may be placed in the cloud.

Prepare the report for Peter Nalley, the managing partner of your firm.

Exercise 11–7 [Auditing]

As a staff member of Norton, Price, and Cummings, CPAs, you have been asked to prepare a report on "Materiality" that will be circulated to all staff as part of the firm's continuing education program. It has been suggested that the report should cover the definition of materiality, why the concept is important to auditing, and how to measure it. You should also discuss any other aspects of materiality you find important.

Write the report as requested.

Exercise 11–8 [Tax]

You are on the financial staff of Governor James Cash, who is governor of a large state. He has been a prominent supporter of the flat tax idea for many years. Now, as governor, he is considering pushing for the adoption of a flat tax to replace the current progressive state income tax. He has asked you to prepare a report for him covering the pros and cons of a flat tax and how, if he decides to pursue the idea, he should respond to critics.

Write the report for Governor Cash.

Exercise 11–9 [Systems]

You are an accounting information systems specialist working for Great Lakes Cargo, Inc. The company's president, LaToya Evans, has asked for your help. Recently she read a news story about the business reporting language XBRL, which, she learned, has greatly changed the way financial data is communicated. She has asked you to research XBRL and write a short report to distribute to the company's executive committee. The committee will need sufficient information about XBRL to make an informed decision about the potential use for Great Lakes.

Write the report for the committee. The transmittal document should be addressed to Ms. Evans. Remember that neither she nor the other committee members have specialized knowledge about accounting information systems.

Exercise 11–10 [General]

As a staff member of Swobe, Deal, and Grace, CPAs, you have been asked to prepare a report on the *FASB Accounting Standards*

Codification® that will be circulated to all staff as part of the firm's continuing education program. It has been suggested that the report should cover why and how the Codification has come about and how and when to use it. You may also include other aspects of the topic you believe to be important.

Write the report as requested.

Exercise 11–11 [Financial/Auditing/International/ Current Professional Issues]

You are a partner in a regional CPA firm, Crawford & Simmons, with fourteen offices covering the Eastern United States. Your firm has several large multinational and domestic clients that are publicly traded. To better serve clients and to keep the firm's staff well informed, the partners have decided to produce a report covering changes in the accounting profession that may occur over the next two years. This would include:

- Projects the FASB is working on that may result in new accounting standards.
- Announced activity of the SEC, IRS, Congress, and the Public Company Accounting Oversight Board (PCAOB) that may result in required changes in how your clients or your firm conduct their financial or auditing activities.
- Activity of the International Accounting Standards Board (IASB) and the International Auditing and Assurance Standards Board (IASSB) that may affect your clients or your firm.

Do the necessary research for this project and write the report.

NOTE

1. Alvin A. Arens, Randal J. Elder, and Mark S. Beasley, *Auditing and Assurance Services: An Integrated Approach*, 15th ed., 139. Reprinted and electronically reproduced by permission of Pearson Education, Inc., Upper Saddle River, New Jersey.

CHAPTER

E-Communication and Social Media

12

With the explosion of information technology, online media have become almost universal for business as well as personal communication. Email, the Internet, social media; online research and computer-assisted composition: These are just some of the tools that have become part of our everyday communication. Earlier chapters discussed ways we can use technology to research accounting literature and then compose and revise the documents we send. This chapter focuses on how you will use electronic media to communicate with others, both within the organization where you work and to those outside your firm or business, such as clients, other professionals, and agencies. The chapter also discusses how you can use online media in your search for employment.

Electronic communication takes a variety of forms. Email is now used almost universally for both personal and business purposes. In recent years we've seen the advent and development of other media, such as social networks, instant messaging, text messaging, blogging, podcasting, and online video. Many of these media were originally developed primarily for personal communication, but they are now becoming more common in many business settings, including the profession of accounting.

Although online media can make the communication process quicker and sometimes easier than before their widespread use, they should be used carefully to prevent mistakes—even social or professional disasters. As an illustration of the latter possibility, recall situations you've heard of where an embarrassing email was sent to an unintended recipient, or confidential material was sent accidentally to someone with no right to the information, causing a security breach.

This chapter discusses the effective use of email in business, with a look at social media and their role in the life of a professional accountant. We will see that the principles of effective writing stressed throughout this text for traditional forms of communication apply to messages sent via online media as well. You should plan what you write to achieve your intended purpose in a way that is appropriate to your audience; write in a style that is clear and concise, with main ideas that are easy to spot; and review what you've written to ensure that it is both correct and professional.

The chapter also includes a section on telephone etiquette, which may seem a surprising topic to include in a discussion of online communication and social media. But we might think of the telephone as one of the earliest modern examples of social media, one that in its day revolutionized the conduct of business and interpersonal communication. And like the more recently developed online communication media, telephones must be used with care to ensure that they contribute to professional success.

EMAIL

In many businesses, emails have replaced paper memos for much of the written communication that takes place within the organization. Like hard-copy memos, emails may be brief or lengthy, formal or informal. An email may announce a meeting or arrange a lunch, request help on a project or provide detailed information about a business's activities. Emails may also be used to communicate with clients or other people outside the organization, as substitutes or supplements to hard-copy letters. You should give the emails you write to all your business associates the same care and attention you use whenever you write.

Composing the Email

When you write an email, follow the guidelines for effective writing discussed throughout this text. Think carefully about the purpose of the email: Do you want to respond to a request, make your own request, or provide information? Who will your readers be, and what will they expect from your email? Write the email in a concise, clear writing style and structure so that main ideas are easy to spot. Emails also call for a number of special considerations. Keep the following guidelines in mind as you compose the email.

Address Messages Carefully
We've all heard stories of messages being sent to unintended recipients. This often occurs when a memo is sent using a distribution list or some general address, rather than to an individual. The results are sometimes funny, as when an employee invites the entire corporation to lunch; or they can be disastrous, as might occur when the plans for a new product are sent by mistake to the firm's competitors. The lesson is to "think twice and click once" when addressing an email.

When replying to an email that was sent using a distribution list, remember that if you click on the "reply to all" button instead of the "reply" button, your reply will be sent to the entire distribution list. Is that necessary or what you intend?

Finally, when you reply to an email, consider whether you need to include previous email exchanges with your current email message—a series of replies to replies. Some email programs allow you to choose to include or not include previous email exchanges as part of a reply. But the default mode for many email programs reproduces and thus continues old email exchanges, which can go on for pages. If you don't have a good reason to include previous exchanges in your reply, it may be better to reply to your correspondent with a fresh original email.

Write a Strong Subject Line

Write a short, powerful subject line with key words near the beginning, because your recipients' software may truncate the subject line when the message appears in their inbox. You want to catch readers' attention to ensure that they open and read your message. Compare the following subject lines:

Subject: Meeting

vs.

Subject: Required staff meeting May 19, 3 PM

Which subject line is more likely to ensure attendance at the meeting?

Begin with a Salutation

Most of your emails should begin with a salutation, especially if you're writing to only one person. Although email salutations are usually informal, some situations, such as an email that serves as a cover letter for a résumé, call for a more formal salutation. The email shown in Figure 12–1, which is an informal message between colleagues, uses an informal salutation:

Hi Bob,

For a more formal situation, such as email connected with a job search, address your reader with the same formality you would use if you were talking with this person face to face. In some situations, you would use a salutation such as this:

Dear Ms. Allison,

Note that a comma follows the salutation for both formal and informal emails.

As these examples show, the choice between a formal and informal salutation depends on the purpose of the email and your relationship with the recipient. The degree of informality within a firm or office may also reflect the culture of the organization, so you should look for models of customary usage in the emails you receive from others with whom you work.

Put Important Ideas First

The first line of your email should catch the readers' attention so that they will want to read the rest of your message. Begin with the most important information, from the readers' point of view, and progress to ideas of less importance. Remember that people often read email hurriedly, scanning for what is important and closing the email before they read it completely. Short paragraphs with clear topic sentences are especially important for longer emails, because they enable readers to spot important ideas quickly.

If you're replying to an email, your opening paragraph may refer to the email you received. If you're responding to a request, for example, you should mention that request specifically in your opening sentence.

Use Conventional Grammar and Mechanics

Follow conventional usage for grammar and mechanics, including standard spelling, punctuation, and capitalization. Avoid the codes often used for text messages sent via cell phone, such as all lowercase letters or abbreviations for frequently used words and phrases. As one practicing CPA has said:

> The Internet has single handedly destroyed all of the rules for proper speech online but your customers will appreciate that you are above trendy, Internet jargon. Compose all of your status updates, tweets and other online messages with proper grammar.[1]

Use an Email Signature

Your email system will enable you to create a file with an automatic signature that you can use at the end of your emails. This signature will include such information as your name, position, firm or business, and contact information.

Use Attachments Carefully

Sometimes you may attach another document to an email, especially if you're conveying a great deal of information, or if you're transmitting a more formal or technical document, such as a report. When you use attachments, the cover email should be brief: Tell the recipient what is attached, and why it's important.

Attachments require some caution. First, be sure that the file you attach is the file you intend to send. Open the attached file from the email you've composed before you send the email to check that it is the correct file. Also review the name of the file: Will it clearly identify the attachment's contents, and be suitable for your reader? Another safeguard is to follow up with your recipient to ensure that the attachment was actually received with your cover email. Occasionally, files do not attach successfully or get lost in cyberspace, especially if the attachment is long or contains graphics. Your "Sent" file should indicate that the attachment was successfully sent with the covering email; however, even if the attachment shows up in the "Sent" file, the attachment still may not reach the recipient.

FIGURE 12-1	Example of an Email

From: Jack Wilson <jwilson@whateversite.com

To: Robert Gonzalez <rgonzalez@whateversite.com

Subject: Lunch today?

Date: Jan. 15, 2014

Hi Bob,

Do you have time for lunch today? This would give us a chance to discuss the Fairweather audit. I should be free by 12:30, and we could try the new brew pub down the street. Let me know if this works for you.

Jack

Uses for Email: Informal or Formal?

Accountants use email for such a wide variety of purposes and in so many situations that the difference between formal and informal is more a question of degree than a clear-cut distinction. Email used for business will likely be more formal than purely social email, however, so you should write in Standard English, as clearly and concisely as possible, in a friendly, respectful tone that is appropriate to your reader.

As an example of an informal email that might be common within a business or firm, consider the email in Figure 12–1. It is being sent to one person only, but emails may be sent to several people or even an entire distribution list, if the information is relevant to a group. Figure 12–2 shows an example of an email that might be sent to several departments, or even an entire organization. You will notice that this email seems more formal than the lunch invitation in Figure 12–1, in keeping with the purpose of the second email and its wide distribution. The second email also contains an email signature at the close of the email.

Email within an Organization

You probably recognize that standard email headings resemble the format of a memo: sender's name, recipient's name, subject line, and date. In fact, email has largely replaced paper memos for interoffice communication in many business settings. However, the guidelines for effective memos discussed in Chapter 10 apply as much to email used within an organization as they do to paper memos.

FIGURE 12–2   Example of An Email

From:	Mary Ellen Parker <meparker@othersite.com>
To:	Staff <distribution list>
Subject:	Vacation Requests for Fiscal Year 2015
Date:	May 15, 2014
Attachment:	Vacation Request Form

In order that we may plan our staffing schedules for the upcoming fiscal year, we need to have everyone's vacation requests as soon as possible. Please complete the attached request form and return it to me no later than May 25.

Thank you very much for your help.

Mary Ellen Parker

Director of Human Resources
Big and Little, CPAs
111-222-3333
meparker@othersite.com

External Email

In the past, business correspondence addressed to recipients outside an office was always sent via U.S. mail or some other delivery service. Today some external business correspondence, both letters and memos, is sent electronically. A major advantage of sending these documents as email is of course the speed with which they are transmitted. The recipient can also reply quickly, thus completing the exchange of information in a timely manner.

Business correspondence sent electronically carries risks, however. Security can be an issue. In addition, emails used in business, especially to people outside the writer's organization, are not always written with the care they need in order to be effective. Email writers may not give the necessary attention to detail that marks an effective business document, and they may be tempted to write in a very informal style that is not appropriate in a business environment. As we've already seen, grammatical and mechanical conventions, such as correct spelling and punctuation, are as important for email as they are for documents sent in an envelope.

Email—a Few More Cautions

The use of email, although certainly convenient, requires caution. Be careful to do the following:

Compose Your Message as If It Will Be Read by Everyone

Remember that an email message may be read by people you do not intend to read it. Email messages are not private, and there are no "off-the-record" emails. Emails are sent over computer communications networks, where they can be easily intercepted.

All email messages are saved somewhere and can be used as proof that the communication took place. Usually you are sending the email to record some information for the record, but occasionally people fall into the trap of treating email like a phone call. For example, they may say in an email something like "Steve thinks he's going to exercise his options for $4,000, but it'll never happen as long as I'm the CFO." Imagine how this CFO will feel if Steve turns up with a copy of the email message. Again, the best advice is to assume that every email message you write will be read by everyone else.

One more word of caution: Emails can very easily be subpoenaed as evidence in legal proceedings. And, remember that nothing you post electronically, whether an email, a text message, or a posting on any of the social media sites that are so popular, is ever confidential. You must assume that your postings are permanently available to whoever may have the time and resources to retrieve them. You cannot delete them with assurance that there is no backup somewhere or that what you delete cannot be retrieved with software designed to recover erased or deleted files. Never use emails to circulate gossip or derogatory comments about another person or entity, and think carefully about anything you commit to cyberspace.

Avoid Sending Junk Email

Email resulting from forwarding jokes, humor, and other "items of interest" that have little if any relevance to the work environment is a form of junk email. You may find those photographs of baby animals absolutely adorable, but they don't belong on the job. Save humor and other non-business items for people with whom you correspond socially. Even if you are tempted to forward serious news items about some topic related to your work, consider very seriously whether the intended recipient will find them useful or have the time to read them.

You should also remember that email used for social correspondence, such as the email you exchange with family or friends, can cause problems if you write or receive it on the job. The computer on your desk, along with its supporting hardware and software, is the property of your employer, and you should use it only for communication related to your professional responsibilities. You should not, therefore, write or respond to personal email using the business's equipment. Recall also that all emails, even those you delete, are saved somewhere in your employer's system. You don't want records of your personal life available for business associates to access, even accidentally.

Many businesses have formal policies for the uses of email by their employees. If your business has such a policy, you should, of course, follow the rules carefully.

Think before You Send
The ease and speed with which emails can be exchanged can be a hazard if writers send a hastily composed memo that contains emotional or politically volatile content. Don't use email to express anger or frustration.

USE OF ELECTRONIC MEDIA IN JOB SEARCHES AND JOB APPLICATIONS

Electronic media have become an important tool for those seeking employment. In fact, some prospective employers require electronic submission of résumés, making paper résumés almost obsolete in some cases. You may also use the Internet, including business networking sites, to locate jobs for which you will apply. These sites may ask you to submit your résumé electronically, or they may require you to complete a profile that will be used to match your credentials and job objectives with prospective employers. Electronic media can help you find a good job, if you use it with care.

Use of Social Media for Job Searches

Electronic media enable you to access information about many jobs available in almost any location, and you can easily and quickly apply to the positions that interest you. In addition, electronic placement agencies and networking sites may enable prospective employers to identify you as someone they wish to interview. It has been reported that 90% of companies use social media and networking sites, such as LinkedIn, to find qualified candidates for employment.[2] However, electronic media also carry serious risks for people seeking employment.

Employers have the same access to the Internet that you do. That means that they have access to what you've posted on the Web in other contexts, such as your postings to blogs, Twitter, YouTube, and Facebook. Many employers surf the Web to find out more about prospective employees than the information written on the résumé. Remember that for professional employment purposes you need to project a professional image. Also remember that it is difficult, if not impossible, to separate your social image from your professional image on social media. This means that you should never post anything on social media that could conflict with your image as a professional.

Electronic Submission of Résumés

A prospective employer may ask you to submit your résumé via email. If you encounter this request, send the résumé as an attachment, using the cover email as a short letter of application. The cover email should identify specifically the position for which you're applying, summarize briefly your credentials, and refer to the complete résumé that you've attached. This cover email should be carefully composed, using a courteous, professional tone; it should also be written in Standard English using the guidelines discussed earlier in this text. Proofread the cover email carefully to make sure it's free of errors. Remember that this cover email may be your first opportunity to impress the prospective employer with your communication skills.

Because you will have prepared your résumé carefully, you will have a computer file that you can use for email submissions. You can also tailor your résumé to match the particular position for which you're applying.

Some employers, placement agencies, or networking sites may scan the résumés they receive into computer-searchable databases, which they then search using industry- and job-specific key words in order to match applicants to specific positions. So include as many of those words as possible.[3] Examples of key words you may wish to include when submitting a résumé for an accounting position include CMA, CPA, auditing, tax, systems, cost, managerial, and locations you may be interested in, such as Atlanta, Chicago, Los Angeles, and New York.

Chapter 14 provides additional information on the creation of an effective résumé and letter of application.

LinkedIn Profiles

One of the most widely used networking sites for business, including job searches and recruiting, is LinkedIn, and its use by companies seeking to hire accountants is on the rise.[4] Creating a LinkedIn profile that will attract the notice of potential employers may be part of your search for employment.

The LinkedIn website specifies the information required for a profile. You will find much of the required information on your résumés, such as education, work experience, and skills. You will also be asked to supply a profile photograph. As you might imagine, the photograph should project a professional image.

It's important to follow the instructions for creating your profile. It should be as complete as possible, and you should update it often. Complete, current profiles are much more likely to result in job offers. You should also proofread your profile carefully to ensure that it is written in Standard English and is free of errors.

SOCIAL MEDIA USED IN THE ACCOUNTING PROFESSION

Social media, which many people now use daily for personal communication, have become increasingly important in many business settings. Even networking sites that were originally designed for strictly social interaction, such as Facebook, have been adapted for some business purposes. A business may use a social networking site to recruit new hires and identify prospective candidates for an interview. It may also use social media for a variety of other purposes, such as training, customer/client relations, and market research.

An article in the *Journal of Accountancy* discussed the use of social media within the accounting profession. According to CPAs interviewed for this article, sites such as Facebook, Twitter, and LinkedIn will be "essential parts of the CPA's work tool kit in the years to come." In fact, some accountants assert that "CPAs looking to grow their firms and engage clients have 'no choice' but to embrace social media."[5]

Not all companies, including accounting firms, embrace social media with such enthusiasm, however, and the profession may remain ambivalent about its use. Some believe the profession will see "a split among CPA firms, with some embracing social media and others avoiding it and touting that fact to clients and potential clients."[6] It may be, however, that companies reluctant to use social media now will become more receptive to its potential and eventually adapt and expand their use of these media.

If you are employed by a firm that embraces the use of social media, you should use it carefully. Compose written messages posted on social media with the same attention to detail you use for all business writing, putting into practice the guidelines for effective writing stressed throughout this text. This advice includes the use of Standard English.

Social Media Policies

Many companies have policies about their employees' use of social media. These policies specify the information and opinions that employees may, and may not, share via the Internet. Some of the prohibited material is obvious, such as classified or proprietary information about the business or its clients or associates. Some businesses also caution employees about saying anything negative about the business itself or the people who work there. This means that if you're upset about something that has happened on the job, or angry with your boss, you should not vent through email, Facebook, Twitter, or any other form of social media. Violation of a business's social media policy can result in termination, so you should become aware of its policy and, as well, use discretion about what you say on the Internet.

Once you are working in an accounting position, you may need to adjust your use of social media to be even more careful of potential misuse. Some companies may require their employees to maintain separate accounts for their personal and professional communication. They may also caution their employees to be especially discreet in making social connections so that they will maintain a professional public image.

Blogs

In recent years blogs (a shortened word for *weblogs*) have become more common within the profession of accounting. Blogs, which may be hosted by an organization or by an individual, enable users to communicate in a timely way on topics of common interest. They can be updated frequently, and many blogs allow readers to respond to the information and opinions posted, thus generating a conversation. Examples of blogs dealing with accounting topics are included among the online accounting publications shown in Figure 15–2 on page 272.

Writing for a blog may be a good way for you to network with other accountants and business professionals who share your interests. If you decide to write a blog posting or join in a blog conversation, remember to review your employer's policy on social media, as we've already discussed. In addition to following your employer's policies, take care that what you say, and how you say it, projects a professional image. Remember that once something is posted to a blog, it is available to everyone and will last forever.

Once you've decided to write for a blog, keep these general guidelines in mind:

Review What Has Already Been Written on the Topic

Read what other people have already written on your topic so that what you write for the blog will be timely and responsive to what others have said. You may also want to review recent publications on the topic that have appeared in other news outlets, both print and electronic publications. Remember to document any sources you use to give credit for ideas and information that are not your own.

Plan What You Want to Say

As with other forms of professional writing, you should first consider the purpose of your writing and the main ideas you want to convey. An outline will help you organize your ideas.

Consider Your Audience

Analyze the readers of the blog so that you write about topics that they will find interesting and relevant. Write in a style that is appropriate for your readers, at a technical level they will understand. As a general rule, blog postings are written in an informal, conversational style.

Organize Your Thoughts

When you write a blog posting, begin with a brief introduction to introduce your main idea(s). Short paragraphs with strong topic sentences and transitions, as needed, will ensure that readers find your posting easy to read and understand.

Write Clear, Descriptive Headlines

You want to catch your readers' attention so that they read your blog posting.

Keep It Short

Blog postings are meant to be brief. Consult previous postings at the site you're using to get an idea about the preferred length for that site.

Edit Your Blog Posting before You Post

Be sure that you've written in a clear, readable style. Like all professional writing, blog postings should be written in Standard English and should be proofread carefully before posting.

Instant Messaging and Texting

Like blogging, instant messaging and texting are becoming more common within the accounting profession, though they are not used universally. The extent to which you use them for professional communication will depend on your particular situation.

Instant messaging, in which brief messages appear automatically on users' computer screens, may be used for both internal and external communication. It may be a stand-alone program or embedded into social networks, office software, or other platforms.

When you write a message that will be posted as an instant message, use the same principles of effective communication you use for all your writing. Many business people expect instant messages to be written in Standard English, rather than with abbreviations, acronyms, and other jargon more typically found in the messages exchanged in personal communication.

Instant messages are not the place for exchanging confidential information, unless you're using a secure server. Nor should you use them for personal communication as long as you're working in a business setting.

Texting, which uses a cell phone network to transmit brief written messages, is widely used socially and may be acceptable for some business uses. However, some people regard texting as too informal for professional use, and the language often used to text, with its many abbreviations and acronyms, may lead to a lack of clarity and detract from a professional image.

As with all forms of electronic communication and social media, you should evaluate your particular work environment to see if texting is consistent with its culture. Recall the tip stressed throughout this text: Write with your audience in mind. If your audience expects you to text, then that's what you should do. But take care in composing even the briefest text to ensure that it's courteous and clear and maintains a professional image. Recall too that some professionals, including accountants, may expect texts to be written in Standard English. Here again you should write according to your reader's expectations.

You no doubt realize that you should never read or send texts while you're in a conversation with a client, co-worker, or other professional.

It's also worth noting that as in the case of email, text messages do not disappear when deleted. So many of the same cautions relating to the use of email also apply to text messaging.

TELEPHONE ETIQUETTE

Telephone conversations are an essential component of business, including the business of an accountant. Well-conducted telephone conversations can ensure smooth working relationships with clients, fellow professionals, and others within the business community. At the same time, careless, discourteous phone calls can ruin professional relationships. Here are some tips for using the telephone effectively.

Making a Call

- Before you call, know what you need to say. For some conversations, you may outline the questions you want to ask or the information you're looking for. If necessary, you can write notes in your outline as you're talking so that you remember what's important.
- When you've reached the person with whom you wish to speak, introduce yourself and the company or firm for whom you work.
- Speak with courtesy and respect, in a pleasant tone of voice.
- If you're not sure you've understood something completely or correctly, paraphrase what you've heard so that the person can repeat or modify the information, if necessary.
- Thank the other person for taking the time to talk with you.

Receiving a Call

- Give your caller your complete attention, and listen carefully. Don't try to accomplish some other task, such as working on your computer, during the call.
- Take notes so that you'll remember important points.
- Speak in a courteous, respectful manner with a pleasant, professional tone of voice.

Conference Calls

- When you speak during a conference call, always identify yourself by name before you speak, every time you speak.
- When you're not speaking, mute your phone so that other callers won't hear the background noise from your office.
- Listen carefully as others speak, taking notes as necessary.

Cell Phones

Cell phones are another great convenience, but like most social media, they can cause problems in a business environment—most of which result from their use at inappropriate times. As a general rule, you should turn the phone off if you're having a conversation with a client, co-worker, or other professional. In most cases, this means turning the phone completely off, not just setting it on "vibrate." When you're talking with others, they deserve your undivided attention. Even the vibration of a silent phone can distract you, so that you don't listen carefully to what the other person is saying.

The advice to leave your cell phone turned off will have exceptions. If you're expecting an urgent call on a business matter, you may need to leave the phone in its vibrating mode. The polite way to handle a situation where you may have to take a call is to alert the person with whom you're meeting that the call may come, and apologize if you have to interrupt the conversation. In truth there are very few situations that justify letting a phone call interrupt a face-to-face conversation.

A FINAL WORD: SOMETIMES FACE-TO-FACE IS BETTER

In spite of the advantages and widespread use of electronic communication, it may be better to convey some messages in person. This may be particularly true if the communication involves a disagreement or is in some other way sensitive or difficult. If you communicate in person, you will be able to read the other person's body language. Facial expressions or other body movements that aren't detectible over the phone or through a text message or email can alert you to how the other person is reacting to what you've said, as well as whether you've been understood. This may give you the chance to adjust your message or tone and avoid unintended complications, such as offending a client or damaging a working relationship with an employee or colleague.

EXERCISES

Exercise 12–1 [General]

You are preparing the federal income tax returns for Elaine and David Ellis and find you need some additional information: receipts for contributions to their church, the name and social security number of their youngest child, and the name of the day care center where the child is enrolled.

Write an email to Mr. and Ms. Ellis in which you request this information

Exercise 12–2 [General]

You are a partner in the local firm of Mueller, Britt, & Little, CPAs. It has come to your attention that several employees, both professional and support staff, have recently begun wearing political buttons and displaying political posters in the office.

Write an email to be circulated to all personnel in your firm explaining that such activity should cease and explaining why it is inappropriate.

Exercise 12–3 [General]

You are a partner in the CPA firm of Gregory & Rush. Recently you have noticed that your "inbox" on the local area network in your company accumulates ten to fifteen messages a day that are jokes and humorous stories downloaded from the Internet. Most of these messages are not very funny, but they all take time to delete, and sometimes in the process of deleting them, you delete important messages by mistake. Clearly the situation has gotten out of hand. Write an email to the staff about the problem and ask that the practice of distributing humorous email messages be discontinued. Be sure to explain your reasoning so you won't come across as dictatorial.

Exercise 12–4 [Systems]

Assume you are a newly hired staff accountant in a local accounting firm, Johnson, Park, and Gonzalez (JPG). One of JPG's partners, Francis Park, stopped you in the hall with a question. He said he has read something about "cloud accounting," and he wants to learn more about what this term means. He's heard a rumor that some accounting firms are using this technology in their practices, and he wonders whether JPG should get on board—what the advantages would be, if any, as well as the risks. "After all," Park says, "if we store data in 'the cloud,' wouldn't we lose it if the wind blows the cloud away?"

Mr. Park asks you to research his questions and send him your findings by email. Depending on the amount of information you find in your research, you may decide to summarize your findings in a report and send it as an attachment, with an appropriate cover email. You will need to be especially careful when you analyze the reader of your email (Mr. Park), so that you write at a level that is appropriate to his interests and needs, while being respectful.

Exercise 12–5 [Financial]

You are newly hired as an accountant for the Chase Condominium Association, a condominium owners association with approximately

200 condo units. The Association is currently using the cash basis of accounting. The president, Brenda Galina, has asked that you explain what the accrual basis of accounting is, how it differs from the cash basis, and whether the Chase Condominium Association should switch from the cash basis to the accrual basis.

Write an email to Ms. Galina that answers her questions. You will need to identify the facts and issues the association should consider before making the decision. Invent any facts necessary to do this. If you find that your explanation will be lengthy, consider writing it as an attachment, with a cover email.

Exercise 12–6 [Systems]

Your company, Florodex, intends to contract with a systems consulting firm to develop a new database system. You are responsible for explaining to the consulting firm exactly what your company needs the system to do. However, you have very little understanding of database systems and think you should know more before you talk with the consultants. You have received a brochure that announces a two-day database overview seminar to be given by the local university and think it would be worthwhile to attend.

Write an email to your boss, Peter Tolan, requesting that your company send you to the seminar. Invent any facts you think necessary. You may decide to attach a copy of the brochure to your email.

Exercise 12–7 [Auditing]

You are the managing partner of a medium-size CPA firm with several publicly traded clients. One of your partners, John DeFries, has served as lead partner for the audit engagement of Rousch Industries, a publicly traded client, for the past five years. He has just gotten the word that he will be replaced in that capacity by another partner beginning with next year's audit and is quite upset over this situation. He has emailed you arguing that he has invested years getting to know Rousch's business operations and is therefore the best qualified partner to lead the audit. He feels he is being penalized for some reason he does not understand.

Write an email to Mr. DeFries explaining the requirements of the Sarbanes-Oxley Act and the SEC regarding audit partner rotation and assuring him that he is not being penalized for anything.

Exercise 12–8 [Auditing/Ethics]

You are an audit partner of a small CPA firm. One of the audit managers who works for you, Alan Robinson, has emailed you about a prospective audit client, Stanley Thornton, with whom he has been talking. Mr. Robinson is concerned because the prospective client has made it clear that if he hires your firm he will expect your firm to be his advocate and always act in his best interests. In other words, Mr. Thornton expects your firm to be in a relationship with him similar to the relationship he has with his attorney. Alan Robinson is a little uncomfortable with that expectation, but does not know how to respond. He is seeking your advice. Reply to Mr. Robinson's email advising him to discuss the necessity for independence in the audit, the broader responsibilities of a CPA firm, and how CPA firms differ from other professionals in that regard. Elaborate on these issues, giving Mr. Robinson some ideas of how to explain them to Mr. Thornton.

Exercise 12–9 [Managerial/Ethics]

As the newly appointed CFO of Celebrity Manufacturing, Inc., a medium-size publicly traded company doing business in North America and Europe, you have decided to further the development of a code of ethical conduct for accounting and finance employees in the company. Write an email to members of upper management encouraging them to attend a meeting on September 12th to organize a task force that will write the code. Explain why you think the development of such a code is desirable.

NOTES

1. SueEllen Brantley, "Social Media Etiquette Tips for CPAs," AICPA Insights, 22 August 2012. http://blog.aicpa.org/2012/08/4-social-media-etiquette-tips-for-cpas.html (28 January 2013).
2. Alison Doyle, "How to Get Started with Social Networking: Social Networking Tips for Job Seekers," About.com. 2013. http://jobsearch.about.com/od/socialnetworkingtips/a/social-networking.htm (15 January 2013)
3. Alison Doyle, "Resume and Cover Letter Guide: Drafting Descriptions," About.com, 2013. http://jobsearch.about.com/od/resumes/a/draftdesc.htm (15 January 2013)
4. Alexandra DeFelice, "Social Media Trends: Where Does Your Firm Stand?," accountingWEB. 2013. http://www.accounting-web.com/article/social-media-trends-where-does-your-firm-stand/220655 (15 May 2013).
5. Jeff Drew, "Technology and CPAs: Visions of the future," *Journal of Accountancy*, June 2012. http://www.journalofaccountancy.com/Issues/2012/Jun/20114844.htm (28 January 2013).
6. Ibid.

CHAPTER

Writing for Exams: CPA, CMA, and Academic Exams

The importance of writing skills to the successful practice of accounting has been clearly documented, as we saw in Chapter 1. Because writing skills are essential for success in an accounting career, accounting certification exams evaluate writing skills as well as technical competencies. The American Institute of Certified Public Accountants (AICPA) has tested writing skills on the Uniform CPA Examination since 1994. Since 2013, written communication tasks have comprised 15% of the total score for the Business Environment and Concept (BEC) section of the CPA exam. Moreover, since 2012 the IMA (formerly the Institute of Management Accountants) has tested writing skills on the Certified Management Accountant (CMA) exam; candidates complete four 30-minute essays as part of the exam.[1] Thus, your professional future as an accountant depends on your ability to write well.

This chapter will look at these professional exams, including the criteria used to test candidates' mastery of effective writing. The chapter will suggest ways you can write responses to exam questions that show your mastery of the technical content as well as your writing skills. The advice given for the certification exams will work equally well for your academic courses, when exams in those courses call for a written response. You will see that the criteria of effective writing tested on professional and academic exams are the same qualities stressed throughout this text: coherent organization, with main ideas that are easy to identify; adequate development of main ideas; a clear, concise writing style; precise vocabulary; and Standard English.

WRITING FOR THE CPA EXAM

Since 2013, three tasks requiring written responses have been included in the Business Environment Concepts (BEC) section of the CPA exam. The AICPA calls the written responses asked for on the exam

241

"constructed responses."[2] Each question specifies the specific format the constructed response should take, usually that of a typical business document such as a memo or letter. For each of these tasks

> candidates must read a scenario and then write an appropriate document relating to the scenario. The instructions state what form the document should take (such as a memo or letter) and its focus. The candidate's response should provide the correct information in writing that is clear, complete, and professional.[3]

The specific writing skills tested on the CPA exam include these:[4]

- **Organization:** Structure, order of ideas, and connecting ideas, including using an overview or thesis statement, unified paragraphs, and transitions and connectives.
- **Development:** The use of supporting evidence and information to clarify thoughts, including using details, definitions, examples, and rephrasing.
- **Expression:** The use of Standard English including grammar, punctuation, word usage, capitalization, and spelling.

The AICPA has also specified that the writing should be accurate, clear, and concise.[5] Moreover, the AICPA expects exam candidates to respond directly to the topic identified in the question. You will not receive credit for your answer if you write a response that is off-topic.[6]

You will write your constructed responses on the CPA exam using a word processor with a spell-checker. The spell-checker will help you identify and correct some misspelled words, but not all of them; for example, a spell-checker will not discriminate between homonyms such as *their* and *there*. The word processor will also make your editing and revision easier and quicker to do.

You should recognize from the preceding description of the exam that a successful response to a writing task requires skills that go beyond the ability to write well or understand the relevant accounting concepts. Specifically, you will need to read the question carefully and follow directions. In addition, you will need to use your critical thinking skills. In fact, your ability to read carefully, follow directions, and think critically will affect your ability to succeed on the CPA exam in questions and tasks that don't explicitly evaluate writing skills.

The AICPA has identified problem-solving skills, among others, as important for success on the CPA exam.[7] Candidates should be able to

- Apply professional skepticism, which is an attitude that includes a questioning mind and a critical assessment of information or evidence obtained.
- Identify and solve unstructured problems.
- Develop reasonable hypotheses to answer a question or resolve a problem.

FIGURE 13–1   Sample CPA Exam Question Requiring a Constructed Response[8]

SkyView Inc., a small startup company, has hired you as a consultant to assess its financial systems and related processes. During your review, you learn that the company's accountant is responsible for providing general ledger access to others in the company, processing all financial transactions in the general ledger, and printing checks. The president of the company must authorize write-offs in the system, but the accountant has access to the president's username and password.

Prepare a memo to SkyView's president assessing these responsibilities in the context of segregation of duties. Also address the possibility of the accountant committing fraud.

Type your communication in the response area below the horizontal line using the word processor provided.

REMINDER: Your response will be graded for both technical content and writing skills. Technical content will be evaluated for information that is helpful to the intended reader and clearly relevant to the issue. Writing skills will be evaluated for development, organization, and the appropriate expression of ideas in professional correspondence. Use a standard business memorandum or letter format with a clear beginning, middle, and end. Do not convey information in the form of a table, bullet point list, or other abbreviated presentation.

- Formulate and examine alternative solutions in terms of their relative strengths and weaknesses, level of risk, and appropriateness for a given situation.
- Develop creative ways of thinking about situations, problems, and opportunities to create insightful and sound solutions.
- Develop logical conclusions through the use of inductive and deductive reasoning.

The ability to analyze problems, think critically, and make sound judgments will thus be essential to your success on all parts of the CPA exam, not just the sections requiring written responses. These skills are stressed throughout this text, especially in Chapter 7, "Critical Thinking," and Chapter 8, "Accounting Research."

Figure 13–1 shows a sample question provided by the AICPA, typical of those that might appear on the CPA exam. This question requires a constructed response. Several features of this question, and the accompanying instructions, are worthy of note. The question appears in the form of a hypothetical business case scenario. The answer must be written in the form of a typical business document to a specific reader, in this case a memo addressed to the president of a company. The answer must be helpful to that reader and specifically address the issues raised in the question. The answer must also illustrate writing skills the AICPA has identified as important: "development, organization, and the appropriate expression of ideas in professional correspondence."

But note this restriction: The instructions state that you should not use a table or bulleted list to present the information in the memo. Although bulleted lists and tables are often effective in business writing, the AICPA does not want them on the CPA exam. Therefore, you should follow the AICPA's instructions precisely.

By way of contrast, however, bulleted lists may be appropriate on the CMA exam, as we will see in the following section.

WRITING FOR THE CMA EXAM

Writing skills and critical thinking skills are also essential for success on the CMA exam. According to the Director of Exam Administration for the IMA, William Cordes, the essay section of the CMA exam evaluates a candidate's ability "to analyze, evaluate, and communicate,"[9] as well as a candidate's mastery of accounting concepts and technical skills. As you will surely recognize, analysis and evaluation are components of the critical thinking process, so the IMA is stressing both critical thinking and writing as essential to the successful practice of management accounting.

Candidates for the CMA designation will answer four essay questions on the CMA exam. The IMA has stressed that each answer must be relevant to the question asked. Thus, your ability to read carefully and follow directions will be essential to receiving credit for your answer. In addition, the IMA will evaluate these specific writing skills:[10]

- Use of Standard English: proper grammar, punctuation, and spelling
- Organization: logical and coherent arrangement of ideas
- Clarity: clear communication of analysis and recommendation(s), if any, with well-constructed sentences and appropriate vocabulary

Figure 13–2 shows a sample question from a CMA exam, with two possible answers that would receive full credit. Study these examples to see how they fulfill the requirements of the exam:

- Both answers are relevant to the question asked.
- Both answers are arranged logically and coherently, and main ideas are easy to identify. Each answer begins with a thesis statement that summarizes the answer and directly answers the question. Additional paragraphs form the body of the essay; each paragraph begins with a topic sentence and explains one part of the answer.
- Sentences are clearly and correctly constructed, with appropriate word choices. They have been edited and proofread so that they are free of misspelled words and other errors.

FIGURE 13–2   Sample CMA Exam Question Requiring a Written Response[11]

Sample Question

Identify and describe the two fundamental types of internal audits, and give two examples of each.

Sample Answer #1

The two types of internal audits are operational audits and compliance audits.

An operational audit is a review of the functions within an enterprise to evaluate the efficiency of operations and the effectiveness with which those functions achieve their objective. An example would be an audit to assess productivity. Another example would be an evaluation of processes to reduce rework.

A compliance audit is the review of both financial and operation controls to confirm that they conform to established laws, standards, and procedures. An environmental audit would be an example of a compliance audit. An examination of the company's investment portfolio to assess whether the credit ratings of issuers conform to investment policies would be another example of a compliance audit.

Sample Answer #2

There are two types of internal audits: operational and compliance audits.

Operational audits are reviews of operations to ensure efficiency and effectiveness. Examples include:
- Process efficiency review.
- Productivity review.

Compliance audits review controls to ensure compliance with regulatory guidelines, policies, and procedures. Examples include:
- Review of legal contracts to ensure compliance with contractual obligations.
- Review of bond covenant agreements to make sure the company is meeting requirements.

- Sample Answer #2 also uses a technique of document design—set-off lists. Notice that these lists are constructed with parallel grammatical structure; that is, all items in the lists are noun phrases.

Written responses to CMA exam questions should take five to ten minutes to complete. Some questions can be answered in one or two well-constructed sentences. Other questions may require candidates to write brief essays, such as the answers shown in Figure 13–2. Candidates will type these written responses into a text box on a computer screen.

PREPARING FOR AND TAKING THE CPA EXAM OR CMA EXAM

Preparing for professional certification examinations such as the CPA exam or the CMA exam is much more involved than studying for an exam in an academic course. You will study many long hours, perhaps with the help of an exam review text or course. The types of questions you are asked on the written portions of those exams may resemble those in your course exams, perhaps to explain a concept, describe a process, analyze a situation, or solve the problem of a hypothetical client. Exam questions may also resemble the writing assignments you completed as part of your coursework, or possibly some of the more technical writing assignments included in this text.

Taking a certification exam may cause you anxiety, and the written responses asked for may seem especially daunting. We offer tips below to help you succeed in the examination, including ways to reduce the stress through time management. We'll also discuss strategies for reading the questions and planning your response, writing your answer, and editing for correct language. You can learn how to write an answer so that you receive full credit for what you know.

Manage Your Time

The pressure caused by the time constraints in a professional examination poses a challenge. You can meet this challenge, and reduce stress, if you manage the time you have to complete the required response. The key is to budget your time so that you can plan, write, and revise your answer.

First, take a few minutes to read the question carefully to be sure you know what is being asked. Underline key phrases in the question so that your answer won't overlook something important. Then jot down the main ideas you want to include in the answer. Put numbers by these ideas or draw arrows to arrange them in the most effective order. You might budget one to five minutes to plan your answer, depending on the total time you have for your response.

The next step, writing your answer, should take most of the remaining time. In this stage you will write in well-organized paragraphs with main ideas that are easy to spot. You need an overview or thesis statement for the entire response, which should come at or near the beginning of your response. Then develop supporting paragraphs with relevant details—pertinent facts from the question, definitions, examples, and rephrasing, as the exam specifies. Paragraphs should be unified, devoted to the development of one idea. The main idea of a paragraph will appear at the beginning of the paragraph as the topic sentence, with appropriate transitions that achieve a coherent flow of thought.

As you compose your response, write as well as you can, but don't get stuck looking for the perfect word or phrase if it doesn't come quickly.

The most important objective is to get the ideas down on paper to get credit for what you know. Write as well as you can, and keep going.

Finally, allow time to edit your answer. When you edit, check that all words are correctly spelled and that sentences are grammatically correct and clearly constructed.

Time is a big factor in answering the written components of professional exams, so use it wisely. Budget your time so that you can plan, write, and then revise.

Use the Exam Question to Organize the Response

We saw earlier that you should write in short paragraphs with strong topic sentences, enabling exam graders to identify your main ideas. The question itself can suggest the wording of the topic sentences. The sample question and answers from the CMA exam in Figure 13–2 illustrate this approach to organizing your response.

WRITING RESPONSES FOR ACADEMIC EXAMS

Some of the academic courses you will take in preparation for your career may also require you to write responses as part of a course exam. Sometimes these exams are called essay exams, or discussion questions. The writing you do for these exams will help prepare you for the certification exams you will take later.

Preparation

Although much of your studying for an objective examination will also help prepare you for questions requiring a written response, such as an essay or discussion question, you need to do a different kind of studying as well. Remember that these questions will require that you show a mastery of ideas. You may be asked to explain a concept, compare or contrast two methods of doing something, evaluate alternative treatments for a given situation, or justify a recommendation. Therefore, when you are studying for an exam, you should note concepts and explanations that would lend themselves to this type of question.

When you prepare for an exam, outline topics that may be subject to questions that call for a written response. When your outlines are ready, review them and try to guess questions that might appear on the exam. Then outline the information you would include in your answers to those questions.

Taking the Exam

Actually composing a written response is easier if you have a strategy for using your time and composing your answer. For some exams you may hand write your answers, or you may answer the exam question on a computer. This strategy works for either situation.

Budget Your Time

Managing your time well is a crucial part of your strategy. You may not have as much time as you would like to accomplish the three steps of the writing process: planning, writing, and revising. But you should make the time you have work to your advantage. Budget the time you have to compose your answer. For example, if you have 30 minutes, allow 5 minutes to read the question carefully and plan your response, 20 to write, and the final 5 minutes to revise.

Organize Your Answer

The goal for organizing your answer is to help the grader read it easily so that you will receive full credit for what you know. Thus, you should apply one of the primary recommendations emphasized throughout this text: Use summary sentences so that your main ideas stand out. The key is to begin the answer with a thesis statement and to use topic sentences at the beginning of each paragraph.

The thesis statement should echo the question and summarize the main ideas of your answer. Suppose you find this question on an exam:

Explain the matching concept in accounting.

Your answer to this question might begin this way:

The matching concept is used to determine what expense amounts should appear in the income statement for a particular period.

For short discussion questions, your answer might be only one paragraph long. In this case, the thesis statement for the answer would also function as the topic sentence for the paragraph. For more extensive questions, organize your answer into several paragraphs, each discussing one aspect of your answer. Each paragraph will have a topic sentence that provides a transition from the last paragraph, where needed, and that summarizes the main idea to be discussed in the new paragraph. Suppose you're asked this question on an exam:

Discuss how the definition of an asset changed after the Accounting Principles Board was replaced by the Financial Accounting Standards Board.

Your answer might be organized like this:

Thesis (first paragraph of your answer):

When the Financial Accounting Standards Board replaced the Accounting Principles Board, it switched the focus of income determination from the Expense/Revenue View to the Asset/Liability View.

Topic sentence for paragraph 2:

Under the Expense/Revenue View previously taken by the Accounting Principles Board, assets were merely debit balances left over after deciding the proper amount of expenses to match with revenues in the income statement.

Topic sentence for paragraph 3:

Under the Asset/Liability View favored by the Financial Accounting Standards Board, net income is determined by directly measuring changes in the value of net assets adjusted for changes resulting from owners' equity transactions.

One final reminder about organization: When deciding how many paragraphs to use for your answer, remember that readers usually find shorter paragraphs easier to read, as long as you provide adequate transitions so that they can follow your train of thought.

For a further discussion of organization, review Chapter 3.

Use Document Design

Sometimes the best way to include several points in your answer in a minimum amount of time is to use the document design principles explained in Chapter 6, especially set-off lists and headings. One of the sample answers to a CMA exam question shown in Figure 13–2 uses set-off lists. (Remember, however, not to use a set-off list on the CPA exam!) For a longer written response especially, headings may be a good way to divide your answer into its main components. If you are required to produce a memo or letter, be sure to follow the design principles discussed in Chapters 9 and 10.

Qualities of a Good Written Response

The discussion so far has already suggested several qualities of an effective answer to a question requiring a written response. Here is a summary of those qualities, plus a few additional pointers:

- If you hand write an answer, your handwriting should be legible and your pages neat and easy to read. Corrections, additions, and deletions should be made as neatly as possible.
- Main ideas should be easy to identify; the flow of thought should be easy for the grader to follow.
- Answer the question directly and completely. Supply adequate details and examples to support your assertions.
- Sentences should be concise, clear, and readable. Grammatical and mechanical errors should not distract the reader.

EFFECTIVE WRITING AND TECHNICAL MASTERY: BOTH IMPORTANT

To succeed in an exam that asks for a written response requires that you master technical accounting content, of course. Success also depends on your mastery of the effective writing and critical thinking skills stressed throughout this text.

Like business document readers, exam graders want written responses to be coherent (main ideas easy to identify, flow of thought easy to follow), concise (no wasted words), and clear (no guesswork about meaning, no distractions caused by grammatical and mechanical errors). Thus, the writing skills emphasized in this text apply to professional certification and academic exams as well as to more common forms of business writing.

When you are studying for a professional certification exam, you may find it helpful to review the chapters of this book that discuss these qualities of effective writing. These chapters will probably be the most useful to you:

- **Chapter 2:** Writing appropriately for the reader and responding to the requirements of the questions
- **Chapter 3:** Organizing for coherence
- **Chapter 4:** Writing with a style that is clear and concise
- **Chapter 5:** Writing in Standard English
- **Chapter 6:** Formatting techniques
- **Chapter 7:** Critical thinking

EXERCISES

Exercise 13–1 [Managerial]

Compare and contrast traditional and activity-based costing (ABC) systems. How do ABC systems provide value to a business's management?

Exercise 13–2[12] [Auditing]

Auditors provide "reasonable assurance" that the financial statements are "fairly stated, in all material respects." Questions are often raised as to the responsibility of the auditors to detect material misstatements, including misappropriation of assets and fraudulent financial reporting.

Write an essay on one of the following topics:

- Discuss the concept of "reasonable assurance" and the degree of confidence that financial statement users should have in the financial statements.
- What are the responsibilities of the independent auditor in the audit of a financial statement? Discuss fully, but in this part do not include fraud in the discussion.
- What are the responsibilities of the independent auditor for the detection of fraud involving misappropriation of assets and fraudulent financial reporting? Discuss fully, including your assessment of whether the auditor's responsibility for the detection of fraud is appropriate.

Exercise 13–3 [Auditing]

The International Auditing and Assurance Standards Board (IAASB) has been actively involved in recasting old standards and casting new standards in a form that is intended to be clearer, basing standards on objectives rather than procedures and using the word "shall" to indicate requirements that must be followed. Other improvements are intended to make standards easier to read and understand.[13] Write an essay discussing the relationship between the IAASB and the Auditing Standards Board (ASB) in the United States and how this effort of the IAASB may affect the output of the ASB. Your essay should be long enough to completely cover the important issues involved.

Exercise 13–4[14] [Systems]

One morning, the computers at U.S. Leasing Company began acting sluggish. Computer operators were relieved when a software trouble-shooter from IBM called several hours later. They were more than happy to help the troubleshooter correct the problem they were having. The troubleshooter asked for a phone number for the computers as well as a log-on number and password.

The next morning, the computers were worse. A call to IBM confirmed U.S. Leasing's suspicion: Someone had impersonated an IBM repairman to gain unauthorized access to the system and destroy the database. U.S. Leasing was also concerned that the intruder had devised a program that would let him get back into the system even after all the passwords were changed.

Write an essay discussing what techniques the imposter might have employed to breach U.S. Leasing's internal security and how U.S. Leasing might avoid these types of incidents in the future.

Exercise 13–5 [Tax]

Write an essay discussing the important tax and legal advantages and disadvantages in organizing a business as a partnership, an S Corporation, or a Limited Liability Company.

Exercise 13–6 [Financial]

Write an essay discussing the various valuation bases used in GAAP, such as historical cost, fair market value, liquidation value, replacement value, and depreciated or amortized cost. For each basis in your discussion, cover its definition, describe in general terms when it is proper to use it, and critique the advantages and disadvantages of its use. Also address the issue of why we should (or should not) use so many different valuation bases in GAAP. Is it really fair to claim that GAAP is still based on historical cost?

Exercise 13–7 [Financial/International]

Write an essay discussing the advantages and disadvantages of adoption of International Financial Reporting Standards (IFRS) in the United States. Assuming IFRS are adopted, include in your essay a discussion of the pros and cons of using a convergence approach versus a "condorsement" approach to adoption.

NOTES

1. See "Become a CMA®," http:// www.imanet.org/cma_certification/ become_a_cma.aspx (10 May 2013).

2. American Institute of Certified Public Accountants, "Written Communication" 2006–2013. http:// www.aicpa.org/BecomeACPA/ CPAExam/ForCandidates/ HowToPrepare/Pages/ WrittenCommunication.aspx (6 June 2013).

3. American Institute of Certified Public Accountants, "The Uniform CPA Examination Candidate Bulletin: Information for Applicants," January, 2013. http://www.nasba.org/files/2013/01/ Candidate_Bulletin.pdf (25 January 2013).

4. For a complete guide to overall content of the exam, see American Institute of Certified Public Accountants, "Content and Skill Specifications for The Uniform CPA Examination" May, 2009; Updated October, 2011, Effective January, 2013. http:// www.aicpa.org/BecomeACPA/ CPAExam/ExaminationContent/ ContentAndSkills/ DownloadableDocuments/ CSOs-SSOs-Effective.Jan2013.pdf (24 January, 2013). You may also want to look at American Institute of Certified Public Accountants, "Written Communication," 2006–2013. http://www.aicpa.org/ becomeacpa/cpaexam/forcandidates/ howtoprepare/pages/writtencommunication.aspx (25 January 2013).

5. American Institute of Certified Public Accountants, "Content and Skill Specifications for The Uniform CPA Examination" May, 2009; Updated October, 2011, Effective January, 2013. http:// www.aicpa.org/BecomeACPA/ CPAExam/ExaminationContent/ ContentAndSkills/ DownloadableDocuments/ CSOs-SSOs-Effective.Jan2013.pdf (6 June 2013), 39.

6. American Institute of Certified Public Accountants, "Written Communication," 2006–2013. http://www.aicpa. org/BecomeACPA/CPAExam/ ForCandidates/HowToPrepare/ Pages/WrittenCommunication.aspx (6 June 2013).

7. American Institute of Certified Public Accountants, "Content and Skill Specifications for The Uniform CPA Examination" May, 2009; Updated October, 2011, Effective January, 2013. http:// www.aicpa.org/BecomeACPA/ CPAExam/ExaminationContent/ ContentAndSkills/ DownloadableDocuments/ CSOs-SSOs-Effective.Jan2013.pdf (6 June 2013), 37–38.

8. American Institute of Certified Public Accountants, "CPA Examination Tutorial and Sample Tests," 2006–2013. http:// www.aicpa.org/BecomeACPA/ CPAExam/ForCandidates/ TutorialandSampleTest/Pages/ exam_tutorialllel.aspx (6 June 2013).

CHAPTER 13

9. William Cordes, personal email (15 May 2013).

10. William Cordes, personal email (15 May 2013).

11. William Cordes, personal email (15 May 2013).

12. Alvin A. Arens, Randal J. Elder, and Mark S. Beasley, *Auditing and Assurance Services*, 15th Ed., © 2014, pp. 168, 212. Reprinted and Electronically reproduced by permission of Pearson Education, Inc., Upper Saddle River, New Jersey.

13. Glenn Cheney, "International auditing standards may get clearer," *Accounting Today*, 8 January 2007. http://www.webcpa.com/article.cfm ?articleid=22985&pg=acctoday (24 January 2013).

14. Marshall B. Romney and Paul J. Steinbart, *Accounting Information Systems*, 11th Ed., © 2009, p. 178. Reprinted and Electronically reproduced by permission of Pearson Education, Inc., Upper Saddle River, New Jersey.

CHAPTER

14

Writing for Employment: Résumés and Letters of Application

Finding a job after graduation is a concern for most accounting students and some accountants who already have their degrees. Your communication skills can be a tremendous asset in finding that job. In fact, an applicant's communication skills may be the *single most important factor* in employers' hiring decisions. This chapter focuses on several important skills you need to get a good job: researching a targeted company, preparing a résumé and letter of application, and writing a thank-you letter to follow an interview.

STARTING THE JOB SEARCH: RESEARCHING POSSIBLE EMPLOYERS

The way you begin your job search depends to some extent on where you are when you start. If you are still a student in a large university, you will probably work with your school's job placement office, its faculty, and the recruiters who visit your campus. If you are a student in a small school, opportunities for on-campus interviews may be more limited, and you may find it helpful to work with the accounting faculty to identify potential employers. If you have already graduated, then you may be on your own in locating potential jobs and establishing initial contacts with employers, although the placement office of the school from which you graduated may still work with you.

Whether you're a student or already a practicing professional, you may also look for positions on networking sites, such as LinkedIn. Chapter 12 discusses the use of electronic media to locate and apply for employment, including the email submission of résumés and the creation of profiles that some networking sites, such as LinkedIn, require.

Regardless of how you begin your job search, you will need to write certain documents to secure the job, including a letter of application, a résumé, and a thank-you letter after you have had an interview. For all these documents, knowledge of the prospective employer is important because you will want to tailor what you write to that employer's needs. You will also want to show the people who read these documents that you are familiar with the company and that you did the preparation necessary to make a good impression. You should be very familiar at least with the content of the company's Web site, but additional research into the company's operations is desirable. At an interview, you may be asked whether you have questions about the company; it can be very embarrassing to ask a question the answer to which is readily available on the company's Web site or some other material to which you've had access.

Thus, you may begin your research by studying the organization's Web page. It may also be that the company publishes a blog or some other online publication; you should become thoroughly familiar with the information you obtain from these sources. You can also search the Internet for articles and news items in the financial press, and you can talk with business faculty about the organization. Your school's job placement office may also have an information file on the company. Perhaps you will also be fortunate enough to meet recruiters from the organization on campus at accounting club meetings or at job fairs. If you have this opportunity, listen carefully to what the recruiters say about their organization and ask appropriate questions. Show with polite, attentive listening that you are interested in what the recruiters have to say, and remember the names of the people you meet!

You should also find as much information as possible about the particular job for which you are applying. If there is a specific job opening, you will probably have general information about the position in a job announcement. Read the announcement carefully so that you learn as much as possible about the position's requirements and the credentials the employer is looking for. This information can guide you when you prepare your résumé and application letter.

PREPARING YOUR MATERIALS

All the information you gathered in your research will be important as you prepare the materials you will use for your job application. These materials may include a résumé, letter of application, thank-you letter, and possibly other materials as well.

Follow Instructions

Before you begin the actual process of applying for a job, take time to read any instructions the employer has provided for the application process, including instructions relating to written materials the employer requests. Some employers specify the electronic submission of the résumé, for example. If you submit a hard copy rather than an electronic version, your résumé will likely be ignored.

Similarly, the employer may specify that you include particular information in your application, such as your experience or training in a specific area. You should provide requested information *exactly and in the form and manner requested*. For example, if you are asked to describe in your cover letter how your credentials may fit the position for which you are applying, be sure to (a) provide a cover letter, and (b) describe *in your cover letter* how you may fit the position. Don't ignore the request for a cover letter, and don't just assume that whoever reads your résumé will figure out how you may fit the position.

Not following directions precisely is one of the biggest reasons job applicants are rejected. Prospective employers are very likely to assume that if an applicant is careless in following application directions, he or she will likely be careless in following directions on the job.[1]

Prepare Your Résumé

Preparing a résumé may be one of the most important steps you take in finding a good job. Remember this tongue-in-cheek advice: "An ounce of image is worth a pound of performance." This quip actually has some truth when applied to résumés. Your performance in school and in previous jobs is, of course, essential, but if the résumé doesn't project a professional, competent image, your application won't be considered seriously. Prospective employers will identify and interview applicants who show the qualities they are looking for. Initially, these qualities will be determined by a careful reading of an applicant's cover letter and résumé.[2] So take the time and the care necessary to do a good job when you prepare these documents.

Figure 14–1 illustrates an effective résumé. This example is not the only way to prepare a good résumé, however, and you may find other models in business communication texts or in materials supplied by your school's job placement office. We will consider the résumé in Figure 14–1 as a generic model that you can adapt to your own situation.

Format
First of all, look at the document design of the résumé in Figure 14–1. Notice the placement of text on the page and the pleasing use of white space, headings, fonts, and bullets. The résumé is arranged so that it has an attractive, professional appearance; it is also easy to read because it's not crowded, and important information is easy to find. You'll see how these design techniques can be used with the various parts of a résumé.

Name and Address
Center your name in bold print at the top of the page. On the next line, put your address at the left margin and your phone number (including your area code) at the right margin, as shown in Figure 14–1. Place your email address below your phone number. Place a horizontal line under this portion to separate your identifying data from your qualifications.

FIGURE 14–1   Sample Résumé

Shane W. Brown

1324 Horsetooth Road   Phone: (970) 435-1234
Fort Collins, Colorado 80125   email: sbrown@csu.edu

CAREER OBJECTIVE	An accounting position that will allow me to build on my academic and employment background and provide opportunities for professional growth and development. Willing to travel.
SUMMARY OF QUALIFICATIONS	Degree in accounting; honor student; experience with corporate staff; experienced in customer service.
EDUCATION	Bachelor of Business Administration, University of Georgia, June 2014 Major: Accounting GPA: 3.55/4.0

WORK EXPERIENCE

June 2013–September 2013	**Jaymart, Inc.; Executive Offices,** Norcross, Ga. *Accounting Internship* • Assisted in the preparation of year-end audit work papers. • Worked on depreciation schedules; updated property, plant, and equipment accounts. • Participated in the preparation of the 2013 corporate tax return work papers, and set up schedules for the 2014 corporate return. • Prepared 2014 income tax projections for individual corporate officers.
March 2012–June 2013	**University of Georgia Language Laboratories,** Athens, Ga. *Laboratory Assistant* • Supervised foreign language students using the laboratory. Worked an average of 15 hours per week.
June 2011–September 2011	**AT&T Information Systems,** Atlanta, Ga. *Support Services* • Assisted AT&T employees with their mailroom needs.
June 2010–September 2010	**Food Giant,** Atlanta, Ga. *Courtesy Clerk, Produce Department* • Promoted to Produce Department Manager in July 2010. Assisted customers.
HONORS AND ACTIVITIES	Association of Students of Accounting; Beta Alpha Psi Initiate (Accounting Fraternity); University Honors Program, Recipient of Junior Division Honors; Program Certificate; Beta Gamma Sigma (Business Honor Society); Dean's List (seven of eleven quarters); Phi Eta Sigma; Tau Epsilon Phi (Social Fraternity); Finance Club; College Republicans; Intramural Softball, Volleyball.
INTERESTS	Racquetball, current events, travel, music.

Career Objective

Be as specific as possible about the kind of job you're looking for so the employer can easily determine whether your goals match any available openings. You might indicate an accounting specialty such as tax, auditing, or systems, for example. At the same time, you don't want to close any doors you will later wish you had left open, so consider describing your objective in a way that will allow for all reasonable possibilities of employment for which you're qualified. Even better, you can edit your résumé so that your objective fits specific openings for which you're applying.

Summary of Qualifications

Employers often receive a large number of résumés and do not have time to study the detailed information the résumés contain. Therefore, you should provide a "snapshot" of your qualifications that will immediately catch the employer's eye.

Notice Shane Brown's Summary of Qualifications section in Figure 14–1. In one quick set of phrases he sums up why the employer should pick him for the job.

Education

Beginning with your most recent degree or school, provide information in reverse chronological order about your education to show your qualifications for employment. Include the following information:

- Degree(s) you have completed or are working on.
- Complete name of the school granting this degree.
- Date of the degree, or expected graduation date.
- Your major and, if applicable to the job, your minor.
- Grade point average, if it is above 3.0 on a 4.0 scale. (Figure your GPA several ways to try to reach at least a 3.0—for example, cumulative GPA, GPA in your major coursework, GPA in upper level courses, and so on—labeling it accordingly.)
- Approximate percentage of your college expenses you financed yourself, if this amount is significant.

If you have attended several colleges or universities, include information about all of them, especially if you received a degree. If you attended schools without completing a degree, give the dates of your attendance.

You don't need to include information about your high school education, unless that information is relevant to a potential employer. If you're applying for summer employment, but still have some time before you graduate from college, then you might list your high school and date of graduation.

Work Experience

Again in reverse chronological order, provide information about the jobs you have held, both full- and part-time. You can also list volunteer work if it's relevant to the job for which you're applying. For each job you list, provide the following information:

- Dates of employment. You may decide to put the dates in the left margin, as in the sample résumé.
- Name and location of the organization for which you worked.
- Your position.
- A description of your responsibilities, with emphasis on the ones that show you are qualified for the job you are now seeking. Note any promotions or honors you received. Whenever possible, describe your responsibilities using active voice verbs such as *assisted, completed, prepared,* and *supervised.* Quantify your accomplishments, if possible. In the example résumé in Figure 14–1, Shane Brown notes that he worked in the language lab an average of 15 hours per week.

Honors and Activities

List the organizations you have belonged to, the honors you have received, and any other activities that show you to be a well-rounded, active person. List these activities from most important to least important, *from the potential employer's point of view.* If you held an office in an organization or had significant responsibilities, add this information as well. Finally, if an organization or honor is not self-explanatory, explain it briefly, as illustrated in the sample résumé in Figure 14–1.

Interests

Information about your hobbies and interests is optional on a résumé. The advantage of including this information is that it can show that you are a well-rounded person with interests that might help you relate to other people, such as your co-workers and clients.

References

If you provide the names, addresses, and phone numbers of your references on your résumé, the employer can contact them easily. However, you run the risk that an employer will call your reference at an inconvenient time, or that the reference will not immediately recall detailed information about you. As a general rule, do not include a list of references or letters of reference with your résumé unless they are specifically requested. However, you should prepare a list of references in advance of any interview you may have and give the list to your interviewer.

In addition, it is generally not necessary to include a statement on your résumé that "references are available upon request," as this is generally considered obvious. However, if you are enrolled or have recently graduated from a college or university, you may be able to place reference letters on file with your school's job placement office. Then your résumé or reference list can include a line such as this one:

References available upon request from:

Placement Office
University of Manhattan
Manhattan, Georgia 30678

Although placing reference letters on file with school's placement office may be useful, most employers will prefer to contact your references directly.

One final word about references: Never list people as references without first asking their permission. Ask people to be references who are likely to remember you well and have favorable things to say about you. Former instructors and employers are good candidates.

What *Not* to Put on a Résumé

Remember that there are laws against hiring discrimination on the basis of age, sex, race, religion, marital status, or national origin, so do not put information of this nature on a résumé. Also, when preparing your résumé, avoid phrases such as these:

- gets along well with co-workers
- pleasant disposition
- always eager to please

These phrases make you sound as if you were applying to be a pet rather than an employee! "Fluff" phrases like these are guaranteed to send your résumé straight to the bottom of the pile.

Generally, employers hiring for accounting positions are interested in two things: what you know and what you can do. Therefore, your résumé should specifically state what you know and what you can do.

Write a Letter of Application

Often you will send your résumé to a potential employer with a formal letter of application, or you will write to follow up some earlier communication. Like the résumé, the letter must be professional and well researched.

Your letter should follow the general advice for letters discussed in Chapter 9, including these guidelines:

- Address the reader by name. Get the appropriate name over the telephone or by other means, if possible.
- Give your letter an attractive, professional appearance. Use good stationery and a high-quality printer. The letter and résumé should be printed on matching paper and both should match the envelope.
- Write in short, concise paragraphs and clear sentences. A courteous, conversational tone is best.
- The spelling, grammar, and mechanics of your letter should be perfect.

The content of your letter will depend on your particular situation. The letter will typically have three paragraphs. The first paragraph will identify the specific position for which you're applying. It will also provide a context for your application, such as how you learned about the position. If you have already discussed the job or possible employment with an employee of the company, you should refer to this person by name and say exactly why you're sending the résumé. You might write a sentence such as this one:

> Sara Evans suggested that I write you about a possible opening in your auditing department. I had the pleasure of talking with Ms. Evans at a meeting of our Accounting Club here at the University of Central California.
>
> As you will see in my enclosed résumé, . . .

After the introduction to your letter, use your second paragraph to show the reader two things: that you are familiar with the organization doing the hiring and that you have the credentials the organization is looking for. Thus, you can briefly refer to what you've learned about the company from your research and highlight the information on your résumé that shows you to be especially interested in, and qualified for, the position. In other words, you use the letter of application to sell yourself as the best person for the job. The following paragraphs show examples from two different letters:

> As you will see on my enclosed résumé, I will graduate from the University of Northern Idaho in June with a Masters of Accounting degree and a specialty in tax, so my training should qualify me for an entry-level position in your tax department. In addition, I have worked as a tax assistant with the Smith Company during the past two summers.
>
> * * *
>
> While at the University of Tempe, I have worked an average of twenty hours a week to pay approximately half my college and living expenses. At the same time I have maintained a cumulative GPA of 3.3 and have been active in a number of campus organizations. I believe this record shows that I am a conscientious worker with an ability to organize my time and achieve goals in a deadline-intensive environment.

The final paragraph should include a courteous closing and suggest a response from the reader or follow-up action you will take. You might suggest that you will call in a week to see if the employer needs additional information. At the least, express enthusiasm for the position and a hope that you will hear from the employer soon:

> I hope that you will find my education and experience suitable for this position and that we can set up an interview soon to discuss the position further. I look forward to hearing from you.

Figure 14–2 shows a letter of application.

Mail your letter of application and résumé in a flat business envelope so that you won't have to fold your documents. Alternatively, some employers may ask for applications and résumés to be submitted by email, as we discuss further in Chapter 12.

FIGURE 14–2 Letter of Application

FIGURE 14–2 Letter of Application

2134 Roxboro Road
Atlanta, GA 30378
January 15, 2014

Ann Bradbury, Partner
Bradbury, Ellis, and Gomez, CPAs
33 Hightower Building
Atlanta, GA 30391

Dear Ms. Bradbury:

It was a pleasure meeting you and George Ellis last week at the Accounting Club meeting here at Fulton University. As you suggested, I am sending you my résumé because you anticipate having an opening soon for which I would be qualified.

As my résumé shows, I will graduate from Fulton in May with an MACC degree and a specialty in auditing. As an intern with Brown and Hill, CPAs, I participated in several audits in the north Georgia area. I hope you will find that my education and experience make me a good candidate for an auditing position with Bradbury, Ellis, and Gomez.

I would very much appreciate the opportunity to talk with you further about possible future employment. I will call your office next week to see whether we might set up a time for an interview.

Sincerely,

Carla Brown

Carla Brown
Enclosure

Write a Thank-You Letter

With an impressive résumé and application letter, good credentials to support them, and a little luck, you will probably have one or more interviews for jobs. After the interviews, you need to write letters to the people who met with you to thank them for their hospitality and to show enthusiasm for what you learned about the organization and the position for which you're applying.

This letter need not be long; a letter of two or three short paragraphs is usually long enough. Again, you need to address your readers by name and refer specifically to your meeting and to one or two

FIGURE 14–3   Thank You Letter

FIGURE 14–3   Thank You Letter

2134 Roxboro Road
Atlanta, GA 30378
April 23, 2014

Ann Bradbury, Partner
Bradbury, Ellis, and Gomez, CPAs
33 Hightower Building
Atlanta, GA 30391

Dear Ms. Bradbury:

Thank you very much for meeting with me last week to discuss the possibility of my working for Bradbury, Ellis, and Gomez after my graduation next month. I enjoyed the opportunity to visit your office and meet the other members of your auditing staff. The lunch with June Oliver and Richard Wang was particularly pleasant and informative because they were able to share their experiences as first year auditors.

I would very much welcome the opportunity to work as an auditor with your firm, so I hope that you will decide my qualifications meet your needs. Please let me know if I can provide any additional information.

Thank you once again for your hospitality. I look forward to hearing from you.

Sincerely,

CarlaBrown

Carla Brown

of the topics you discussed. If you met any of the firm's other employees, you should express pleasure at having had that opportunity. End your letter with a courteous closing and express the hope that you will hear from your reader soon.

This letter, like the application letter, should follow the guidelines for letters covered in Chapter 9. A sample thank-you letter is shown in Figure 14–3.

Electronic Submissions

For some jobs, you will submit your résumé and application letter electronically. Some job announcements request an electronic submission, or you may find it an advantage to submit your materials quickly. In situations such as these, you can attach your résumé to an email. The email itself will be your formal letter of application, with your résumé as an attachment. Select the rich text option for your email in order to preserve the formatting of your application letter.

A word of caution about email submissions, including the email itself: Take the same care you would for any professional document, including careful editing and proofreading. Remember that this submission is your first chance to make a good impression on your prospective employer. Chapter 12 provides more information on the use of electronic media for job applications, including the email submission of your résumé.

EXERCISES

Exercise 14–1 [General]

Imagine that you are an employer who received the résumé shown in Figure 14–4. How would you react to the résumé? Would you be likely to give the applicant an interview? Why or why not?

Examine the résumé closely, noting the applicant's accomplishments and experience. Does this person have credentials that might make him a good employee?

Rewrite this résumé so that the applicant's credentials show to good advantage. You may have to make up some details so that the résumé is complete.

Exercise 14–2 [General]

Visit your school's placement office to find out about jobs for which you will soon be qualified. If you're close to graduation, consider positions that require a degree. If you still have a year or more before you complete your degree, identify internship positions.

Draft a résumé suitable for submission for a position that interests you.

Exercise 14–3 [General]

Locate an accounting position online for which you may soon be qualified. Write a résumé to respond to this job announcement.

Exercise 14–4 [General]

Exchange résumés with one or more of your classmates. Critique the résumés, checking for effective organization, wording, and page design.

FIGURE 14–4   Résumé to Accompany Exercise 14–1

William H. Bonney

PRESENT ADDRESS   PERMANENT ADDRESS
745 Main St.   1634 Scaffold Lane
Athens, GA 30600   Highnoon, Ga 31200

EDUCATION   DEGREE   CUM
                              GRAD. DATE   MAJ. GPA   GPA
University of Georgia   6/13   3.4   3.5
Oconee Springs High School   6/09   3.9

MAJOR COURSES
Principles of Accounting I and II; Financial Accounting I, II, III;
Systems I.

WORK EXPERIENCE

	TITLE	FROM	TO
Auto Stores, Inc. Clarkstown, Ga.	Cashier	7/12	9/12
Hamilton's Coldwater, Ga.	Cashier	5/12	9/12
Tulips Discount Stores Roosevelt, Ga.	Clerk	6/11	9/11
Sam's Market Athens, Ga.	Salesperson	11/10	1/11
Esops, Inc. Athens, Ga.	Office/Customer svc.	6/10	10/10
Telemarketing, Inc. Athens, Ga.	Telemarketer	7/12	Present

HONORS AND ACTIVITIES
Honors Program
Dean's List
Golden Key
Outstanding College Students of America
Phi Chi Theta Business Fraternity
Association of Students in Accounting
James E. Cassidy Scholarship

PERSONAL
Date of Birth - October 20, 1994; excellent health; prefer to work in the
north Atlanta area.

Proofread each other's résumés to be sure there are no mechanical or typographical errors. After you receive suggestions from your classmates, revise your résumé accordingly.

Exercise 14–5 [General]

Imagine that you find the following job announcement at your school's placement office. Prepare an application letter for this position to accompany your résumé.

> ACCOUNTANT Entry-level staff accountant for a mid-sized business services firm. Degree required. Send résumé to Hugh Lee, Director of Human Resources, North Carolina Systems Consultants, Durham, NC 60314. An equal opportunity/affirmative action employer.

Exercise 14–6 [General]

The application letter you prepared for Exercise 14–5 was so effective and your résumé looked so impressive that you had an office interview with North Carolina Systems Consultants. At the interview, you met the company's president, George Owen, and several other accountants in the accounting department. You had lunch after the interview with Mary Wilson, a senior accountant in the firm, as well as the controller, Robert Wages. You learned that the company has been in business for six years, but that it is now expanding into a larger market and adding additional services for its customers.

Write a thank-you letter to follow up on your interview.

Exercise 14–7 [Financial/Auditing]

The job listing for Johnson & Peters, CPAs, shown in Figure 14–5, is a typical listing of an entry-level job opening in a small to medium-size CPA firm. Assume you have all the qualifications for this job. Write your résumé and a letter of application to respond to this listing. Invent any facts you may need to complete this assignment. Address your letter to James Sorbon, Director of Personnel.

Exercise 14–8 [Tax]

The job listing for a tax analyst for National Chemical Corp., shown in Figure 14–6, is typical of many job listings for this type of job. Assume you have all the qualifications for this position. Write your résumé and a letter of application to respond to this listing. Address your application to Susan Charon, Director of Human Resources. Invent any facts you may need to complete this assignment.

FIGURE 14–5   Typical Entry-Level Job Listing for a Medium-Size CPA Firm

Johnson & Peters, CPAs
1231 Main St.
Houston, TX 77001

Opening for Audit Associate

Johnson & Peters provides an excellent opportunity for advancement and development of a life-long career. The firm is committed to the development of our future leaders. Associates may report to and receive instruction from staff, managers, principals, and partners with all levels of experience.

Audit Associate Specific Duties

- Become familiar with accounting and auditing procedures and perform them in accordance with Johnson & Peters' standards in an accurate, thorough, and timely manner.
- Work on preparation of financial statements, lease testing, payroll testing, cash disbursement testing, auditing accounts payable, searching for unrecorded liabilities, maintaining confirmation logs, and preparing audit files.
- Understand clients' accounting systems.
- Resolve audit issues by obtaining evidence and making inquiries of clients.
- Apply concepts of materiality and audit risk.
- Prepare audit file content that is informative, indexed, cross-referenced, and easily understood.
- Manage daily client workflow and multiple client projects.

Personal and Professional Development

- Pursue and pass the CPA Exam.
- Earn confidence, trust, and respect from clients and colleagues.
- Continually develop technical skills and industry knowledge.
- Demonstrate initiative, resourcefulness, creativity, independent thinking, and sound business judgment.
- Represent Johnson & Peters in a positive and professional manner.
- Develop an ability to motivate and train staff.
- Actively participate in Johnson & Peters' internal development programs, including staff training courses.

Requirements

- Bachelors degree in accounting.
- Excellent written and oral communication skills.
- Ability to work in a team environment.
- Ability to learn in a fast-paced environment.
- General computer literacy including proficiency in Microsoft Word® and Excel®.

Please apply directly to James Sorbon, Director of Personnel.

FIGURE 14–6   Typical Entry-Level Job Listing for a Tax Analyst in Industry

National Chemical Corp.
756 Petro Lane
Tulsa, OK 74103

<u>Opening for Tax Analyst</u>

National Chemical Corp. (NCC) produces a broad range of specialty chemicals and fibers that are marketed globally in over 80 countries. In 2013, NCC had revenues of approximately $4.2 billion. The company is based in Tulsa, OK, and employs more than 10,000 people worldwide.

<u>Job Responsibilities</u>
- Assist with preparation and filing of Sales and Use tax returns in numerous jurisdictions.
- Assist with external Sales and Use tax audits.
- Assist with various special projects.
- Assist with management or issuance of customer and vendor exemption certificates.
- Assist with preparation of property tax returns, and monitor tax assessment notices and bills.
- Assist in preparation of monthly journal entries, reconciliation of applicable general ledger accounts, monthly and quarterly tax payments, returns, and submissions to various jurisdictions.

<u>Requirements</u>
- Degree in accounting or related field.
- Demonstrated analytical and problem-solving skills.
- Ability of communicate effectively, both orally and in writing.
- Ability to work in a team setting.
- Detail oriented and strong research and analytical skills.
- Ability to use tax research software.
- Proficiency in computer skills using MS Office.
- Willingness to learn new computer software.
- Knowledge of accounting principles and corporate tax law.
- Ability to multi-task and work under tight deadlines.
- Strong interpersonal skills.

Apply directly to Susan Charon, Director of Human Resources.

Exercise 14–9 [Managerial]

The job listing for a corporate accountant, shown in Figure 14–7, is typical of many job listings for this type of job. Assume you have all the qualifications for this position. Write your résumé and a letter of application to respond to this listing. Address your application to Thomas Lombardo, Director of Human Resources. Invent any facts you may need to complete this assignment.

FIGURE 14–7   Typical Entry-Level Job Listing for Corporate Accountant

Allegheny Industries
8005 Allegheny Drive
Pittsburgh, PA 15250

Opening for Corporate Accountant

Allegheny Industries is an international, publicly traded company manufacturing heavy equipment for the construction and shipping industries.
The equipment it manufactures is marketed globally. In 2013, NCC had
revenues of approximately $2.3 billion. The company is based in Pittsburgh
and employs more than 6,000 people.

Duties

- Prepare financial statements and various financial reports for internal
  and external use.
- Perform accounting activities relating to the maintenance of general
  ledger accounts and the month-end closing process, including journal
  entries and reconciliations.
- Assist with various treasury duties including cash reconciliations, depos-
  its, refunds, vendor and debt payments, and loan compliance.
- Assist with preparation of budgets and forecasts.
- Assist with federal, state, and local tax compliance.
- Assist with other functions as needed.

Job Requirements

- Bachelors degree in accounting.
- Good knowledge of US GAAP and able to research new issues.
- Ability to work with people from all departments.
- Strong written and verbal communication skills.
- Strong problem-solving skills.
- Proficiency in Microsoft Excel® and Word®.

Apply directly to Thomas Lombardo, Director of Human Resources.

NOTES

1. Laura Raines, "Want a job? Write
   a letter," *The Atlanta Journal-
   Constitution,* 8 April 2012. H1.
2. For a good discussion of the
   process employers go through
   before interviewing an applicant,
   see George Violette and Douglas
   Chene, "Campus Recruiting: What
   Local and Regional Accounting
   Firms Look for in Hew Hires," *The
   CPA Journal* (December 2008): 67.

CHAPTER

Writing for Publication

15

As a practicing accountant or business services professional, you may decide at some point in your career to write an article for publication. This might be a short article for a newsletter, perhaps published by the organization you work for, or it might be a longer article for a professional journal, such as the *Journal of Accountancy* or the *Management Accounting Quarterly*. You might also write a blog related to your work or respond to an article you find online. Most of the techniques discussed in this book apply to writing for publication, but in this chapter, we consider some additional pointers.

PLANNING YOUR ARTICLE

To plan your article, start by considering the publication that you want to write for and the topic you want to write about. Most likely, you'll be writing about your experience in practice, such as a better way to approach an accounting procedure or solve an accounting problem. You may also write a position paper to express your opinion on some controversial accounting or business issue currently under discussion in the profession.

Whatever the topic you've chosen, target your writing to the editorial practices and readers of the publication to which you're submitting the article. One of the best ways to have an article published is to write on a subject that is interesting and relevant to a wide range of the publication's readers.

Consider the type of writing typically published by the targeted publication. You will probably want to write for a journal that prefers practical articles about the practice of accounting. The *Journal of Accountancy*, *The CPA Journal*, and the *Management Accounting Quarterly* publish articles on practical concerns shared by accountants. Journals and newsletters published on the state or local level might publish articles of general interest to accounting professionals, but they also include articles of local interest. Other publications such as the *Accounting Review* prefer academic articles on scholarly research. Figures 15–1 and 15–2 show some accounting journals of

FIGURE 15–1   Some Accounting Publications Available Online and in Print

CA Magazine
This is the leading accounting publication for Canadian Chartered Accountants. http://www.camagazine.com/index. aspx.

The CPA Journal
This journal is a publication of the New York State Society of CPAs. It publishes articles on accounting and auditing, taxation, finance, management, responsibilities and leadership, and technology. http://www.cpajournal.com/.

The International Journal of Accounting (IJA)
The IJA is published by the University of Illinois and publishes articles explaining international accounting practices including theoretical justifications and criticisms. http://www.sciencedirect.com/science/journal/00207063.

Journal of Accountancy (JOA)
The JOA is published by the American Institute of Certified Public Accountants (AICPA). It contains articles on auditing, career development, consulting services, ethics and independence, financial management, financial reporting, forensic and valuation services, fraud, internal controls, personal financial planning, practice management, risk management, tax, and technology. Available to members of the AICPA, or you can just subscribe to the journal. http://www.journalofaccountancy.com.

Journal of Accounting Research (JAR)
The JAR is an academic journal focused on academic research. It is published by The Accounting Research Center at the University of Chicago Booth School of Business. http://onlinelibrary.wiley.com/journal/10.1111/(ISSN)1475-679X.

Accounting Review (AR)
The AR is published by the American Accounting Association and contains articles "reporting the results of accounting research and explaining and illustrating related research methodology." http://aaajournals.org/loi/accr.

The New York Times (NYT)
The NYT has a special section devoted to accounting at http://topics.nytimes.com/topics/reference/timestopics/subjects/a/accounting_and_accountants/index.html.

The Wall Street Journal (WSJ)—Accounting
The WSJ has a special section devoted to accounting at http://online.wsj.com/public/page/news-accounting-industry.html.

FIGURE 15–2   Some Accounting Publications Available Online Only

accountancylive
This journal is published in the UK. It publishes articles on international accounting in addition to those more focused on the UK. http://www.accountancylive.com.

Accounting Today
This is a good source for all news and opinion aimed at the CPA. Two blogs— *Accounting Tomorrow*, which deals with the future of the accounting profession, and *Debits&Credits*, which deals with the latest developments in accounting, tax, and client advisory services— are also published by this journal. http://www.accountingtoday.com.

AccountingWEB
This is a very good source for news on topics that include tax, accounting and auditing, technology, practice, and education. The Web site also has links to several useful blogs including the IMA Young Accounting Pros Blog, on which members of the IMA's Young Professionals Committee discuss advice and experience highly useful to entry-level accountants. http://www.accountingweb.com.

Big 4
This is a useful blog covering career opportunities and significant developments in larger accounting firms and other companies. Its contributors are current employees or alumni of those companies, but it is not affiliated with any company or group of companies. http://www.big4.com/blog.

CPA Trendlines
Published by Bay Street Group LLC, this publication contains useful articles on tax, accounting, and finance. http://cpatrendlines.com.

Management Accounting Quarterly (MAQ)
The MAQ is published by the IMA (formerly the Institute of Management Accounting) and contains articles "by and for academics and practitioners of accounting and financial management." Topics include (among others) "cost/management accounting techniques, ABC/ABM, RCA, GPK, statistical process controls, target costing, theory of constraints, methods of calculating stock options, techniques to improve accounting and finance education, new theories in finance and accounting, and much more." http://www.imanet.org/resources_and_publications/management_accounting_quarterly.aspx.

Smart Brief
This is a source for several useful newsletters that publish articles dealing with their respective topics, including the following AICPA publications: *CPA Letter Daily* (for accounting news), *IFRS Report* (for global accounting news), *InfoTech Update* (for information technology in accounting), *Forensic & Valuation Reporter* (for forensic valuation in accounting), *Financial Planning Digest*, *BusIndNews*, and the *Global CPA Report*. http://www.smartbrief.com/news/accounting.

interest to practicing accounting professionals. Figure 15–1 lists publications that are available both in print and online; Figure 15–2 shows accounting publications that are available only online.

Blogs on topics of interest to accountants have become common, and their use will likely become even more prevalent in coming years. Chapter 12 discusses writing for blogs more fully, but most of the suggestions you find in this chapter will also help you write effectively when you publish online.

Here are other questions to consider about the publication in which you hope to publish your writing:

- Who are the readers of the publication? What are their interests and concerns? How much technical expertise on your topic are they likely to have?
- What format, organization, and length do the publication's editors prefer? You can learn this either from an editorial policy statement or by studying articles already published.
- What style of documentation does the publication use? If the publication doesn't specify a documentation style, follow the guidelines for documentation given in Chapter 8 of this text.
- What writing style do the editors prefer? Articles in professional accounting publications may be written either in a serious, scholarly style or in a light, conversational one. A blog will usually be informal, though it should be written clearly and correctly. All publications prefer prose that is clear, readable, and concise, with little, if any, unnecessary accounting jargon.

RESEARCH

After you've chosen a topic and publication to target, find out what else has been written on the topic lately, especially if you are hoping to publish the article in a national or regional journal. You can search the Internet or visit a good library to find this information. This research will help in several ways:

- You'll find out what has been published recently on the topic so your article will not repeat what has already been done.
- You'll find out what issues or approaches are of current interest in the profession.
- You may find references that you can use in your article to support your position. Alternatively, you may find positions taken by other people that you want to refute.

In addition to this background research to find out what has already been published on the topic, you may need to do original research to back up your writing with sound observations and reasoning, and perhaps with authoritative accounting pronouncements as well. You may find it helpful to review Chapter 8 of this handbook, which discusses accounting research in more detail.

DRAFTING AND REVIEWING THE ARTICLE

After you have planned the article and done any necessary research, you're ready to begin writing. Draft and revise your article according to the guidelines discussed throughout this text. Chapter 3, which discusses document organization, may be especially helpful. When you feel reasonably satisfied with the article, ask colleagues to critique it. People who have successfully published may be particularly helpful.

For the final manuscript you will submit for publication, pay particular attention to a professional presentation, including accurate and complete documentation of any sources you have used, prepared according to the guidelines of the publication to which you're sending the article. Professional appearance of the document pages is also important, and grammar and mechanics should be flawless.

SUBMITTING THE ARTICLE

When you're finally ready to submit your article to the targeted publication, send it along with a cover letter addressed to the editor by name. If you submit the article electronically, you will send it with an email that functions as a cover letter. This cover letter or email should be concise and courteous and should mention the title of your article. Explain briefly why you think the article would interest the publication's readers.

Be sure you have complied with the publication's submission requirements; for example, the publication may require that you write the article in Microsoft Word and submit it electronically. A publication may also require that you submit multiple hard copies of the article. Whatever the submission requirements are, follow them precisely.

After all this preparation, your article should have a good chance of acceptance for publication. However, be prepared for the possibility that your article will be rejected by the first publication you send it to. If your article is rejected, turn it around and send it somewhere else. Be sure to revise it to suit the readers and editorial policies of the new journal: type of articles published, interests and needs of the readers, length and style of writing, and style of documentation.

Writing for publication can be a rewarding component of your professional accounting career, but like all the writing discussed in this book, it requires planning and attention to detail, including a concern for the readers.

EXERCISES

Exercise 15–1 [General]

Obtain a recent issue of several professional business publications. For each of these publications, answer the following questions:

1. What type of writing do these publications publish? Possibilities include academic research, practical accounting applications for public or managerial accountants, articles of organizational or local interest, or articles addressed to some special-interest group.
2. Who writes the articles for these publications? They may be written by members of a sponsoring organization, professional writers, professors, or other accounting professionals.
3. Analyze the specific articles published. Are they all the same length, format, and style? Some publications may publish a variety of articles, such as short notes and longer essays and articles.
4. What are the standard editorial practices, such as article length and style of documentation?

Exercise 15–2 [General]

Identify a topic that has recently been in the financial news, such as a news item from *The Wall Street Journal*. Select one of the periodicals you identified in Exercise 15–1. Summarize the news item in a way that would be relevant to the readers of that periodical. Remember to document your sources properly and prepare your article according to the submission requirements for the targeted journal.

Exercise 15–3 [Tax]

Identify a tax article that has appeared in the *Journal of Taxation*. Summarize the article in a style that would be appropriate for the readers of *The Wall Street Journal*. Remember to document your sources properly and prepare your article according to the submission requirements for *The Wall Street Journal*.

Exercise 15–4 [Financial]

Identify a recent FASB Accounting Standards Update (ASU). Summarize the Statement in a style that would be appropriate for the readers of *The Wall Street Journal*. Remember to document your sources properly and prepare your article according to the submission requirements for *The Wall Street Journal*.

Exercise 15–5 [Financial]

Identify a recent FASB Accounting Standards Update (ASU). Summarize the Statement in a style that would be appropriate for the readers of the U.S. edition of *The Economist*. Remember to document your sources properly and prepare your article according to the submission requirements for *The Economist*.

Exercise 15–6 [Auditing]

Prepare an article for *Bloomberg Businessweek* on the role of auditing in helping to protect investors. In your article, explain how an audit is undertaken, the reliance on internal controls put in place by management, and the responsibility of management for the financial statements.

Remember to document your sources properly and prepare your article according to the submission requirements for *Bloomberg Businessweek*.

Exercise 15–7 [General]

Choose an article from a recent edition of an accounting journal such as the *Journal of Accountancy* or *The CPA Journal*. Analyze the effectiveness of the writing using the "Tips for the Effective Writer" shown in Figure 1–2 in Chapter 1. Then summarize your evaluation in a short memo to your instructor. Alternatively, your instructor may ask you to prepare an oral presentation of your analysis. Whether you present your analysis in written or oral form, back up your findings with specific examples from the article you analyzed.

CHAPTER

Oral Communication: Listening and Speaking

16

Communication is a multifaceted process. It includes verbal skills such as reading, writing, listening, and speaking, as well as various forms of nonverbal communication—gestures, facial expressions, and other forms of body language. Moreover, all of these types of communication are interactive, making communication a complex process indeed.

So far in this text we've focused primarily on the writing skills you'll need as a professional accountant. This final chapter examines two important oral communication skills, listening and oral presentations, both of which will play an important part in your professional success.

LISTENING SKILLS

In Chapter 1, we pointed out that listening skills are an important part of effective communication. What you hear from other people often provides much of the information you need to perform your job well. When you listen carefully, you'll find out what other people may know about the situation you're involved in, what their expectations are, what their attitudes are, and ideas they have about the work in progress.

In addition, the willingness and ability to listen carefully to what others say contributes to good relationships between you and your colleagues. In fact, listening attentively to what other people are saying might even be considered an ethical issue, because it involves respect for others. Here are some guidelines to keep in mind as you learn to be a good listener. Some of these skills apply to one-on-one or small-group communication, and some apply to listening in a larger group setting, such as a meeting. Many of the guidelines apply to all situations in which good listening is important.

For Conversations with Another Person or in a Small Group

- Focus your attention on what the speaker is saying and don't let your mind wander to other topics. In particular, don't rehearse your own response to what is being said while the speaker is still talking.

- Don't interrupt the speaker. If you must interrupt for clarification, wait for a pause and then apologize: "I'm sorry to interrupt, but I want to be sure I understand this point before we move on. Did you mean... ?"
- Look at the speaker, maintaining good eye contact. Your face should express sincere interest and, where appropriate, empathy with what the speaker is saying.
- Leave your cell phone or other electronic equipment turned off and put away.
- Avoid distracting gestures or movements, such as playing with a pen. When the speaker has finished talking, ask questions for clarification or for additional information, if needed.
- When the situation requires that you understand and remember precise, accurate information, summarize what the speaker has said and ask whether you've understood correctly.
- For some more formal situations, such as an interview, prepare topics for discussion or questions in advance. Anticipate what questions you'll be asked, and have answers in mind. Think also about the questions you'll want to ask. Take your notes with you to consult as the discussion progresses. Leave space in your notes to record important information.

For Large Group Discussions, Lectures, and Meetings

- Depending on the situation, take notes so you won't forget important information. This advice applies especially to an interview, meeting, or lecture.
- In a meeting or large group discussion, as with a smaller group, listen attentively. Maintain steady eye contact with the speaker. Sit quietly and avoid distracting others. Leave electronic equipment turned off and out of sight.
- Don't become involved in side conversations during a meeting, for example with the person sitting next to you, even if the side conversation relates to the topic of the meeting. These side conversations are distracting to others, including to the speaker.

When you master listening skills such as these, you'll have much better information to use as the basis of further work. You'll also have contributed to a respectful, professional environment and better relationship with your colleagues.

ORAL PRESENTATIONS

Speaking before a group, like writing, is often an important part of an accountant's professional responsibilities, yet public speaking creates anxiety for many people. If you learn a few strategies for public speaking, however, and practice as often as possible, your fear of these situations will diminish. With guidance and practice comes mastery, and with mastery comes control. In the remainder of this chapter, you'll see that effective oral presentations, like writing, result from a process: preparation, practice, and delivery.

Preparing to Speak

The time you spend preparing for your oral presentation will help ensure your success. Preparation involves several steps, as the following sections will discuss. You will analyze your purpose and audience; conduct any necessary research; compose your speech; prepare your notes and visual aids; and—perhaps most important—practice your presentation.

Planning the Presentation: Analyzing Purpose and Audience

The first step in planning your presentation is to analyze its purpose. Perhaps you need to inform the listeners about the progress you've made on a project, or propose that the decision makers in the group approve a new project. You may want to convince senior management to invest in a new computer system or explain to co-workers how to implement the system already adopted. Remember that no matter what the primary purpose of your presentation is, it has an important secondary purpose as well: your desire to impress your listeners as a competent professional.

As you analyze the presentation's purpose, think also about the audience. How many people will you be speaking to? Will they be a fairly homogeneous group, or will you be speaking to people with different degrees of knowledge about your topic and different interests? An important consideration about the audience is which decision makers will be present. In planning your presentation, the needs and interests of these decision makers should be a primary concern.

Critical thinking techniques apply just as much to an oral presentation as they do to a written document. Think in advance about the questions the audience will have about the topic, whether or not there will be a formal question-and-answer session as part of the presentation. By anticipating listeners' questions, you can explain your ideas in a convincing way. Anticipating listeners' questions and having the information ready to answer them also shows the audience that you are thoroughly prepared, credible, and professional.

Throughout the planning and preparation of the speech, always think about the audience: what they know about your topic, what they need to know, what their concerns and interests are, and what their attitudes may be toward your point of view and the information you'll present.

Other Things to Consider

In addition to analyzing your purpose and audience, you need to determine how much time you'll have for the presentation. Find out also how you will be speaking to your audience: formally from a podium, or perhaps informally from your seat in a conference setting.

Yet another consideration is whether to illustrate your speech with visual aids, such as charts or other graphic material. If you decide to use visual aids, consider the room where the presentation will be made. Will the space and facilities allow you to use the visual aids you prefer? A later section of this chapter discusses how to prepare effective visual aids. For now, the important point to remember is that you need to start planning visual aids early.

Finally, budget your time so you can complete the work needed to gather information, compose the speech, make notes, prepare visual aids, and practice the presentation. All these steps take time, particularly if your topic requires much underlying research.

The key to handling all these tasks is to make a schedule with dates for completing each step. It's important to plan your work and budget your time.

Gathering Information

The next step in preparing the presentation is to gather the necessary information. Be thorough in your research so that you can answer any questions the audience may raise. When you are thoroughly prepared, you'll seem competent and professional, and your presentation will have an excellent chance of success.

Before you begin the research for your presentation, you may want to review Chapter 2, which discusses how to generate ideas, and Chapter 8, which covers accounting research..

Composing the Speech

After you've gathered the information you need, organize the material into an outline. Keeping in mind the purpose of the speech and the interests of your audience, identify the main points you want to make. *Your speech should contain no more than three to five main points.* These main points, with an introduction and conclusion, are the outline of your presentation. Let's look now at how to fill in that outline.

Introduction. The introduction should do two things: get the listeners' attention and preview the main points you will cover.

When you plan the opening sentences of the presentation, consider the listeners' point of view. Why should they listen to what you have to say? Will your speech be meaningful to them, perhaps helping them solve a problem or accomplish a goal? What do you and your listeners have in common that would make them interested in your presentation? What makes your topic particularly timely and relevant to your listeners? Why are you qualified to speak on this topic? Questions such as these can help you compose the opening sentences of your presentation to get your audience's attention. Here are a few additional suggestions:

- Begin with an interesting story or example to introduce your topic.
- Cite a startling statistic.
- Ask a rhetorical question—one that you don't expect your audience to answer, but that will start them thinking about the topic.

After your opening sentences, provide a brief preview of what the speech will cover. If you tell the audience what the main points will be, you'll help them remember what's important as you progress through your presentation.

Body of the Presentation. In the body of the presentation, you present again your main points and develop them in detail. Be specific and concrete: Use facts, examples, and, where appropriate, statistics.

As you move from one main point to the next, you can help your listeners remember main ideas with two techniques: internal summaries of what you've already said and clear transitions that lead into the next main topic. For example, you might say something like this:

> So one advantage of this new software is that it would reduce the time needed to process customer accounts. [This is an internal summary. We know it's a summary because of the word *so*.] The second advantage is that the software would provide us with better records for our sales managers. [This sentence provides a transition into the next major section of the speech and identifies the second main point for the listeners.]

By providing internal summaries and obvious transitions, you can help your listeners remember main ideas as you give your presentation.

Conclusion. The last part of the formal presentation is the conclusion. Once again, you will help the listeners if you summarize the main ideas you want them to remember. Your presentation will be most effective, however, if you end with a forceful closing. Here are some suggestions:

- Ask your audience to do something. This call to action may be low key—a request that they consider your recommendation, for example. However, you may want to be more forceful, and sometimes even dramatic, if you think the topic warrants this approach and if this tone is suitable for your audience.
- Refer again to the opening sentences of your presentation. If you used a story, example, or statistic, suggest how the ideas expressed in your speech relate to these concepts.
- Remind your audience of the benefits they will receive if they follow your recommendations.

For additional help in composing your speech, review Chapter 3, which covers the principles of coherent organization.

Making Notes

After you have gathered your material and completed the outline, you are ready to put your notes in final form—the form from which you will actually speak. Notice that this section is not called "Writing Your Speech," and for a very good reason. Most experienced speakers find it unnecessary to write down every word they want to say. In fact, having a word-for-word manuscript of your speech could lead you to make two mistakes in your presentation: reading the speech or trying to memorize it (more about these pitfalls later).

The most helpful way to prepare notes is in outline form. You should already have this outline because you prepared it as you gathered information and organized your materials. Your job now is to put this outline into notes you can speak from. Here are a few pointers:

- Transfer the outline to note cards or standard-size paper. Write large enough that you can see what you've written at a glance.
- Include main points, as well as supporting details and examples.
- Write out the opening sentences and the conclusion. (This is the exception to the advice not to write out the speech word-for-word.)
- Indicate in your notes where you will use your visual aids.
- As you review your notes, highlight or underline key phrases in a contrasting color of ink. When you make the presentation, these underlined phrases will remind you of the points you want to make.
- Number the notecards or pages and clip them together.

When we discuss practicing and delivering your presentation, you'll see how notes prepared in this way will help you make a smooth presentation.

It would also be possible to display your notes on the screen of a laptop or tablet computer. This approach is convenient, but it carries some risk. You might experience some technological glitch that would interfere with your presentation. For this reason, if you use a computer in this way, it may be prudent to carry a printout of your notes as a backup.

Preparing Visual Aids

To appreciate how visual aids can contribute to an effective presentation, consider your audience's point of view. When people read, they have a number of visual cues to help them identify and remember main ideas. They have titles and headings, paragraph breaks to signal a shift in topic, and often graphic illustrations. If they need to review something that has already been covered, they have only to turn back the page to see that material again.

Listeners to an oral presentation have none of these visual cues to help them follow the flow of thought, unless the speaker provides them with visual aids. A major advantage of visual aids is that they help listeners identify and remember main ideas. They offer another advantage as well, because well-constructed, attractive visual aids make the presentation more interesting.

Visual aids appeal to the audience by making the presentation easier to follow and more interesting. What are the best kinds of aids to use?

To some extent, your choices depend on where you'll be speaking. If you are making a classroom presentation, for example, you can prepare handouts; write on the chalkboard, whiteboard, or easel pad; prepare posters and charts; or use electronic slides created by Microsoft PowerPoint, Apple Keynote, or similar programs.

You may decide to use more than one kind of visual aid. For example, handouts give your listeners something to take with them to reinforce what you've said, especially when you want to give them lengthy or detailed information. However, you don't want them reading the handout instead of listening, so illustrate your presentation with posters, charts, or electronic slides, and distribute the handouts after the presentation.

Let's look more closely at guidelines for preparing visual aids that you can use during your presentation:

- Be selective in planning your aids, and limit the amount of information you present visually to key ideas. If your audience is constantly occupied reading material presented visually, they may not listen to what you're saying.
- Keep your aids simple. Use key words and phrases rather than sentences, and limit each aid to about five or six lines.
- Be sure the writing is legible and large enough to be read from the back of the room.
- If possible, use bright colors to make your aids more attractive. (Avoid yellow, which is often hard to see from a distance.)
- Make your aids neat and professional looking. A computer with a graphics package will help you achieve a professional appearance. You might even consider having the aids professionally prepared.

You can include any information on your visual aid that will help your listeners understand and remember your message, but visual aids are particularly helpful in identifying your main points, summarizing your recommendations or conclusions, or providing a vivid illustration. You can also summarize statistical information in a table or graph. (Chapter 6 provides additional information on the preparation and use of charts and graphs.) Yet another technique is to reproduce cartoons to amuse your listeners as you illustrate a point.

After you have prepared your visual aids and notes, you are ready for the next important step in the preparation of the oral presentation: practice.

Practicing the Presentation

Practicing the presentation is essential for several reasons. For one thing, the more often you review the speech, the more familiar you become with it, so that when you speak before an audience, you will appear knowledgeable and convincing. You'll also feel more confident that you have mastered the ideas you want to present. When you practice, especially before other people, you also identify in advance any potential problems that could occur, such as a presentation that is too long or too short for the allotted time.

Here are some strategies that will make your practice time most useful:

- Practice the speech out loud. Pay attention to your voice, posture, and gestures.
- Time the presentation to make sure it is the appropriate length.

- Practice using the visual aids, including any equipment you will be using, such as equipment for an electronic slide presentation.
- If possible, practice in the actual room you'll be using for the presentation.
- Practice before a live audience, such as friends, family, or co-workers. Ask them to be critical of the content and delivery of the speech.
- If you have access to video recording equipment, ask someone to record the presentation so that you can identify and correct any problems.

Finally, avoid this common pitfall:

Never read or try to memorize your speech!

The only exception to this guideline is that you may find it helpful to memorize your opening and closing sentences.

Checking the Arrangements

For some oral presentations, preparations include arranging for a room and equipment. Even if someone else is responsible for these duties, it may be a good idea to check them yourself. Be sure that the room will be unlocked in time for the early arrivals at the presentation and that the equipment will be delivered and set up in working order.

Check again on these arrangements a short time before the presentation begins. If there is some unforeseen problem, such as malfunctioning equipment, you'll have time to correct it.

Appearance and Dress

A final consideration in the preparation for your presentation is appearance and dress. As in any professional situation, your grooming should be impeccable. The clothing you wear will depend to some extent on the situation, but professional styles and colors are almost always preferable. If you are in doubt, it's better to err on the side of conservatism.

In summary, thorough preparation for the presentation—your appearance, the arrangements, your visual aids, and the speech itself—will ensure good results when you speak before a group.

Making the Presentation: Poise and Confidence

Earlier, we discussed the steps of preparing an oral presentation before you actually give it: planning, composing, and practice. Now we'll look at the qualities of effective delivery and strategies to help you become an accomplished public speaker.

The effect you should create on your audience is one of poise and confidence. With adequate practice and preparation, you are well on your way to reaching this goal. Let's look at techniques of actual delivery that contribute to an effective presentation.

Eye Contact

One of the secrets of public speaking is eye contact between the speaker and the audience. When you look your listeners in the eye, you involve them in the topic and help ensure that they listen carefully.

Establish eye contact when you first stand before the audience: stand straight, smile with confidence, and look around the room. Look directly at various people at different locations. This initial eye contact should last for a few seconds.

As you begin the presentation and progress through it, continue to maintain this eye contact. Hold the eye contact with each person for several seconds, perhaps the length of a complete phrase. Shift the contact from one side of the room to the other, front to back, and at various points in the middle. If your audience is small, you may be able to make eye contact with everyone in the room several times.

Regardless of the size of your audience, it's essential to establish eye contact with one important group of listeners: the decision makers. They will be judging the ideas you present and your effectiveness as a speaker. Good eye contact will help you keep their attention. You'll also seem confident and in control of the situation.

You may also find it helpful to look frequently at the listeners who seem most interested and supportive of what you are saying. You can recognize this group by their expressions of interest and attention, or perhaps even nods and smiles. Their enthusiasm can give you extra energy and confidence.

Here's a final word about eye contact and the use of visual aids, including electronic slides. When you refer to your aids, don't turn your back on the audience except briefly if you need to locate and point to something specific. Maintain eye contact as you refer to the aid so that your audience will listen to your explanation.

When you think about the importance of maintaining good eye contact with the audience, it's obvious why you shouldn't read your speech and why you should be so familiar with your notes that you only glance at them from time to time.

Body Movement and Gestures

Poised, natural use of your body and gestures also contributes to an effective presentation. Stand still, with good posture, and look directly at the listeners. Don't move about, except to use your visual aids (for example, to point to something on a chart or to change a slide).

Natural, expressive use of your hands is an effective way to emphasize ideas and feelings. For this reason, it's better to place your notes on a table or lectern so that your hands are free for gestures.

Voice

Three elements of your voice contribute to a presentation's effectiveness: pitch, volume, and speed. Pitch is the high or low tone used for speaking. Most people's natural pitch is fine and requires no modification for public speaking. A few people need to pitch their voices a little lower than normal, especially if they are nervous when they speak.

Volume and speed may require more attention. The key to speaking at the correct volume is to speak loudly enough so that people in the back of the room can hear you. Be consistent; don't let your voice drop at the ends of sentences, for example, so that your audience misses the last words or must strain to hear you.

When you practice the presentation, pay particular attention to the speed at which you are speaking. You should speak slowly enough to enunciate each word clearly. Some speakers have a tendency to speak more rapidly when they are nervous. If you fall into this category, make a conscious effort to slow down.

Managing Stage Fright

Now that we've introduced the topic of nervousness, let's think for a minute about how to manage what for many speakers is the worst part of public speaking: stage fright. Notice that the heading for this section is "*Managing* Stage Fright," not "*Eliminating* Stage Fright." Even the most experienced, effective speakers may have some stage fright; in fact, they use this emotional energy to help them make a more effective presentation. The emotion, if kept in control, can give you the extra charge to make an energetic, enthusiastic, and convincing presentation.

Of course, too much stage fright is counterproductive. Let's look at some strategies you can use to manage stage fright before and during your presentation.

Prepare Well in Advance. One advantage of thorough preparation and practice is that they help prevent stage fright. When you know you thoroughly understand the topic, and when you have thought in advance about the questions and interests of the listeners, you will *feel* prepared, and thus competent. A feeling of competence, in turn, gives you confidence in your ability to do a good job.

Actual practice, especially before a live audience, will also increase your confidence.

Just before You Speak. Two tricks may be helpful in the last few minutes before you are scheduled to speak. The first is to use this time to go over your notes one last time to be sure your main points, as well as your opening and closing sentences, are fresh in your mind. The second trick is this:

Don't think about how you're feeling!

If you think about being nervous, you'll only increase the feeling. Instead, think about something pleasant that is completely unrelated to your presentation. Perhaps you can think about some pleasant activity you have planned for later in the day.

During the Presentation. Most speakers find that their stage fright goes away after the first few minutes of their presentation. When you are speaking, look directly at your listeners with poise and confidence: They'll probably reflect these positive feelings back to you. Notice which of your listeners are most interested and receptive to what you're saying, and make frequent eye contact with these people. Their enthusiasm will add to your feelings of confidence and help to ensure that your presentation is effective.

Special Considerations in Presentations of Financial Information

The standard techniques for presentations given in this chapter apply to accounting presentations, of course, but you should bear in mind a number of special considerations when you are presenting financial information. Most of the time, presentations of financial information contain numbers, tabular data, and charts that may be shown on electronic slides. The following points apply in this type of presentation:

- Make sure your numbers are consistent. For example, if "Sales are expected to reach $7.25 million in 2015" appears on one slide, make sure your other slides don't contain some other number. It's easier to make this kind of error than you might think. When you develop a presentation, you will revise it several times before you produce your final version. When numbers are changed during the revisions, it's sometimes difficult to find all the places in the presentation where they appear. As a result, conflicting numbers end up in the final presentation.
- Make sure your numbers "add up." For example, if your presentation includes a statement such as "Sales are expected to grow 20 percent from their 2013 level of $7 million, reaching $8.4 million in 2014," make sure that $7,000,000 times 1.20 does in fact equal $8,400,000 (which it does in this case).
- Make sure the audience can read the charts or slides in your presentation. This applies to the size of the charts or slides as well as their design. Many audience members would have difficulty making out the slide in Figure 16–1. Although the slide illustrates

---

FIGURE 16–1   Example of a Poor Slide

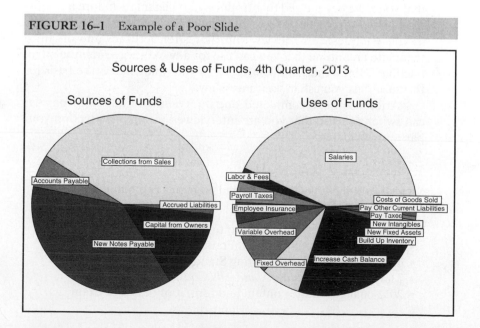

Sources & Uses of Funds, 4th Quarter, 2013

where the company's funds came from and where they went, the labels on the pie slices are too small to read, particularly from the back of the room. Also, there is too much information on the slide to take in at once. In this case, the presenter should separate the charts into two slides and increase the font size in the labels.

- Use computer-assisted presentations wherever possible. Presentations developed in graphics programs look very professional, and they may well make the difference between your recommendations being accepted or rejected.

A FINAL WORD

Public speaking may always fill you with some apprehension. With practice and the mastery of technique, however, you will become much more sure of yourself and your ability to be an effective oral communicator. For that reason, it's a good idea to take advantage of every opportunity to practice your public speaking. The payoff will be greater professional success.

EXERCISES

Exercise 16–1 [General]

Select one of your classmates as a partner for this exercise. Imagine that you have been asked to introduce your classmate before a professional meeting of your peers. Interview your classmate, taking notes as you ask questions. Review your notes for accuracy and organize them into an outline that you can use for a two- or three-minute introduction. (Hint: Analyze the interests of your audience as the basis for the questions you ask in your interview.)

After you have completed one interview, you and your partner can switch roles so that you are interviewed for an introduction your partner will make.

Exercise 16–2 [General]

Select one of the following topics and prepare a five-minute presentation to give to your class:

- Career opportunities in accounting
- The Association of Certified Fraud Examiners
- The International Accounting Standards Board
- The *FASB Accounting Standards Codification*®
- 2011 changes to the content and format of the CPA exam

Exercise 16–3 [General]

The more opportunities you have to speak before a group of people, the more confident you'll be of your abilities. With your instructor's approval, make these informal oral presentations:

- Introduce the classmate you interviewed for Exercise 16–1.
- Explain to the class how to work an accounting problem that was assigned for homework.

Exercise 16–4 [General]

Assume you have been asked to give an oral presentation to a group of local business leaders on the role of ethics in accounting. Your audience will be knowledgeable about business and current events, but they are not themselves accountants. Your presentation, which will be the program of a business luncheon, will be 15 minutes long.

Research the issue of ethics in accounting and prepare an outline for your presentation. Then deliver the presentation to your class or to a group of friends.

Exercise 16–5 [Tax]

Prepare an oral presentation on itemized deductions that may be taken by an individual for tax purposes. Assume the audience for the oral presentation is a group of young people just beginning their careers. Prepare any visual aids needed for an effective oral presentation. Your presentation should be about 15 minutes long.

Exercise 16–6 [Systems]

Prepare an oral presentation on the eXtensible Business Reporting Language, XBRL. In your presentation, discuss what XBRL is, how it is used, and its advantages. Assume the audience for the oral presentation is a group of young people just beginning their financial data management studies in school. Prepare any visual aids needed for an effective oral presentation. Your presentation should be about 20 minutes long.

Exercise 16–7 [Tax]

Prepare an oral presentation for class from a recent article in the *Journal of Taxation*. Remember to adapt your information and presentation to the needs and interests of your classmates. Your presentation should last about 10 minutes.

Exercise 16–8 [Financial]

Prepare an oral presentation for class of a recent FASB Accounting Standards Update (ASU). Remember to adapt your information and presentation to the needs and interests of your classmates.

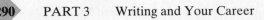

Exercise 16–9 [Auditing]

Prepare an oral presentation for class on the Public Company Accounting Oversight Board (PCAOB) and why it was formed. Remember to adapt your information and presentation to the needs and interests of your classmates. Prepare any visual aids you think may be helpful to your audience.

Exercise 16–10 [Auditing]

In early 2007, the AICPA formed the Center for Audit Quality (CAQ). Prepare an oral presentation for class thoroughly explaining the purpose and structure of the CAQ and why the AICPA probably felt a need for such a group.

Exercise 16–11 [Tax]

Your school's honorary society has asked you to give a presentation at its monthly meeting on "Objectives of the Federal Tax Law." Your audience will be primarily other accounting students, but will also include professional accountants who are in attendance to recruit new hires for their firms. (You hope to be one of these new hires.) Prepare notes to use for your presentation. Your instructor may ask you to make your presentation to the class.

Index

A

accountancylive, 272
Accounting Research Manager (CCH), 141
Accounting Review (AR),
   270, 271
Accounting Standards Codification, FASB,
   139–140, 141
Accounting Standards Updates
   (ASUs), 140
Accounting Today, 272
AccountingWEB, 272
Acronyms, 66–67
   Active voice, 72–74
Ad hominem fallacy, 132
Adverbs, conjunctive, 86
Agreement, pronouns, 90
American Institute of Certified Public
   Accountants (AICPA), 1, 2, 125, 241
   See also CPA exam
   Code of Professional Ethics, 11, 133
   Tax Research Techniques, 169, 181
Antecedents, 42, 90
Apostrophes, 93–94
Appeals to authority, paragraph development
   and use of, 48
Appropriateness for readers, 5
Argument process
   alternatives, identifying, 127
   conclusion, presenting, 128–129
   counterarguments, identifying and responding
     to, 128
   key issues, identifying, 127
   logic, approaches to, 129–131
   reasoning fallacies/mistakes, 131–133
   research and data collection, 127
   steps for, 126
   support, building, 127–128
Attention-getting sentences, 50–51
Authority, fallacies and false, 132

B

Bar graphs, 119
Bibliography style, 165–167
Big 4, 272
Blogs, 234–235, 273
Brainstorming, 24
Bullets, 117

C

CA Magazine, 271
CCH (Commerce Clearing House)
   Accounting Research Manager, 141
   IntelliConnect, 141
   Standard Federal Tax Reporter, 141
   Tax Research NetWork, 141
Cell phones, 237
Certified Management Accountant exam. *See*
   CMA exam
Certified Public Accountants exam.
   See CPA exam

Checkpoint (Thomas Reuters), 141
Chicago Manual of Style,
   The, 145
Clarity
   defined, 5, 66
   jargon, 66–67
   in letters, 170
   in memos, 194
   precision, 67–70
   readable sentences, 72–78
   wording, use of concrete, 70–72
CMA (Certified Management
   Accountant) exam
   example question, 245
   preparing for, 246–247
   writing for, 244–245
Code of Professional Ethics
   (AICPA), 11, 133
Coherence, 5
   discussion questions, 48–49
   essays, 49–54
   paragraphs, 44–48
   pronouns and, 42
   readers' questions, responding
     to, 37–38
   repetition of key words or
     phrases, 41–42
   summary sentences, using, 36–37
   transitions, 38–43
   unified writing, 35–36
Colons, 97–98, 174
Columbia Guide to Online Style (Walker and
   Taylor), 145
Commas
   rules, 94–97
   splices, 86–87
   when not to use, 96–97
   when to use, 95–96
Commerce Clearing House. *See* CCH
Communication
   See also Oral presentations; Social media
   components of, 2–3
   ethics and, 10–11
   face-to-face, 237
   forms of, 8–9
   importance of, 1–2
Conciseness
   defined, 5, 59
   in letters, 170
   in memos, 194
   simplicity, 61–64
   unnecessary words,
     eliminating, 59–61
   verbs and nouns, selecting, 64–66
Conclusions, 37
   in essays, 51–52
   in letters, 169
   in memos, 194
   in oral presentations, 281
   in reports, 210

Conjunctive adverbs, 86
Content, 4, 5
Coordinating conjunctions, 86
Cordes, W., 244
CPA (Certified Public Accountants) exam
  Business Environment Concepts (BES)
    section, 241
  example question, 243
  preparing for, 246–247
  writing for, 241–244
CPA Journal, 270, 271
CPA Trendlines, 272
Critical thinking
  argument, making an, 126–133
  defined, 4, 5, 125
  elements of, 125
  ethics and, 133–134
  logic, approaches to,
    129–131
  reasoning fallacies/mistakes, 131–133
  research and, 147–150
  writing and, 10, 20
Critiquing, 30

D
Dangling modifiers, 68–69, 92
Database services, 141, 159–160
Deductive paragraphs, simple and complex,
    44–47, 49
Deductive reasoning, 129–131
Definitions, paragraph development
    and use of, 48
Details, paragraph development and use of
    descriptive and factual, 47
Discussion questions, coherence and, 48–49
Document design. *See* Format
Documenting research, 145–146
Drafts
  final, 28
  revising, 26–28
  writing, 26

E
Either/or fallacy, 133
Electronic media. *See* Social media
Electronic submissions,
    231–232, 263–264
Email
  addresses, checking, 225–226
  attachments, 227
  composing, 225–227
  examples of, 228, 229
  external, 229
  informal versus formal, 228, 229
  internal, 228
  letters sent by, 184
  memos sent by, 198–199
  salutations, 226
  signature, 227
  tips for using, 229–231
Emotions, fallacies and, 132
Endnotes, 165–167, 146
Engagement letters, 176–178
Essay exams, writing responses on, 247–249
Essays
  attention-getting sentences, 50–51
  coherent, 49–54

conclusions, 51–52
  example of, 52–54
  techniques, applying to other kinds
    of writing, 52
  thesis statements, 51
Ethics
  communication and, 10–11
  critical thinking and, 133–134
  defined, 10
Executive summary, 209

F
Facebook, 233
Fallacies, reasoning,
    131–133
False dilemma, 133
FASB (Financial Accounting
    Standards Board), 11
  Accounting Standards Codification,
    139–140, 141
  Accounting Standards Updates, 140
Feedback/critiquing, 30
Financial Accounting Standards Board.
    See FASB
Flowcharts, 120, 121
Fonts, 114
Footnotes, 165–167, 146
Format
  endnotes or footnotes and bibliography style,
    165–167
  examples of, 110–113
  graphic illustrations, 117–121
  headings, 115–116
  importance of, 110
  for letters, 170–172
  lists and setting-off material, 116–117
  for memos, 194–198
  neatness, 115
  pagination, 117
  paper and print, 114
  for résumés, 256
  type sizes and fonts, 114
  white space and margins, 114–115
Fragments, 86
Fused (run-on) sentences, 87
Future tense, 88

G
Gender, pronouns and, 91–92
Generally Accepted Accounting Principles
    (GAAP), 139–140
Glassman, C. A., 61
Grammar-check programs, 101
Graphic illustrations
  flowcharts, 120, 121
  graphs, 119–120
  labeling and text references to,
    120–121
  pie charts, 118–119
  purpose of, 117
  in reports, 211
  tables, 118
Graphs, 119–120

H
Hard skills, 1
Hasty generalization fallacy, 132–133

Headings, 115–116
Homonyms, 27

I

Ideas
  arranging/organizing, 24–26
  generating, 23–24
Illustrations/examples, paragraph development
  and use of, 47–48
IMA (Institute of Management Accountants), 2,
  241, 272
  See also CMA exam
  Statement of Ethical Professional Practice,
  11, 133
Imperative mood, 88
Independent clauses
  commas, use of, 95
  comma splices, 86–87
  semicolons, use of, 98
Indicative mood, 88
Inductive paragraphs, 47
Inductive reasoning, 129
Information, gathering, 22–23
Instant messaging and texting, 235–236
Institute of Management Accountants.
  See IMA
IntelliConnect (CCH), 141
International Accounting Education Standards
  Board (IAESB), 1
International Journal of Accounting
  (IJA), 271
Internet sources and websites, 140, 155–158
Introduction to Applied Professional Research for
  Accountants, An (Ziebart), 147
Introductory adverbial clauses, 95
Irregular verbs, 89

J

Jargon, 66–67
Job searches/applications
  See also Résumés
  electronic submission of, 231–232,
  263–264
  letter of application, 260–262
  preparation of materials, 255–264
  researching, 254–255
  social media, use of, 231–232
  thank-you letter, 262–263
Journal of Accountancy (JOA), 270, 271
Journal of Accounting Research (JAR), 271

L

Language, fallacies and, 132
Letters
  additional notations, 175
  clarity and conciseness, 170
  engagement, 176–178
  form and appearance, 170–172
  job application, 260–262
  management advisory, 179, 180–181
  organization, 169
  planning, 168–169
  responding to correspondence,
  175–176
  second pages in, 175
  sent by email, 184
  signature, 174

  standardized, 184
  tax research, 179, 181–183
  thank-you, 262–263
  tone, 170
Letters, parts of
  body, 169
  closing, 174
  conclusion, 169
  heading, 173
  inside address, 173
  introduction, 169
  salutation, 173–174
Line graphs, 119–120
LinkedIn, 232, 233, 254
Listening skills, 8–9, 277–278
Lists and setting-off material, 116–117
Logic, approaches to, 129–131
Logical fallacies, 125

M

Management Accounting Quarterly (MAQ), 270,
  272
Management advisory letters, 179, 180–181
Manual for Writers of Term Papers, Theses, and
  Dissertations, A (Turabian), 145
Margins, 114–115
Memos
  basic principles, 192–198
  body, 193
  clarity and conciseness, 194
  conclusion, 194
  examples, 193, 195–197, 198
  formats, 194–198
  introduction, 193
  sent by email, 198–199
  tone, 194
Misplaced modifiers, 68–69, 92
Modifiers
  faulty or misplaced, 68–69, 92
  problems with, 92
Mood, verb, 88–89

N

New York Times, The, 271
Nonrestrictive clauses and phrases,
  commas and, 95
Note taking, 142–143, 144
Nouns, conciseness and use
  of descriptive, 64–66

O

Online database sources
  citing, 146
  description of, 141, 159–160
Oral presentations, 278
  appearance and dress, 284
  audience analysis, 279
  body movement and gestures, 285
  body of presentation, 281
  composing the speech, 280–281
  conclusion, 281
  delivering the presentation,
  284–286
  eye contact, making, 284–285
  gathering information, 280
  introduction, 280–281

Oral presentations (*Contd.*)
notes preparation, 281–282
practicing, 283–284
preparing to speak, 279–284
stage fright, handling, 286
visual aids, preparing, 281–282
visual aids, tips on, 287–288
voice, 285–286

P
Pagination, 117
Paragraphs
appeals to authority, use of, 48
coherent, 44–48
deductive, simple and complex, 44–47, 49
definitions, use of, 48
details, use of descriptive and factual, 47
development of, 47–48
illustrations/examples, use of, 47–48
inductive, 47
length of, 44
structure of, 44–47
Parallel sentence structure, 93
Paraphrasing, 143
Parenthetical elements, commas and, 96
Passive voice, 72–75
Past tense, 88
Personal pronouns, 91
Pie charts, 118–119
Plagiarism, 143–144
Plain English disclosure rule, 4, 61
Plurals, 93–94
Post hoc fallacy, 132
Precision, 67–70
*Prentice Hall Guide for College
Writers*, 143
Prepositional phrases, problem
with using, 76
Prepositions, list of, 76
Present tense, 88
Problem solving, writing and, 9–10
Pronouns
agreement, 90
coherence and, 42
gender and, 91–92
personal, 91
problems with, 90–92
reference and precision, 69–70, 90–91
Proofreading, 28, 101, 115
Publication, writing for
drafting and reviewing article, 274
planning your article,
270, 273
research, 273–274
submitting article, 274
Publications, list of accounting, 271–272
Purpose
identifying, 18–19
statement, 23–24

Q
Quotation marks, placement
of punctuation
in, 99
Quotations
punctuation in direct, 98–99
research and direct, 143

R
Readable sentences
tone, 76–78
variety and rhythm, 75–76
voice, passive and active, 72–75
Readers
analyzing, 20–22
questions, responding to, 37–38
Reading, 8
Reasoning
deductive, 129–131
fallacies/mistakes in, 131–133
inductive, 129
Reference, pronouns and, 69–70, 90–91
Repetition of key words or phrases, 41–42
Reports
appearance of, 211
examples of, 205–206, 212–219
planning, 204, 206–207
style and tone, 211
Reports, parts of
appendices, 210
body, 210
conclusion, 210
graphic illustrations, 211
illustrations, list of, 209
introduction, 209–210
list of, 207–208
notes and bibliography/references, 210–211
summary section, 209
table of contents, 208
title page, 208
transmittal document, 208
Research
basic guidelines, 138–146
critical thinking and, 147–150
documentation style, 162–164
documenting, 145–146
endnotes or footnotes and bibliography style,
165–167
Internet sources and websites, 140, 155–158
note taking, 142–143, 144
online database sources, 141, 146, 159–160
plagiarism, 143–144
printed sources, 141–142, 161
quoting or paraphrasing, 143
revisions, 145
steps, 147–150
writing report or memo, 144–145
Résumés
career objective, 258
education, 258
electronic submission of, 231–232, 263–264
example of, 256
format, 256
honors and activities, 259
interests, 259
letter of application, 260–262
name and address, 256
preparation of, 256–260
references, 259–260
summary of qualifications, 258
what not to put on, 260
work experience, 258–259
Revision, 5
draft, 26–28
research writing and, 145

Rhythm, 75–76
Run-on sentences, 87

S

Salutations
  in emails, 226
  in letters, 173–174
Securities and Exchange Commission (SEC),
    4, 11, 110
Semicolons, 98
Sentences
  comma splices, 86–87
  errors, major, 85–87
  fragments, 86
  fused (run-on), 87
  parallel structure, 93
Series
  colons, use of, 97
  commas, use of, 95
  semicolons, use of, 98
Setting-off material, 116–117
Signature
  in emails, 227
  in letters, 174
Simplicity, 61–64
Skills, hard versus soft, 1
Slippery slope fallacy, 133
Smart Brief, 272
Social media
  in the accounting profession, 232–236
  blogs, 234–235
  company policies, 233
  email, 225–231
  instant messaging and texting, 235–236
  job searches/applications and use of,
    231–232
  telephone etiquette, 236–237
  writing, 29
Soft skills, 1
Speaking, 9
Spell-checkers, use of, 27, 28, 100, 101, 115
Spelling, commonly misspelled or misused,
    100–101
Standard English
  apostrophes and plurals, 93–94
  colons, 97–98
  commas, 94–97
  defined, 85
  modifiers, problems with, 92
  parallel sentence structure, 93
  pronouns, problems with, 90–92
  quotations, direct, 98–99
  semicolons, 98
  sentence errors, major, 85–87
  spelling, 100–101
  verbs, problems with, 88–90
Standard Federal Tax Reporter (CCH), 141
Subject-verb agreement, 89–90
Subjunctive mood, 88
Summary sentences, using, 36–37
Syllogism, 129–130, 131

T

Tables, 118
Tax research letters, 179, 181–183
Tax Research NetWork (CCH), 141

Tax Research Techniques (AICPA), 169, 181
Taylor, T., 145
Telephone etiquette, 236–237
Tense, verb, 88
Texting, 235–236
Thank-you letter, 262–263
Thesis statements, 51
Thomas Reuters, *Checkpoint*, 141
Tone, 76–78
  in letters, 170
  in memos, 194
  in reports, 211
Tradition, fallacies and appeal to, 132
Transitions
  commas, use of, 95
  examples of, 38–39
  problems with, 43
  purpose of, 38
  repetition of key words or phrases, 41–42
  words and phrases, list of commonly used,
    39–40
Transmittal document, 208
Turabian, K. L., 145
Twitter, 233
Type sizes, 114

U

Unified writing, 35–36
Unnecessary words, eliminating, 59–61

V

Variety and rhythm, 75–76
Verbs
  conciseness and use of active, 64–66
  irregular, 89
  problems with, 88–90
  subject-verb agreement, 89–90
  tense and mood, 88–87
Visual aids
  preparing, 281–282
  tips on, 287–288
Voice, passive and active, 72–75

W

Walker, J. R., 145
Wall Street Journal, The, 271
Websites, useful, 155–158
White space, 114–115
Words
  clarity and use of concrete, 70–72
  commonly misspelled, 100
  eliminating unnecessary, 59–61
  precision and use of, 67–68
  simplified choices, 62–64
Writer's block, dealing with, 28–29
Writing
  critical thinking and, 10
  for electronic media, 29
  example of effective, 6, 7
  how to become better at, 6–8
  impact of technology on, 4
  listening and, 8–9
  plain English disclosure rule, 4
  problem solving and, 9–10
  qualities of effective, 4–5
  reading and, 8

Writing (*Contd.*)
  skills, importance of, 2
  speaking and, 9
  spell checkers, problems with, 27, 28
  structure, basic, 25
  under pressure, 29
  unified, 35–36
  what do accountants write, 3–4
Writing process
  critical thinking, 20
  drafts, final, 28
  drafts, revising, 26–28
  drafts, writing, 26
  feedback/critiquing, 30

ideas, arranging/organizing, 24–26
ideas, generating, 23–24
information, gathering,
  22–23
planning, 22
proofreading, 28
purpose, identifying, 18–19
purpose statement, 23–24
readers, analyzing, 20–22
summary of, 18

Z
Ziebart, D. A., 147